# EMPIRE MARINE

# EMPIRE MARINE

## General Littleton W.T. Waller and the Growth of American Imperialism, 1856–1926

### VERNON L. WILLIAMS

FORT WORTH, TEXAS

Copyright © 2024 by Vernon L. Williams

Library of Congress Cataloging-in-Publication Data

Names: Williams, Vernon L., author.
Title: Empire marine : General Littleton W. T. Waller and the growth of American imperialism, 1856–1926 / Vernon L. Williams.
Other titles: General Littleton W. T. Waller and the growth of American imperialism, 1856–1926
Description: Fort Worth, Texas : TCU Press, [2024] | Includes bibliographical references and index. | Summary: "The grandson of a Virginia governor, Littleton W. T. Waller grew up during the post-Civil War years when his widowed mother struggled to provide for her sons. Unable to attend university or a professional military school, Waller elected to pursue a military career. He secured a commission in the Marine Corps in 1880 and began a successful military career, retiring in 1920 as a major general. Empire Marine examines the role that Waller played in the development and growth of the Marine Corps within the emerging empire of turn-of-the-century America. Waller's service corresponded with the growth of the Marine Corps and the exportation of American imperialism in the 1890s and beyond. During those years, his assignments included most of the military actions of his day. Particularly significant were the episodes of US political and military expansion in South America, the Philippines, China, Panama, Cuba, and Haiti. Waller's experiences reflected the emerging role that marines would play in the execution of American policy across the globe. As naval power became the accepted tool of expansion, it became apparent that new tactics and expertise would be required to manage the new responsibilities of imperialism. Increasingly, the marines were called upon to spearhead that policy of expansion and demonstrated the ability to achieve tactical and often, political goals. Gradually the Marine Corps began to compete with the army for budget, personnel, and mission capability. Empire Marine demonstrates these transitions and illustrates the emerging roles of the Marine Corps"— Provided by publisher.
Identifiers: LCCN 2023049274 (print) | LCCN 2023049275 (ebook) | ISBN 9780875658674 (paperback) | ISBN 9780875658766 (ebook)
Subjects: LCSH: Waller, Littleton Waller Tazewell, 1856–1926—Military leadership. | United States. Marine Corps—Officers—Biography. | United States—Foreign relations—1865- | United States—History, Naval—19th century. | United States—History, Naval—20th century. | LCGFT: Biographies.
Classification: LCC VE25.W35 W55 2024 (print) | LCC VE25.W35 (ebook) | DDC 359.9/6092 [B]—dc23/eng/20231107
LC record available at https://lccn.loc.gov/2023049274
LC ebook record available at https://lccn.loc.gov/2023049275

TCU Box 298300
Fort Worth, Texas 76129

817.257.7822

*Design by Julie Rushing*

*For my father and mother*
M/SGT Andrew L. Williams, USAF (ret.), 1920–1995
Mary Ruth Norris Williams, military wife, 1926–1999
*They both are gone away now.*
*They spent most of their adult lives*
*in service to our country.*

*To my brother and sister, a major part of our Air Force family*
Michael Gene Williams, 1950–
Enola Gay Williams Boyd, 1957–2010

# CONTENTS

List of Maps | ix
List of Figures | xi
Preface | xiii
Acknowledgements | xv

CHAPTER 1   Beginnings | 1

CHAPTER 2   The Embattled Old Corps | 34

CHAPTER 3   To the East: The Philippines and China | 70

CHAPTER 4   Samar | 106

CHAPTER 5   Intervening Years | 140

CHAPTER 6   A Virginia Aristocrat in Haiti | 176

CHAPTER 7   The Curtain Closes | 209

Appendix: Waller Chronology, 1856–1926 | 223
Notes | 231
Bibliography | 259
Index | 267

# LIST OF MAPS

MAP 1.1     USS *Lancaster* Cruising Track, European Station | 14
*October 29, 1881–June 6, 1882*

MAP 1.2     Cruising Track, European Squadron | 20
*June 6–July 20, 1882*

MAP 1.3     Bombardment of Alexandria, Egypt | 23
*June–July 1882*

MAP 1.4     Cruising Track, European Squadron | 26
*July 20–August 10, 1883*

MAP 2.1     Cuba Theater of Operations | 62
*June–July 1898*

MAP 2.2     Battle of Santiago de Cuba | 66
*July 3, 1898*

MAP 3.1     The Seymour Expedition | 78
*June 10–27, 1900*

MAP 3.2     Relief of Tientsin, Taku to Tientsin | 80
*June 18–23, 1900*

MAP 3.3     Tientsin and the Concessions | 83
*June–July 1900*

MAP 3.4     Rescue of the Seymour Expedition at the Hsi Ku Arsenal | 85
*June 25–26, 1900*

MAP 3.5     Preliminary Operations at Tientsin | 89
*June 27–July 12, 1900*

MAP 3.6     Defeat of the Boxers at Tientsin | 94
*July 13–August 3, 1900*

MAP 3.7     The Relief of Peking | 100

| MAP 4.1 | USS *New York's* Track from Manila to Samar | 112 |
| | October 22–23, 1901 |
| MAP 4.2 | Coastal Operations Area on Southern Samar | 115 |
| | October 23–November 14, 1901 |
| MAP 4.3 | Sojoton Area Operations | 120 |
| | November–December 1901 |
| MAP 4.4 | Prelude to March Across Samar | 124 |
| | December 8–27, 1901 |
| MAP 4.5 | The March Across Samar | 129 |
| | December 28, 1900–January 20, 1901 |
| MAP 5.1 | Marine Operations Area, Panama | 146 |
| | 1904 |
| MAP 5.2 | Waller & The Cuban Pacification Campaigns | 154 |
| | October 1–November 8, 1906 |
| | March 8–June 21, 1911 |
| MAP 5.3 | Tampico Incident |
| | Veracruz Campaign | 170 |
| | April 9–December 4, 1914 |
| MAP 6.1 | Port au Prince | 180 |
| | 1915 |
| MAP 6.2 | Marine Operations Area, Haiti | 188 |
| | 1915–1916 |

# LIST OF FIGURES

FIGURE 1    Naval Academy Impact on Appointments to the Marine Corps, 1861–1880 | 37

FIGURE 2    Naval Academy Impact on Appointments to the Marine Corps, 1883–1900 | 37

FIGURE 3    Naval Academy Impact on Highest Rank Attained During Career in Marine Corps Officers Commissioned, 1898–1900 | 38

FIGURE 4    Naval Academy Status vs Highest Rank Officers Commissioned, 1861–1900 | 40

FIGURE 5    Naval Academy Impact on Highest Rank Attained (War Era Officers Excluded), Officers Commissioned, 1866–1897 | 42

FIGURE 6    Naval Academy Status vs Geographic Patterns, 1861–1900 | 43

FIGURE 7    Highest Rank vs Geographic Patterns Colonel | 43

FIGURE 8    Brigadier General vs Geographic Patterns | 44

FIGURE 9    Major General vs Geographic Patterns | 44

FIGURE 10    Third Marine Battalion | 73

FIGURE 11    Marine Corps Personnel Increase Proposals Based on the Ratio of Four Officers per 100 Enlisted Men for Federal Year 1917 | 201

# PREFACE

I first encountered Littleton W. T. Waller many years ago during my doctoral work at Texas A&M University. My dissertation focused on naval operations in the Philippines during the Spanish-American War and the U.S.-Philippine War that followed. In my study on the Navy in the Philippines, Waller and the Marines were a small part of the war story that played out in the islands from the first shot fired by Admiral George Dewey and the USS *Olympia* in Manila Bay on May 1, 1898, until end of the U.S.-Philippine War over four years later.

Waller's was a complicated story, one that I wanted to sort out. As I pursued his life and military career, I found that many historians praised him as a great field commander whose career was stymied when he became a scapegoat in the political maelstrom growing out of reactions to torture and abuse during the war. Other historians suggested that Waller was no scapegoat but a failure as a military commander in the field. In the pages that follow, you will find that both assessments require reevaluation. Waller's story proved more complex and the assessment of his military judgement and acumen under fire required a more balanced appraisal. There were times in China, for example, that his leadership, endurance, and commitment to mission and his men bordered on the brilliant. On the other hand, his decisions on the march across the Samar wilderness brought death and disaster to his men and a murder trial for Waller. So where does Waller stand as a military commander? I say let the record speak for itself. In the pages that follow, you can judge for yourself.

**VERNON L. WILLIAMS**
*Abilene, Texas*

# ACKNOWLEDGEMENTS

First, I would like to thank Tony Waller, grandson of General Waller, and Tony's wife, Virginia, for their support and assistance during the long research phase for *Empire Marine*. Early on, they hosted me in their La Jolla, California, home where I found all of General Waller's papers in their basement. Boxes and boxes of unorganized documents, correspondence, and photographs were a treasure trove of General Waller's personal records and materials, collected by him over his lifetime. Most of the Waller papers had not been seen by scholars because they had long been in possession by the family. As Tony explained it to me, parts of the papers were handed down by General Waller's widow, Clara, to their three sons over the years. With the death of each son, the papers gradually were reunited into one collection, including some materials relating to General Waller's sons and their military careers. As a Marine officer himself, grandson Tony Waller received the papers from the other relatives and restored the papers into one collection once again. Thanks to Tony and Virginia Waller, a complete set of copies of everything in their basement became the core foundation of my Waller archives in Abilene and the research that proceeded over the years.

Special thanks to Dr. James Bradford at Texas A&M University, who supervised my doctoral work and dissertation on the Navy in the Philippines at the turn of the twentieth century. In the dissertation's narrative, I encountered Waller and the Marines and their role in the islands for the first time and, thus, began this long journey of discovery that has led to this book, *Empire Marine*. Professor Bradford practiced an old form of mentorship where a student's success signaled credible success for the mentor. He opened opportunities for me as a fledgling historian that helped define what became my career and influenced my own work in mentoring my students. His was a teaching model that I never forgot or abandoned as a practicing historian. For nearly forty years, generations of my students can thank Dr. Bradford for much of what I passed on to them.

Special thanks to Dr. Anne Cipriano Venzon for conversations about her work on Smedley Butler and her knowledge about Littleton W. T. Waller. Early in my research period, Dr. Venzon provided some Butler documents related to Waller and offered advice and consultation on the Waller project. Her book on the papers of Smedley Butler is extraordinary, as were her conversations about her experiences with Butler's son at the family home in Pennsylvania.

Special thanks to Dr. John L. Robinson for editing this manuscript and other projects along the way. John was my department chair and friend for many years, and I benefited greatly from his special talent for editing. His commitment to excellence continues to be an inspiration to me.

During the early years of research and collecting the Waller historical papers, several of my students worked on the Waller papers in my Abilene research office and helped organize the materials. Special thanks go to my graduate students, Dr. Tracy Shilcutt, Dr. Jim Ginther, and Dr. Dawn Alexander Tepe, who have all gone on to careers as historians. In addition to these three, I appreciate my Abilene Christian University undergraduate students and interns who worked on the growing Waller Collection.

Special thanks goes to Julie Witmer's remarkable work on maps. She created my designs and map requirements with precision and artistry.

I am grateful to Raseen Chaudary and her graphic talents for charts, graphs, and tables that clarify and enhance the Waller story.

Early on, I began my research at the Marine Corps Historical Center on the Washington Navy Yard. I am grateful for the assistance of Mike Miller and Evelyn A. Englander, as I first encountered the rich collections held there. Brigadier General Edwin H. Simmons, the director, put me in touch with the Waller family and that led to my trips to LaJolla, California, where I found the extensive Waller Family Collection. Later, the Marine Corps archives moved to Quantico where Mike Miller continued his work with me on the Waller project. He was joined there by my former graduate student, Dr. Jim Ginther, who became an archivist for the Marine Corps. In more recent times, thanks to Kara Newcomer for her assistance on several photographic issues.

Thanks go to the Ellen Schoenrock of Abilene Christian University's Interlibrary Loan program. Her extraordinary work in acquiring difficult and often obscure library materials and microfilm added to my research.

I am grateful to Troy Valos, Kevin Geisert, and the staff in the Sargent Memorial Room, Norfolk Public Library in Norfolk, Virginia, during several research trips to their noteworthy special collection facility.

Special thanks to Mark and Lee Mailander, my neighbors and classmates, from long ago at Amarillo Air Force Base where our fathers were based during the height of the Cold War. Mark and Lee retired from the Navy to Virginia Beach where I remember a pleasant afternoon with Mark, searching the Norfolk Naval Base for evidence of the architectural footprint for Waller's time there. Waller commanded the Marine Barracks several times and, after he returned from Panama, he supervised the construction of new barracks and support buildings for the growing Marine Corps expeditionary force at the turn of the twentieth century. Mark and I found several buildings still there from Waller's time in Norfolk.

I am very grateful for the assistance of Dr. Mohamed Awad, an architect and historian in Alexandria, Egypt. Dr. Awad provided important details on Alexandria during the bombardment of the city in 1882. His emails to me, along with a link to an English copy of his article "The Metamorphosis of Mansheyah" provided important details for my map on the bombardment of Alexandria and my narrative concerning Waller and the American Marines in the city center during their time ashore.

Special thanks to Eman Waheed, reference librarian at the Bibliotheca Alexandrina in Alexandria, Egypt, for providing an early map of Alexandria, "Plan d'Alexandrie comprenant toutes ses fortifications rues et édifices principals." Mr. Waheed's correspondence provided important details on the public square where Waller and the Marines served during the riots in the city.

Dr. Rowena Quinto-Bailon, in the Department of History at the University of the Philippines in Quezon City, put me in touch with Dr. Rolando Borrinaga, a scholar who specializes on Samar and its history. Dr. Borringaga provided assistance on the geography of the Sohoton cliffs and other areas of Samar where Waller mounted his operations into the interior.

Special thanks goes to Raymond Blasingame, a businessman and special friend who has provided editing and proofing on several of my recent projects. Raymond offered many editorial suggestions for improving the manuscript. His reading of this manuscript contributed much to my finished work on *Empire Marine*. I appreciate Raymond's interest in my work as a historian.

I want especially to thank my family, my wife Kay Williams, my daughters Mary Elizabeth Purcell and Minda Jane Ciardi, my son James Andrew Williams, and our five grandchildren. My family has made it possible for me to pursue my career as a historian, a career that has led me to the far reaches of the globe. I am so grateful for each of them, and the journey that we have traveled together.

Finally, I want to thank the TCU Press editorial staff, led by Dr. Dan Williams, for the work and effort that they have made to turn the manuscript on Waller into a finished book.

CHAPTER 1     **BEGINNINGS**

In the midst of World War II, naval Captain John Beresford Wynne Waller[1] cabled the commander of the new destroyer, *Waller*:

> TO CAPTAIN OFFICERS AND CREW CONGRATULATIONS ON
>     COMMISSIONING USS WALLER
> SHE IS NOW YOURS STOP
> IT IS YOUR PRIVILEGE TO MAKE HER A LIVING VIBRANT VIGILANT
>     AND VICIOUS INSTRUMENT TO BE FEARED BY OUR ENEMIES STOP
> THIS I KNOW YOU WILL DO AND THE BEST OF LUCK TO YOU STOP
> THE NAME SHE BEARS IS NOT UNKNOWN IN CHINA PHILIPPINES
>     EGYPT CUBA PANAMA HAITI STOP
> I ENVY YOU[2]

USS *Waller* commissioning ceremony, August 15, 1942, Federal Ship Building and Dry Dock Company, Kearny, New Jersey. Mrs. Clara Waller, widow of the late Major General Littleton W. T. Waller, USMC, christened the ship. *Courtesy of the Waller Family Archives.*

Above and below, USS *Waller* commissioning ceremony, August 15, 1942. *Courtesy of the Waller Family Archives.*

Left to right, Brigadier General Henry T. Waller, USMC; Major General Littleton Waller Tazewell Waller, Jr., USMC; Mrs. Clara Wynne Waller; Rear Admiral John B. W. Waller, USN, August 15, 1942. *Courtesy of the Waller Family Archives.*

By this time in 1942, many Americans had forgotten the old Marine whose name the new destroyer bore, but those still familiar with the American imperial adventures in such locales would never forget the remarkable exploits of Major General Littleton W. T. Waller and his role in the American empire across four decades.

From 1880 until his retirement in 1920, General Waller's service paralleled the growth of the Marine Corps, the advance of United States imperialism, and the birth of modern America. During those tumultuous years, his assignments plunged him into most of the military actions of his day, and Waller's work in the emerging American empire underscored the new role that the Marines would play in the execution of American policy around the globe. As naval power emerged as the dynamic tool of expansion and a necessity for success as a world power, the far-flung tasks of the new imperial responsibility demanded new tactics and expertise. Increasingly, Washington called upon the Marines to spearhead that policy of expansion, and the Corps came to personify the capability of achieving both military and political goals, competing with the Army for mission assignments, budgetary funding, and personnel resources.

Waller marched into this new era, often at the point of the American imperial thrust, confident both of the value of his mission and of his abilities to carry it out. As he did so, Waller's activities came frequently under the scrutiny of anti-imperialist critics as well as imperialist sympathizers, and he occasionally found himself under fire from both groups. An ardent expansionist, Waller aggressively challenged the threshold of the very civilization he served.

Military officers such as Waller not only implemented United States foreign policy but, in these uncharted waters, also executed command decisions based upon their particular cultural origins. The scion of a Virginia first family, whose earliest members held high positions in colonial, state, and federal governments, Waller carried out his duties in a manner consistent with his aristocratic southern mores, approaching his assignments with the confidence and commitments characteristic of his class.

Littleton Waller Tazewell Waller was born in York County, Virginia, on September 26, 1856, grandson of Littleton Waller Tazewell, former member of the House of Representatives, U.S. senator, and governor of Virginia. At the time of Waller's birth, his father, Matthew Page Waller, was a prominent physician and farmer near Williamsburg, but the family moved to Norfolk in 1857, when Waller's aging grandfather's "health became bad and he insisted on Dr. Waller's moving . . . to live and attend to his farming interests" there. During the next four years, one disaster followed another as the Civil War loomed and his grandfather and grandmother both died. In the inheritance settlements, Waller's mother, Mary, along with her brothers and sisters, received the title to

Littleton Waller Tazewell, December 17, 1774–May 6, 1860. Waller's grandfather was a Virginia lawyer, plantation owner, and politician who served as U.S. representative, U.S. senator, and served as the 26th governor of Virginia. *Courtesy of the National Portrait Gallery, Smithsonian Institution.*

Governor Littleton Tazewell's home on Granby Street, Norfolk, Virginia. *Courtesy of the Waller Family Archives.*

the old Tazewell house, located on Granby Street. Mary and two of her sisters then sold their share for $12,500 to siblings John, Sally, and Ella Tazewell, who were living in the house at the time. Mary received just over $3,100, money that proved critical during the coming wartime years in Norfolk.

In addition to the house, Grandfather Tazewell left his children "a handsome fortune but what with the [Civil War] and . . . debts," Mary's share "was greatly reduced." Disaster struck again in 1861 when Mary lost her husband, Matthew, and five-year-old Littleton lost his father. Grappling with an uncertain future, Mary relied heavily on her extended family to provide for her children.[3] Years later she acknowledged that her sisters were "very generous and have . . . helped the boys a great deal," even providing seed funds for her sons' business ventures and money for Littleton "when he first went in the

Matthew Waller, father of Littleton W. T. Waller, who died early in Waller's childhood. *Courtesy of the Waller Family Archives.*

service." She and her children moved into the Tazewell house, paying a third of all house expenses and the cost of her servant and laundry. Mary remained in the house until her death in 1886.[4]

Reflecting on her life, Mary wrote that she was "glad my boys are compelled to work. I think it a great safeguard to a young man," although she confided to her future daughter-in-law, Clara Wynne, that Littleton knew little about economy and living within his means. "He spent much of his younger life with his Aunt Lou who had very extravagant notions herself." Littleton also, she admitted, "inherited much of [his ways of handling of money] from his father who [knew] not how to say no, to anyone who he thought a friend." These words provide some clue to the disappearance of the "handsome fortune" left her by Governor Tazewell, most of which was gone soon after his death.[5]

While financial circumstances limited Mary and her boys, she carefully maintained the cultural foundations valued by the family. Equipped with his aristocratic upbringing, Littleton developed a style of his own during his long military career. Throughout his life, attitudes surfaced that reflected the antebellum world of Governor Tazewell and the mores cultivated in the "best" homes of Tidewater Virginia. Mary and her sons remained linked to the Tazewell family and never abandoned their commitment to the traditional white southern way of life. Mary's writings reflect her convictions on race, class, and status, the same persuasions that eventually marked General Waller's military career.

Like so many antebellum aristocrats, Mary never adjusted happily to the new lifestyle dictated by the South's defeat in the Civil War. "Our summer prolonged so much that cold weather caught us without a carpet down or any of the winter fixings done," she wrote in November 1884, because "we had no butler as they call themselves now." Mary carried forward into the final decades of the nineteenth century her family's struggle with the end of slavery and the adoption of the new social order. It was difficult for her to accept the realities of emancipation and the emergence of the New South. "The negroes [sic] here are so much of gentlemen and ladies that we have to do a good deal of their work," she complained casually, "and they have a way of leaving without notice when they find any extra work is to be done."

Such remarks were not so much a diatribe against freedmen as they were indicative of the reconstructed perspective typical of the era.

Mary passed onto her children the racial presumptions of aristocratic Virginia. "I can't think why our letters are so irregular except that the assistant Postmaster is a negroeman [sic] and there are many other" Black workers in the Post Office as well. She advised that things were about to change since "Cleveland is elected [and] all of [the blacks] will be deposed." Littleton's inherited ideas on race and class remained vigorously fixed during the course of his life, as he routinely reached back to his Virginia roots when making administrative or military decisions involving cultures vastly different from his own. In each of the places mentioned in Captain J. B. W. Waller's World War II telegram to the *Waller* crew, Littleton Waller had made judgments founded on his vision of race and class. His upbringing had not equipped him with the breadth of mind or spirit to do otherwise.[6]

Waller's military career brought him to the Marine Barracks at Norfolk several times, but his residency on Granby Street proved transitory since he served so often at sea. In the 1890s, following the death of Aunt Sally Tazewell, Waller and his brothers received a half interest in the house they shared with Aunt Anne E. T. Bradford. A few years later, the house was sold and moved off the Granby Street lot, and the family members shared the proceeds. For a final time, Waller's wealthy aunts provided for him and his brothers.[7]

Despite family financial support, Mary wrote several times of her concern that she could not provide professional education for her boys. In a letter to a cousin during the last days

Littleton W. T. Waller, in his early twenties, before his commission in the Marine Corps, Norfolk, Virginia, circa 1870s. *Courtesy of the Waller Family Archives.*

of her husband's illness, she worried about the future. "My boys are growing and I will soon have to make some arrangements for them and how I am to do it, I can't tell yet. They will have to go in some store, I expect, for as to studying a profession, I am not able to pay the fees."[8] As his mother predicted, after Littleton attended Episcopal High School in Alexandria, Virginia, he returned to Norfolk to enter business as a clerk, moving among several family businesses. But a career in commerce did not appeal to the restless young Waller, who envisioned a more martial life for himself.[9]

## A MILITARY CAREER BEGINS

Waller's introduction to military service came at home in Norfolk in 1877 at twenty-one years old. At a special meeting of the Norfolk Light Artillery Blues on April 20, its members voted to admit the future Marine Corps major general.[10] Nothing in the record of his service with the Norfolk Blues anticipated his future, for he remained a private until he resigned to accept a Marine Corps commission. The only exceptional mention of the young Waller occurred on March 12, 1880, when he was "appointed to a committee of five men to devise ways and means for the Yorktown Centennial, to be known as the Yorktown Centennial Committee." Even here, Private Waller's name was later crossed out and replaced with another. On June 25, 1880, he resigned to accept an appointment as second lieutenant in the United States Marine Corps, a commission he had earnestly sought.[11]

On April 13, 1880, the young Waller had written prominent Virginia scholar and family friend Hugh Blair Grigsby that he had "been advised to ask you to obtain the influence of Mr. [Robert Charles] Winthrop of Boston in my behalf." His two aunts, who took a great interest in Littleton and in Mary's other children, likely prompted this letter. He told Grigsby that he had applied to the Secretary of the Navy for a vacancy in the Marine Corps, and that he was "working up my influence as rapidly as possible as the examinations comes off about the 10th or 15th of May next." Waller suggested that "if Mr. Winthrop would help me either with the President or Secretary of the Navy, I think I can get one of the appointments."[12]

Winthrop, formerly speaker of the House of Representatives, had a long and distinguished career in the House, followed by a brief stint in the Senate.

Careful not to assume too much and unaware of Grigsby's close relationship with Winthrop, Waller closed his missive with the suggestion that Grigsby "not trouble yourself, sir, or even write to Mr. W[inthrop] if you feel that you do not know him well enough to justify it." Although Grigsby's response does not survive, he clearly intervened on Waller's behalf.¹³ As the deadline for the examination approached, however, Waller wrote Grigsby on May 1 that Winthrop had "either not rec[eived] the letter or he is not willing to ask any favor of the government." Waller then thanked Grigsby for his "kindness" in writing to Winthrop.¹⁴

Waller's despair was misplaced. Winthrop contacted not the president or the Secretary of the Navy but John W. Hogg, the chief clerk of the Navy, who had "much to say in these affairs," and who opened the door for Waller. A week later, Waller confided to Grigsby that "some of my friends think that I have seen the Sec[retary of the Navy], and my supporters have interviewed him enough already that he may think I am pushing matters too far." Waller then explained that the "appointment will be obtained by the man who has the most influence, irrespective of his mental capacity, unless he is an idiot, or by his weakness utterly incapacitated for doing his duty." Waller closed his letter by sending his aunts' "kindest regards and good wishes." Mary Waller's network of family connections would be passed on to Littleton, who would continue to draw upon them throughout his career.¹⁵

On June 5, Secretary of the Navy Richard W. Thompson informed Waller that "you have permission, if of the required age, to report at the Navy Department at 10 o'clock a.m., on the 7th inst[ant] to Medical Inspector B. F. Gibbs, U.S. Navy, President of the Naval Medical Examining Board, for examination as to your physical qualifications for appointment as a second lieutenant in the Marine Corps."¹⁶

Two days later, Thompson sent Waller the good news that he had passed the medical examination and ordered him to report to Colonel C. G. McCawley, Commandant of the Marine Corps, for examination "as to your mental and moral qualifications for appointment as a second lieutenant in the Marine Corps."¹⁷ On June 13, Waller notified Grigsby of his "successful and very creditable examination" score of 895 out of a possible 1000 points. The Senate confirmed his nomination on June 14, 1880.

With new uniforms purchased for him by his wealthy aunts, Waller reported to Marine Barracks in Washington, D.C., for two months training, which included instruction in drill, duties on board ship, and guidance in "making out accounts, muster rolls, ration returns," and other duties expected of the new Marine officer.[18] On August 30, 1880, Waller received orders to report to Marine Barracks at Norfolk, where he lived at home with his mother during his first full year of service.

During that year, Waller performed routine duties, serving under Captain Henry C. Cochrane, a Civil War–era

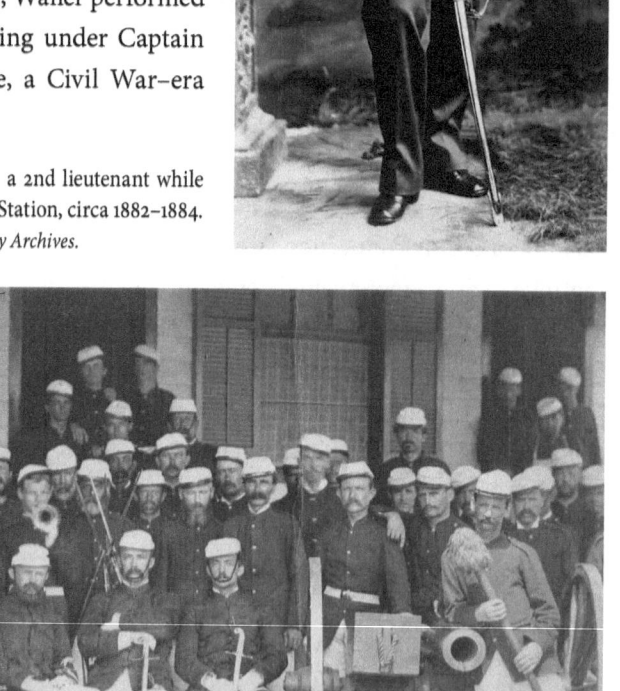

Littleton W. T. Waller as a 2nd lieutenant while serving on the European Station, circa 1882–1884. *Courtesy of the Waller Family Archives.*

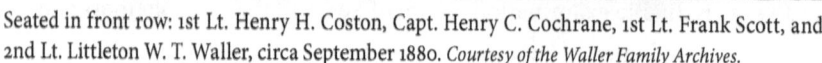

Seated in front row: 1st Lt. Henry H. Coston, Capt. Henry C. Cochrane, 1st Lt. Frank Scott, and 2nd Lt. Littleton W. T. Waller, circa September 1880. *Courtesy of the Waller Family Archives.*

officer who had become increasingly vocal in his calls for reform in the Marine Corps.[19] Cochrane mentored the young Waller, and their paths intersected frequently during Waller's career.[20]

Many years later, another young Marine lieutenant beginning his first assignment in the Marine Corps described Cochrane's reputation from a different perspective. Frederic Wise explained that any enterprising and thoughtful junior officer could usually "avoid social contact" with the Navy Yard commandant, but "the Marine Colonel [Cochrane] was not easily escaped." Wise admitted that under most social occasions, Cochrane was "a gentleman and courteous." Often hosting junior officers at dinners in his home, Cochrane "lived well" and provided "a damned good dinner," but things changed, however, under the duress of duty; Cochrane was "'ornery' and meaner than hell on duty." Wise remembered that he could be "rigidly courteous" in his official demeanor but "cold and sarcastic" at the same time. Wise saw no mentoring in Cochrane's style on the job, but early in his career, Wise was not a mature officer and often found himself in one kind of trouble or another. Cochrane's penchant for discipline remained a part of his technique for accomplishing his mission. "He was a Tartar for discipline" and reserved for himself enlisted men who reported late for duty or arrived slightly inebriated. "A Marine who had been drinking but wasn't exactly drunk came into the Yard" and found himself facing Cochrane, who smelled his breath and promptly limited the hapless Marine to "bread and water for five days—for smuggling liquor into the Marine Barracks—inside himself!"[21]

While Waller found in Cochrane both a mentor and a friend, he too occasionally found himself on the receiving end of a swift and sarcastic barb from his commander. But as the years unfolded, Cochrane assiduously molded the young Virginian into a Marine, taking Waller's natural talent for military affairs and grounding him in the rigors of Marine service aboard ship and on shore at a formative time in Waller's development as an officer.

Barely a year after his arrival at Norfolk, Waller and Cochrane embarked upon an adventure that provided insight into Waller's talent for field work and revealed a glimmer of what Waller's future held. On August 10, 1881, Cochrane and Waller were officially detached from Norfolk and assigned to

USS *Lancaster*, Waller's first sea duty. *Courtesy of U.S. Naval History and Heritage Command.*

The *Lancaster* crew assembles on deck. The Marine Guard is at front right in the picture with Waller standing in from of the Marines, circa 1882–1884. *Courtesy of U.S. Naval History and Heritage Command.*

the 2300-ton sloop-of-war *Lancaster*, with Captain Bancroft Gherardi commanding, outward bound for the Mediterranean. Cochrane handpicked the forty-five-man Marine Guard and wrote the *Lancaster's* executive officer, Lt. Commander C. F. Goodrich, regarding the ship's company and the impending voyage. Goodrich replied that he was "glad to hear that the guard is to be a picked body of men. I wish I could say the same of the crew." The preparations for getting underway soon were complete with the Marines comfortably installed onboard the *Lancaster* at Portsmouth, New Hampshire. The voyage to the European Station cast Waller into his first major expedition, and his service there attracted attention that resulted in a degree of fame for the young lieutenant.[22]

After many delays, on Monday, October 10, 1881, the *Lancaster* hoisted her anchors, and with a slight breeze from the west, eased away from the quay and slowly steamed into New York Bay under the control of the pilot. Ahead lay the Azores, the first port of call after crossing the Atlantic. Two weeks into the voyage, gale force winds and heavy seas suddenly hit the *Lancaster* in a short-lived storm, and a whaleboat was lost overboard with all equipment and supplies. Over the next three weeks, the *Lancaster* made calls at Port Fayal at Horta in the Azores, Gilbrator, and Cartegena on the Spanish southern coast. It proved to be the beginning of an active cruise for the young Marine (see Map 1.1).[23]

New Year's Day, 1882, found the *Lancaster* at anchor at Villefranche-sur-Mer near Nice, France. Under cold, rainy skies, the officers busily prepared for the admiral's reception scheduled for the sixth and argued among themselves concerning the arrangements. Cochrane, irritated that a "row about the invitation cards for [the] reception" broke out, pressured the committee to pare the list to three hundred and drafted Waller and two others to help him send out the invitations to members of the diplomatic and business community in the Nice area. Waller spent the day addressing the invitations, had dinner on board, then joined a "delegation to Monte Carlo" for an evening's entertainment. The diary mentions no training or ship's work with such pressing social duty in the air.[24]

Early the next day, the ship's company drilled at general quarters and mustered on deck to hear a reading of the Articles of War. For the rest of

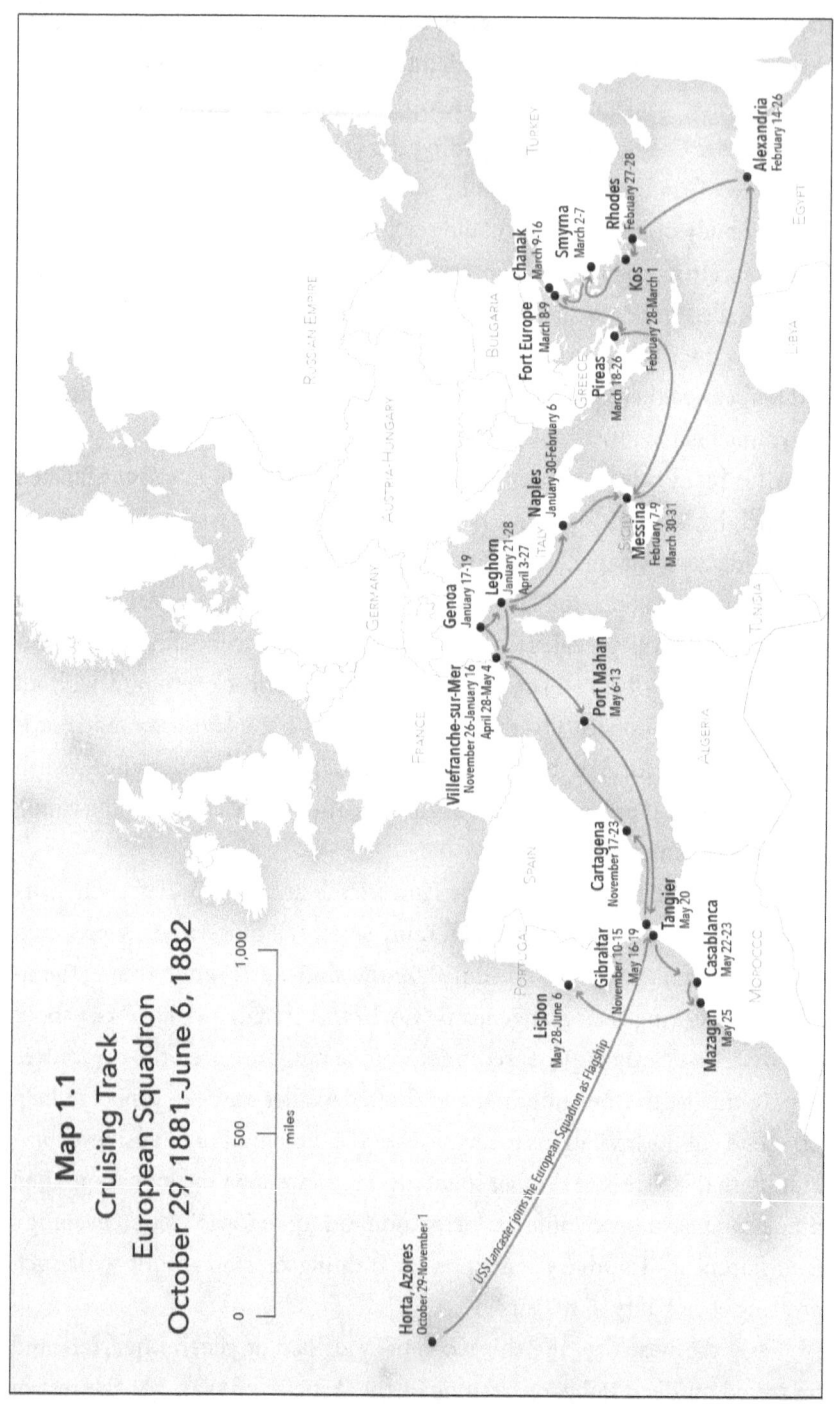

Map 1.1 Cruising Track European Squadron October 29, 1881–June 6, 1882

the day, Waller and the invitation group worked the list "up to 200," and at 4 p.m. Waller joined Cochrane for a jaunt to Nice, calling at Villa Lorenza, and then at Mr. Roger Leigh's, a member of the British parliament, and on to a reception at Mrs. Capt. Stokes-Boyd's. Cochrane then "dined at Restaurant National with Lt. Waller and Chaplain Morrison." After sending a few cables to the United States, they caught the 10:00 p.m. train back to the ship.[25]

The next few days involved more of the same: drill, inspections, social calls, and the admiral's reception. Little changed in the daily routine as Waller and the other lieutenants drilled the Marine Guard under Cochrane's watchful eyes. "Quarters for inspection—the Guard never looked better and now is nearly up to the best possible condition." Cochrane proudly noted that "Captain G[herardi] remarked that the condition was very creditable." Under Cochrane's careful tutelage, Waller learned the basics of handling men, improved his knowledge of drill and tactics, and studied the role of Marines aboard ship as well as the social graces demanded of officers ashore. In the months that followed, Waller refined his talent for leadership and continued to mature as Cochrane groomed the young lieutenant.[26]

Early in the morning on January 16, the *Lancaster* left Villefranche-sur-Mer bound for Genoa, Italy, to the east. The ship "stayed close to the coast," as they cruised past small towns and villages, the view of the snow-capped mountains in the distance, providing a dramatic backdrop for drill. By early afternoon, the ship neared Genoa, and at 3:00 p.m., the pilot came aboard, directing the *Lancaster* to its anchorage fifteen minutes later. "Ran lines ashore" and secured the ship; all hands "saluted the Italian flag with 21 guns." Between touring and diplomatic calls, Waller "drilled the guard" as the shipboard routine continued unabated during the brief stay at Genoa.[27]

The next morning the ship arrived at Leghorn near Pisa, Italy, where the calls ashore resumed. A few days later, Waller accompanied Cochrane, Captain Gherardi, and a party of other officers to the U.S. consul's home for a reception. Waller and Cochrane "took Mrs. Rice [wife of the U.S. Consul at Leghorn] and Mrs. Miller to the theater to see Traviata wh[ich] was well performed." Two days later, the consul general and a large entourage arrived on board the *Lancaster* where the wardroom returned the compliment by entertaining the group for dinner.[28]

Waller nimbly negotiated the social obligations required of a junior officer under the benevolent eye of schoolmaster Cochrane, who often created opportunities for Waller. These social engagements must have been comfortable for Waller, who grew up among his wealthy aunts in the old Tazewell mansion, so long the center of Norfolk's social scene. As a lieutenant of Marines in 1882, Waller still stood at the bottom of the financial ladder, but membership in the officer corps included certain social privileges and access to a formidable network that would have a significant impact on his future as a Marine officer.

As the ship slipped down the Italian coast, Waller enjoyed a variety of activities ashore. At Naples, he visited the ruins of Pompeii, since his education as an officer extended to at least a superficial study of other cultures and their history. Ever the mentor, no doubt Cochrane influenced Waller to value travel and encouraged the study of peoples and their development.

By February 6, the *Lancaster* was underway once again, bound for Messina, Sicily; the sea was "smooth as a mill pond," the journey uneventful, and the ship put into the port for two days. Ships filled the harbor, casks of wine and olive oil lined the quay, and local vendors came aboard to sell their wares: wine, flowers, polished horns, underclothes, opera glasses, painted toys, and a host of other souvenirs. Cochrane "found the city very clean and cheerful, apparently prosperous" as the ship took on coal, and the Marine guard drilled and held inspection, turning out at 1:00 p.m. under arms to receive "the prefect of this province." After two days of shipboard work and requisite calls to the American community, everyone returned to the vessel and the *Lancaster* made way for Alexandria, Egypt, arriving off the coast of Africa on February 14.[29]

Waller found Alexandria a busy place, but happily without the turmoil and unrest that would shake the city later in June when the American squadron would return amid riots and burning chaos. The *Lancaster* remained two weeks at Alexandria. During the fortnight at anchor, the officers spent much time visiting the international community ashore and hosting several dinners aboard their ship. On February 15, Waller and a group of thirteen officers left the ship for an inland excursion to Cairo. The shipboard pattern of drills, inspections, and social calls reached into the month of March, after which the ship sailed for Asia Minor (see Map 1.1). The *Lancaster* worked its way up into the Aegean Sea, calling at Rhodes, Kos, Smyrna, the Dardanelles, and points just short of Constantinople, before returning to Italian waters in April.

During these weeks of cruising, Cochrane's diary occasionally refers to evening chats with Waller concerning drill, tactics, or other professional topics, in which he instructed the young lieutenant as Waller gained more experience with the men and developed as an officer. In spite of his mentor's attention, however, Waller's inexperience and lack of maturity occasionally got him into trouble, testing Cochrane's patience and risking the goodwill the young officer had built up with his commander.[30]

The *Lancaster* had steamed back to Leghorn in early April, and on the sixth, Waller received a three-day leave for a visit to Florence. Waller's "leave expired at sundown on the ninth," but at 9:50 p.m., long after sundown, Cochrane received a telegram "asking for an extension of twelve hours." The next morning Waller still had not arrived, and Cochrane reported him "absent at quarters." Upon his return, Waller explained to a forbearing Cochrane that he had been "left" behind in Florence and stranded. But just two days later, Waller tested his captain's patience once again.[31]

Waller, having arranged to leave the ship and join fellow officers for dinner aboard the *Quinnebaug*, asked Cochrane to remain on the *Lancaster* with the duty until Waller's promised return at 7:00 p.m. Cochrane had planned then to spend the evening ashore at Mrs. Torrey's home. During dinner Waller drank too much, and Cochrane complained in his diary that Waller "got back at 8:45 'flushed.' [He] prevented me from going to Mrs. Torrey's." Waller again survived Cochrane's wrath and soon regained his good graces. Cochrane's diary for the rest of April frequently mentions Waller's social calls and evenings with the American community at Leghorn, but duty still took precedence. A few days later, Cochrane needed a trusted officer to fill a vacancy aboard the *Nipsic*, a 592-ton gunboat. On April 20, Cochrane ordered Waller to the *Nipsic* to head the Marine guard there, the youthful officer's first command.[32]

On the squadron sailed, back to Villefranche-sur-Mer on the French coast and down to Port Mahan and Gibraltar. It continued along the western

USS *Nipsic* (1879–1913), a gunboat of 592 tons that served on the European Station from 1880 to 1883. *Courtesy of U.S. Naval History and Heritage Command.*

coast of Africa to points at Tangier, Casablanca, and Mazagan, before finally setting a course north to Lisbon, Portugal.[33]

Waller wrote that the fleet "sailed for Port Mahon for shore drill and from there we went to Gibraltar and down the West coast of Africa as far as Mogador." At Mogador the *Quinnebaug* left to continue to the Congo and later on to England, while Waller and the rest of the squadron "returned to the Mediterranean visiting the Moroccan coastal ports or towns to communicate with the American consuls." Along the coast of North Africa, Waller found still more adventure and additional danger.[34]

At one of the stops in North Africa, Waller and some fellow officers organized a boar hunt. Waller boasted that during the first drive, a boar crossed his sights, and he downed the animal weighing "two hundred and fifty pounds" with tusks measuring "seven and a half inches from root to point . . . leaving about five inches of formidable weapon." The chaplain of the *Nipsic* "claimed the boar as he had administered the coup de grace," whereupon the local Moors seized the chaplain's rifle and charged him two sovereigns for its return. As for Waller, the Moors "said that I was a brave man, no Jew." In one of his infrequent episodes of humility, Waller confessed that "I let it go at that as I did not want to lose face by telling my feelings when the boar charged."³⁵

After a busy five months cruising along the Mediterranean and African coasts, the *Lancaster* arrived at Lisbon where Cochrane and Waller made one of many obligatory social calls on members of the American community, continuing the practice since arriving on station. The two officers visited the home of John Beresford Wynne, formerly of San Francisco and residing in Lisbon for health reasons. Wynne, the son of a British army officer, had sailed from Lisbon in 1850 "as supercargo [aboard a] ship loaded with wine for California and settled there." But by July 1881, he had returned to Europe, living in Lisbon with his wife and "two daughters at his sister's, Mrs. Hutchens." The meeting with the Wynne family proved fateful for Waller, but at the time duty soon sped him from Lisbon.³⁶

The Lisbon port of call was but the continuation of a long voyage designed to show the flag throughout the Mediterranean region. On his first cruise as a Marine officer, Waller experienced firsthand life aboard an American flagship engaged in supporting American interests abroad. Marine officers on ships faced long periods of tedious work in training, administrative duties, and balancing the political nuances of a Marine serving under the command of a naval officer who rejected the notion that Marines shared any special jurisdiction on ship. Yet, the journey proved of immense value for Waller, for ahead lay many more months of cruising during which he absorbed the fundamentals of leadership from the experienced Cochrane. On the *Lancaster,* Waller practiced the craft of managing men, and from Cochrane, he learned the most important lesson of his career—always look after your men, Cochrane decreed, make sure they come first, and they will look after you. For Waller, it proved a lasting lesson and a guiding principle for the rest of his career.

Cochrane's diaries give a detailed narrative of the voyage beyond Lisbon, and during this period, from the early days of 1882 until the *Lancaster* arrived in Alexandria in June to support British efforts to restore order, provide a sharp snapshot of life aboard an American warship. Waller received periodic mention in Cochrane's diary, and the activities of shipboard Marines offer a candid overview of Waller's life on the European Station during the next two years.

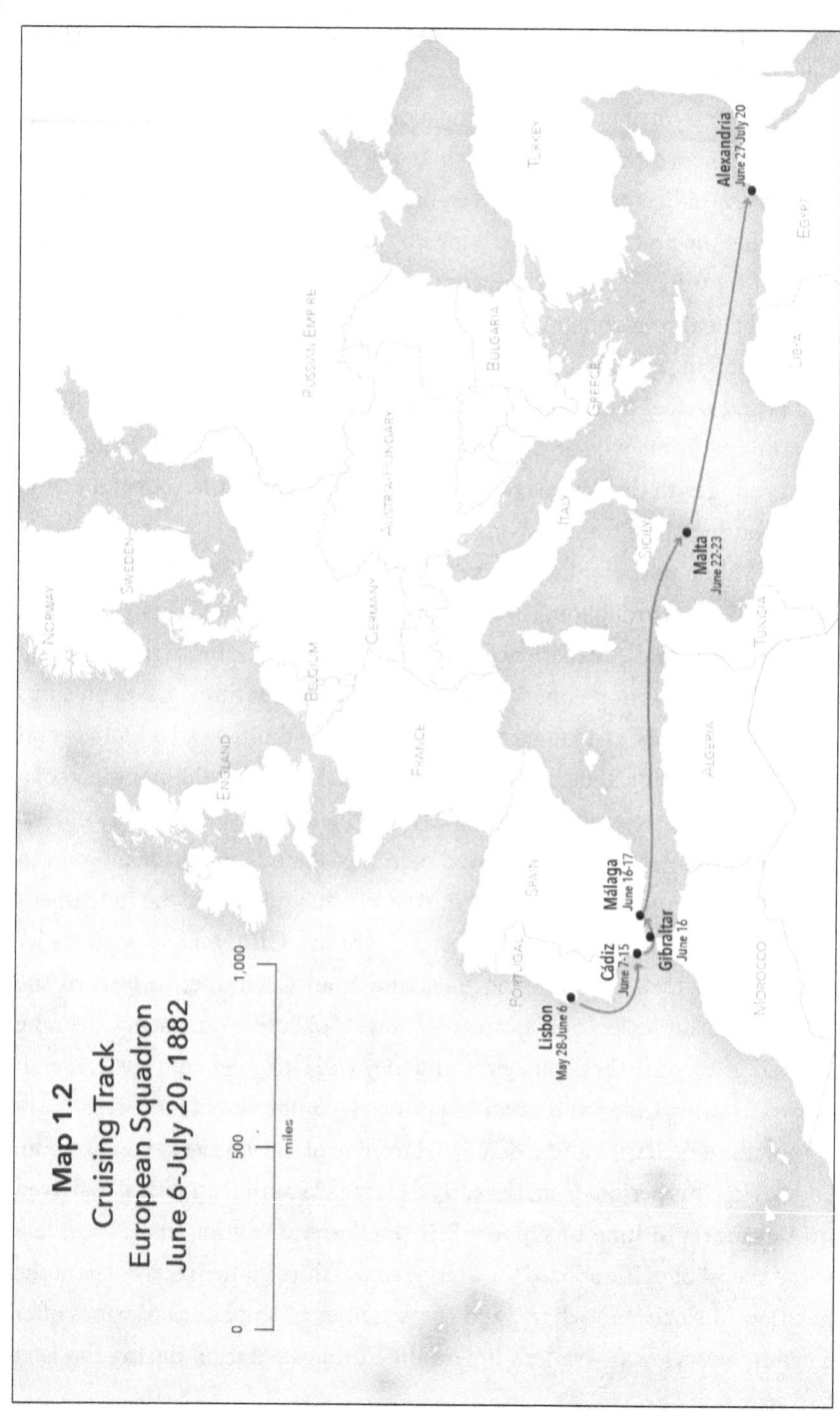

Map 1.2
Cruising Track
European Squadron
June 6–July 20, 1882

In the early morning hours on June 6, the squadron fired their boilers, getting up steam in preparation for departure. Under the cover of darkness, the ships slipped out of Lisbon harbor, setting course for Cadiz. In the days ahead, the work of the squadron continued with more routine visits to Cadiz, Gibraltar, Malaga, and Malta (see Map 1.2). Soon events would call the small American fleet to action, and the Marines on board the three ships would find themselves tested under extreme conditions and provide Waller and the shipboard Marines with a test of arms. They would not be found wanting.[37]

## BOMBARDMENT OF ALEXANDRIA, EGYPT

Meanwhile, a crisis was brewing in Alexandria that soon enveloped the international community. Worried about the growing nationalist movement within Egypt, and its possible threat to the Suez Canal and the mounting Egyptian debt, both the British and the French dispatched squadrons to Alexandria. They hoped that a show of force would undercut the strong nationalist movement within the Egyptian Army and ensure Anglo-French control of Egyptian financial and trading institutions and agencies. Unrest and the deteriorating conditions in Alexandria prompted the Secretary of the Navy to order American vessels on the European Station to make for Egypt with all possible speed, throwing American support behind the imperial powers.[38]

As American citizens and businesses in Alexandria came under increasing danger from the riots in the city, the *Lancaster* arrived off Alexandria on June 27, 1882, followed by the *Quinnebaug* on July 1 and the *Nipsic* on July 12. The three vessels in the squadron immediately became a haven for foreign nationals fleeing the city's havoc, "full of men[,] women[,] and children who were camped on the quarter-deck." Public order deteriorated ashore as riots and looting quickly escalated to include arson, rape, and murder. On July 14, squadron commander Rear Admiral J. W. A. Nicholson ordered Marines from the three vessels ashore to protect American lives and property.[39]

Cochrane commanded the detachment of Marines, which included "Lieutenants F. L. Denny and L. W. T. Waller, and sixty non-commissioned officers, musicians, and privates," the first neutral troops to land. Cochrane

*Judge*, a satirical magazine published in New York, vol. 2, n. 42, August 12, 1882. *Courtesy of U.S. Naval History and Heritage Command.*

led his men through the burning city, advancing to the American consulate located on the Grand Square of Mohamed Ali, often referred to as the Place of Mohamed Ali.⁴⁰ The Marines quickly occupied the consulate building as Cochrane posted patrols to protect American property and to "assist in extinguishing the fires that were raging in that vicinity." The Marines, the first troops to arrive in the area, "which was the centre of the European part of the city and the scene of the greatest part of the pillaging's [sic]," swiftly restored order and established their "headquarters in the St. Mark's buildings," which included the Anglican "St. Mark's Church and the adjoining St. Mark's Building, which belonged to the English community" (see Map 1.3).⁴¹

A journalist "visited the American Consulate" and "found it occupied by sixty American Marines and twenty sailors with a small gun." When the fires in the area threatened to spread to the consulate, Cochrane decided to blow up nearby buildings to halt the spread of flames to save the consulate, but the reporter marveled at "how the Americans managed to get gunpowder into the square" with the air "literally full of sparks." The Marines razed the surrounding buildings, holding the fire at bay, and at the same time, mounted patrols and set up guard posts in the surrounding streets and alleys. During the night arsonists approached the Marines' headquarters, planning to torch

BEGINNINGS | 23

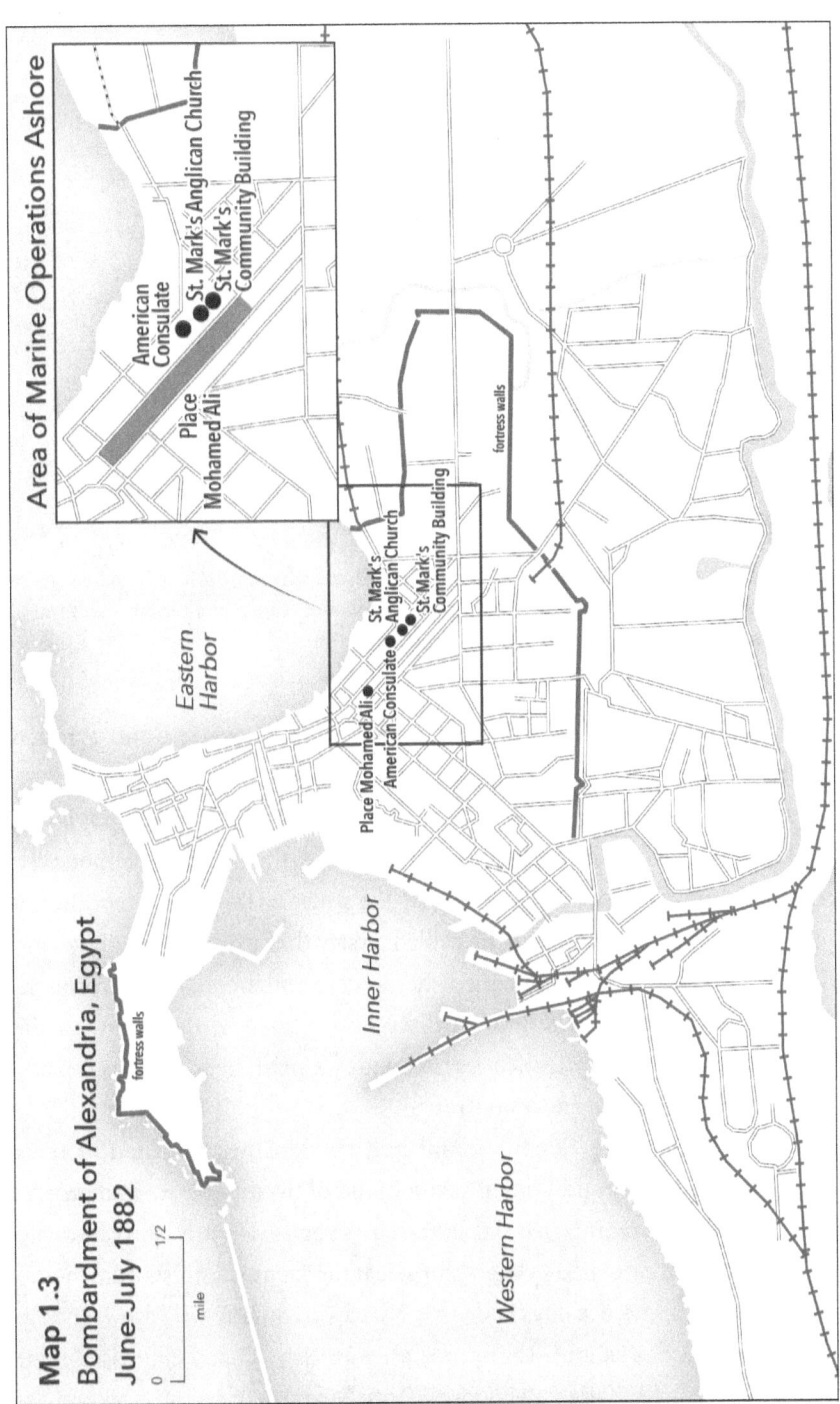

The center plaza at Alexandria, Eygpt, known at the Place Mohammed Ali or Grand Square of Mohammed Ali. This postcard photograph was taken several years before the bombardment of Alexandria. *Vernon Williams Archives.*

the building and the men inside, but they were discovered and arrested before they could set the fires.

As the events unfolded, the correspondent for the London *Telegraph* sent two cables to his editors back home. An early morning dispatch announced that "four graves have just been dug in the square, ready for the bodies of plunderers." Later that evening he cabled tersely that "three of the graves are now filled." The reporter explained that looters and arsonists are "brought in every few minutes. The utmost discretion is used in dealing with the accused." The summary justice carried out by Cochrane's Marines quickly brought the city center under control.[42]

The next morning Cochrane and half the Marines returned to their ships, leaving Denny and Waller in command of twenty-five men to protect the consulate and maintain order in the city's center. On July 18, Waller and most of the men returned to their ships, leaving Denny with six Marines to guard the consulate. Six days later, this guard also quietly withdrew, ending Marine operations ashore. The appreciative British quickly expressed their gratitude. "Lord Charles Beresford [British commander at Alexandria] states that without the assistance of the American Marines, he would have been unable to discharge the numerous duties of suppressing fires, preventing looting, burying the dead, and clearing the streets."[43]

This first brush with danger deeply etched itself in Waller's mind. Years later, as American Marines voyaged to yet another American intervention, this time to the Philippines and China under Waller's command, Marine Lieutenant Frederic M. Wise remembered that "at meals on the *Solace*, we listened respectfully to [Waller's] never-ending accounts of when he was ashore with Admiral Sir Charles Beresford at the taking of Alexandria in Egypt in 1882." Wise then echoed a theme common among Waller's junior officers over the years. He was "the only small man I ever knew who talked a lot about himself, but who could always deliver the goods."[44]

Following the action at Alexandria, Waller remained on the *Nipsic* as the squadron left the British fleet behind and set a course for Sicily and the Italian coast. Ahead, the squadron faced a long cruise that would take them back to familiar ports of call and on to Greece and Turkey. Later in November 1882, Waller rejoined the *Lancaster* and over the next year, Cochrane, Waller, and the Marines would find themselves crisscrossing the northern Mediterranean, North Africa, and finally departing

2nd Lt. Littleton W. T. Waller, circa 1882–1884. *Courtesy of the Waller Family Archives.*

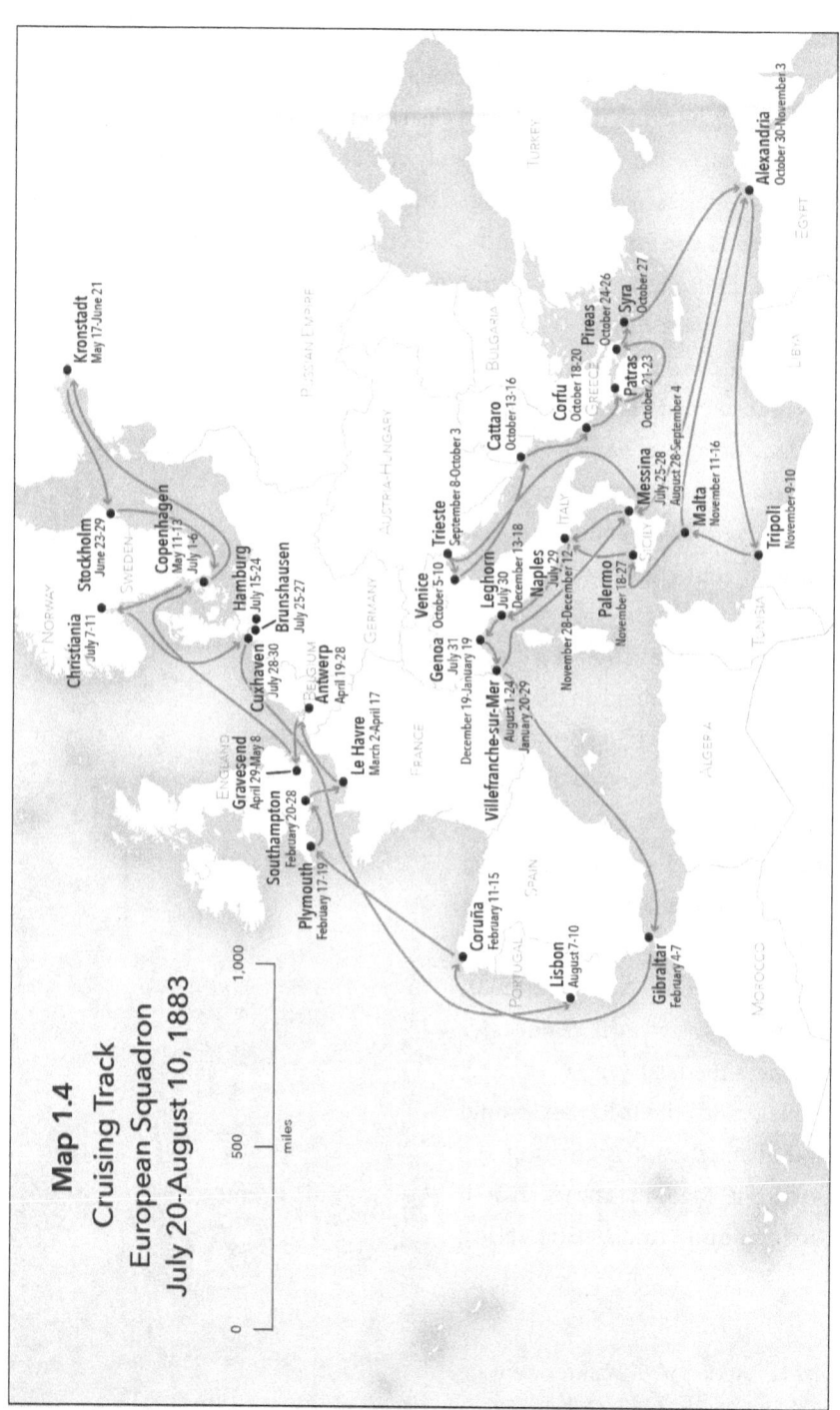

Gibraltar in February 1883 for a six-month cruise to England and Northern Europe. In August 1883, Waller returned to Lisbon for a few days' reunion with Clara and the Wynne family (see Map 1.4).[45]

After a brief stopover in Lisbon, Waller and the *Lancaster* departed for a final cruise to familiar ports in Mediterranean waters. On August 15, 1883, the *Lancaster* steamed out of Lisbon harbor bound for Cadiz and points east (See Map 1.5). Over the next year, Waller continued his service under Cochrane and the Marine guard in what would be his last service on the European Station. His long and varied career over the next thirty-six years would take him to assignments in the Philippines and China, and on various tours of duty in the Caribbean and South America. Waller would never serve on the European Station again.

Waller remained with the European Squadron until the end of July 1884, when a replacement contingent of Marines arrived in Lisbon aboard the sidewheel steamer *Powhatan*. Time in port proved busier than usual with packing to be done, crating up two years of purchases, inventory and transfer of government property to the new Marine guard, and, for Waller, some special personal arrangements with Miss Clara Wynne.[46]

On July 16, 1884, Captain Cochrane received orders transferring the Marine guard to the *Powhatan* effective the next day. Leaving the noncommissioned officers and sentinels at their post on the *Lancaster* "until relieved by the new guard," Cochrane and his lieutenants led the other Marines to the *Powhatan*, passing the relief contingent on the way. The men left behind soon rejoined the Marines on the *Powhatan* and with the transfer complete, Cochrane ordered Waller and Denny to rotate duty on a "day on and day off basis." While Cochrane busied himself with the paperwork and transfer obligations with the arriving Marine commander, Waller and Denny were "to inspect the companies, visit sentinels, and look after the prisoners, etc." With every other day off, the arrangement afforded Waller time to see Clara Wynne and persuade her to marry him.[47]

On July 21, Cochrane "went with Lt. Waller and Ensign Quinby to call on Mrs. Wynne and daughters and spent a very pleasant evening." All three returned to the ship by 10:00 p.m. The visit began a pattern of calls that coincided with Waller's days off. On the twenty-third, the three men once again

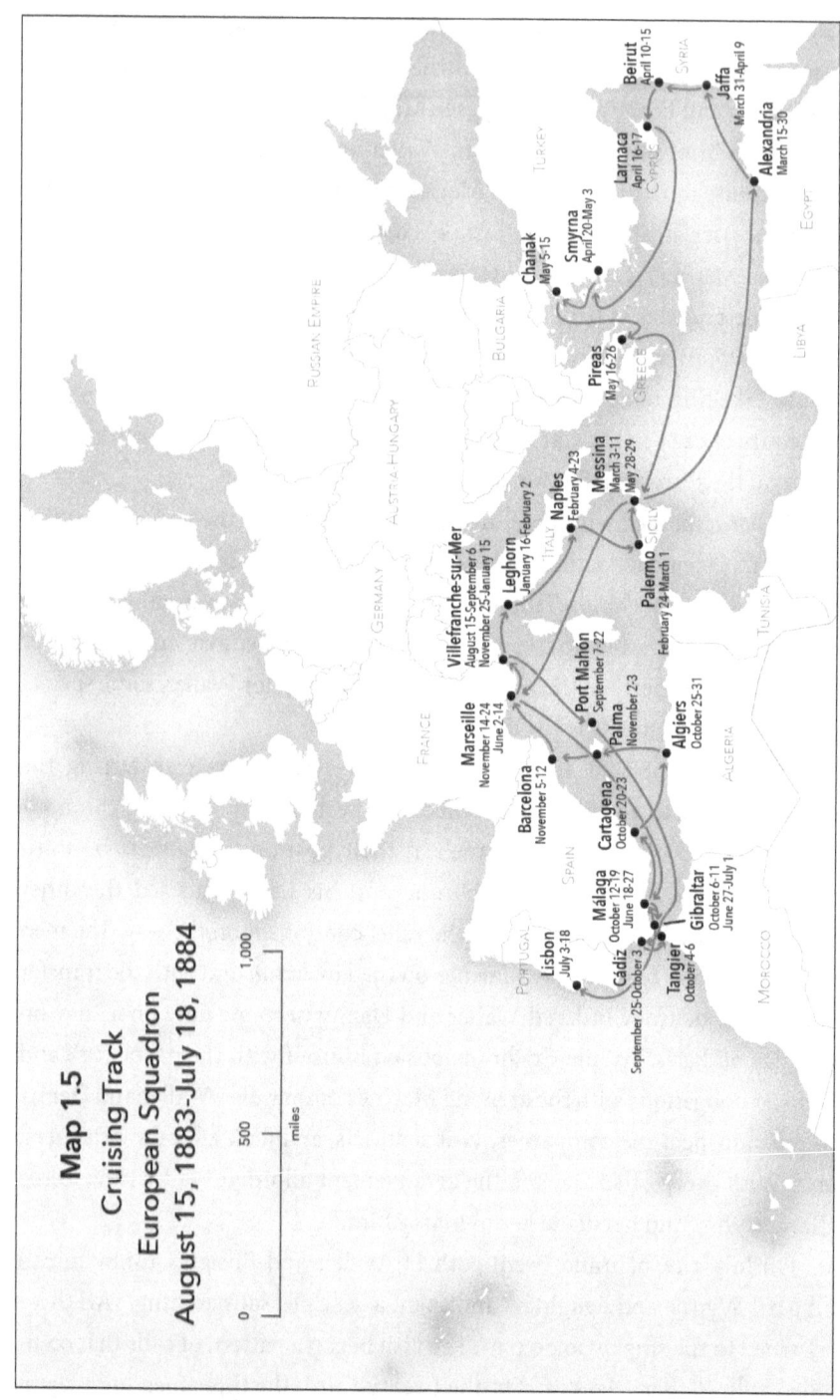

Map 1.5 Cruising Track European Squadron August 15, 1883–July 18, 1884

2nd Lt. Littleton W. T. Waller is seated on the left in the front row, others not identified, somewhere on the European Station, circa 1882–1884. *Courtesy of the Waller Family Archives.*

went ashore to see "Misses Wynne—Lulu and Clara," and since time was growing short, Waller spent as much of it as possible with Clara, knowing his departure for home was but days away.[48]

The coaling of the *Powhatan* reached the final stages on the next day. With the holds full, the men placed the remaining fuel in bags for deck stowage and completed the refueling. At 1 p.m., John Wynne arrived on board with his two daughters for a last visit, since the nearing departure limited Waller's free time. Later that evening Cochrane summoned his two lieutenants and had a "long talk with Lts. Denny and Waller on tactics in my room."

Original orders stipulated that the *Powhatan* must put to sea on July 26, but a "storm delayed sailing," giving Waller more time to work up the courage to ask Clara to marry him.

The following day during drill, Cochrane received a request from Mrs. Wynne to call at the family home. Later in the day, he found his way to the Wynne home where "Miss Clara smiling" welcomed him. Clara called her parents and sister Lulu to the door and the four of them "took me to the parlor where a most businesslike conversation ensued regarding Waller's offer of marriage to Miss Clara."⁴⁹

Two years later, Clara Waller reminisced about the Lisbon episode in a letter to Cochrane, written on occasion of Cochrane's recent marriage: "I hope I shall have the pleasure of meeting your wife before long. I shall have to tell her what an important part you played in a little affair in Lisbon some few years ago." Cochrane later wrote Clara's mother in Lisbon that he was "very glad to learn that you are yet in the cozy and tasteful home where we of the good ship *Lancaster* had the pleasure of meeting you, and delighted to be assured that my connection with the romantic family event was an incident

Painting of Lula Wynne by Clara Wynne at the home place in Lisbon, circa 1884. *Courtesy of the Waller Family Archives.*

that contributed to a great deal of happiness all around. Sunday afternoon, July 27, 1884, often recurs to me and the council then held is a most pleasant memory."[50]

Cochrane had played his part well, and Littleton Waller married Clara Wynne at the Church of the Ascencíon in New York on February 17, 1885. Cochrane later confided to Mrs. Wynne that he had seen "the contracting parties" since the Wallers had "attained the dignity of parent[hood]" and "had to accept as strictly correct the most marvelous accounts of the greatest baby on record."[51]

Cochrane remained a close family friend as well as a reliable mentor for Waller in the Corps. Waller served with Cochrane for four years, "an unusually long time" for officers in that era, and Cochrane wrote in 1887 that he was "greatly interested in [Waller] and hope someday to have him with me again, wife, baby, and all." Clara forever connected Cochrane to the "little affair in Lisbon" and would turn to him at least once for sympathy and perhaps to gain an ally in obtaining a shore assignment for her husband.[52] In 1887, Clara poured out her feelings to Cochrane as she struggled with life as the wife of a Marine officer away at sea much of the time. "I am not happy just at present, for Mr. Waller is at sea, as you probably know, and it is simply terrible to have him away." Lonely for her husband and homesick for her parents, she was "disappointed all around for at one time, it seemed so sure that he would go to the Mediterranean that I allowed my heart to be set upon going back to Lisbon. Now you know what a bitter disappointment this was," she lamented. "I got ready to start for San Francisco . . . and just as I was ready, off went the *Iroquois* to South America. So here I am, and sometimes, I just nearly die of the blues."[53]

While many of the Marine officers of the time remained unmarried, a few elected to wed early in their careers, forcing their wives to endure the difficulty most Navy officer wives confronted.[54] The Wallers were no different, and both came eventually to accept their fate. As the years passed, and despite Waller's higher rank, duty kept him and Clara apart for long periods of time as he commanded expeditions in the field and enjoyed no protracted tours in Washington or other staff assignments assuring a stable home life.

Cochrane's correspondence and diary entries during the 1880s reveal that the "social season" in Europe provided brides for several of his protégés apart from Waller. One such letter, written to Cochrane just four days before Waller's wedding, reveals the social network on the European station. "Hope that Waller has kept his promise [to Clara Wynne] . . . , she is a very nice girl, and Waller would do well to get her. By the way, the Coxes are flourishing in Nice and one inquired particularly about Waller's fiancée."[55]

Military duty, of course, proceeded regardless of any social or familial considerations, and the day finally arrived for the *Powhatan* to depart Lisbon for the United States. On July 30, Waller and Denny drilled the men in the morning while the rest of the ship's company prepared for sea. At 4:00 p.m., they "got underway and dropped down to Belem," where the *Powhatan* received powder and ammunition at 6 p.m., and at 7 p.m. the ship left Europe, bound for Madeira. Cochrane remembered that Madeira "was the first land that we saw in 1881 and the last in 1884."[56]

Upon their arrival home, Cochrane took command of the Marines at Philadelphia, and Waller returned to the Marine Barracks at Norfolk, Virginia. Waller's tour on the European Station had been a pivotal experience for him personally and professionally. Cruising into Mediterranean waters as both a bachelor and military neophyte, the young lieutenant had laid the foundation for a family as well as for an exemplary military career. Waller and Clara began a long marriage and had three exceptionally successful sons who in turn would reach flag rank in the Marines and the Navy. During the ensuing years, Waller began shaping his reputation as an officer of singular competence and courage. He had fallen into the tutelary hands of Captain Henry C. Cochrane, a commander both willing and able to trim Waller's rough edges, launching him successfully into marital and martial waters.[57]

The decade of the 1880s was indeed a defining time for Littleton Waller, as he began his career in the Marine Corps, developing early potential as an officer destined for command and greater things. But times were changing in the Corps, and Waller soon ran up against two intertwined problems destined to plague him throughout his career—his lack of a Naval Academy education and competition from the technocrats just entering the new Corps.

In 1883, just two years after Waller received his commission, a new breed of officers began arriving on the scene. Convinced that they heralded a new, modern Marine Corps, founded upon technology and professionalism, these new officers intended to relegate traditional bush fighters like Waller to the past. In his baptism of fire in Egypt, Waller had acquitted himself admirably under fire, but as the smoke cleared at Alexandria, his battles were just beginning.

CHAPTER 2

# THE EMBATTLED OLD CORPS

In 1884, Waller returned to Norfolk, Virginia, where he began his Marine Corps career. Over his forty-year career, Waller would often be ordered to Norfolk's Marine Barracks, and he found it pleasant to work at home with family nearby. After four years at sea, Waller eagerly renewed acquaintances in his hometown and got down to the business of garrison duty. The Marine officer corps remained small before the turn of the century,[1] and advancement continued to be competitive within the organization. Frank L. Denny, with whom Waller served in the Mediterranean, had been posted to the Marine Barracks at Portsmouth, New Hampshire, and had been promoted to first lieutenant ahead of Waller. So Waller had his professional work cut out for him, but his first concern was for his fiancée, Clara Wynne, who would sail from Lisbon in late January, and preparing for their wedding scheduled for February 16, 1885, in New York City.[2]

Waller's mother, Mary Waller, had been making plans for the new couple for months. Two months before Clara's expected arrival in New York, Mary wrote her a lengthy mother-to-daughter letter. Mary described herself as a "very plain matter of fact old mother" and revealed to Clara that "I expect to spend much of my time with you until you get used to our ways." Her letter detailed the plans underway for Clara's arrival in Norfolk. "Littleton and I have had many talks of you and are planning for your reception." Waller had been looking for a suitable place for their first home and found an "entire floor" two blocks from the Granby house, close so "that when he is on duty, I can be with you or you with me." Mary described the house in detail, which included "four rooms, the kitchen, and a cellar room." Close to a number of Waller's relatives, the house "is near the church and over Dr. Linstall's office and the street cars run not far off." As for servants, Waller planned to hire only one for his wife, and Mary assured her that "I think I can get a good one, that one will be all" she would need, "and when you come to know the worry of these same darkies, you will be glad to have no more."

Mary's letter made clear that Clara soon would enter the southern aristocracy's way of life, founded on the culture of the antebellum past. In the years that followed, Clara adapted to the life of the southern military wife, moving in and out of Norfolk society where she fell easily into the rhythm of the changes that the Marine Corps brought to her and her family. Little is known of Clara's reaction to Mary's premarital counsel, but in the short time she lived under Mary's wing, she grew to admire and care for her mother-in-law.³

Clara Wynne took passage from Lisbon, crossed the English Channel, and eventually reached Liverpool. There she boarded the three-masted barque *Gallia*, a Cunard passenger vessel accommodating 300 first class passengers in "luxurious two-berth" staterooms, with limited space available for "1200 steerage passengers and 2,000 tons of cargo." Despite the lavish appointments, the *Gallia* "was fitted with only two baths for the entire ship," making life aboard ship difficult in the best of times. Clara and her fellow passengers faced a long winter voyage through ice-infested waters in the

S.S. *Gallia* at sea. *Courtesy of the Waller Family Archives.*

Clara Wynne, circa 1884. *Courtesy of the Waller Family Archives.*

North Atlantic where disaster often lurked just below the surface. Not long after they left the British Isles, "a series of violent westerly gales set in." In the days that followed, conditions grew worse as the ship encountered "another heavy gale, which came with scarcely any warning and increased into a perfect cyclone." As the *Gallia* struggled through heavy seas for the next twenty-four hours, "the cyclone raged with great fury." As the vessel cut through the blustery waves, nearby ships sighted icebergs across the westerly route, but Clara's vessel reported no such sightings and sailed through the danger zone without mishap. The captain reported later that "after the storms came extremely cold winds with sleet and snow." The *Gallia* "became covered with a coating of ice three inches thick, and the passengers were obliged to remain below" for most of the journey. Arriving in New York on February 12, two days late, Clara and the other passengers disembarked while Cunard officials quickly made ready for a return voyage.[4]

Five days after arriving in New York, Clara Wynne married Littleton Waller at the Church of the Ascension, and the couple spent the next four weeks honeymooning and then settling into their new home in Norfolk. Before leaving for Virginia, Waller and his new bride called on Captain Cochrane at his home in Chester, Pennsylvania. "I have only seen the contracting parties [Waller and Clara] once since [serving with him on the *Lancaster*] and that was en route from New York to Norfolk the day of the wedding," Cochrane later wrote Clara's mother, Martha Wynne. Over the next several years, Cochrane continued to mentor the young Waller from a distance. Cochrane maintained correspondence with Waller on professional matters and with the couple as a close family friend and confidant.[5]

## CHANGING CAREER PATTERNS IN THE CORPS

During these first five years of his career, Waller had need of an advisor, for the Navy and the Marine Corps had entered a period of transition. Perhaps the most striking change came with the shift in commissions to the Corps from the Naval Academy,[6] producing two sharply defined groups of officers (Figures 1 and 2).[7] No Academy graduates had been commissioned in the Marine Corps from 1861 to 1880.[8] Although a few students who failed to complete the Annapolis course of study did receive commissions in the Corps, the bulk of the appointments went to men unconnected to the

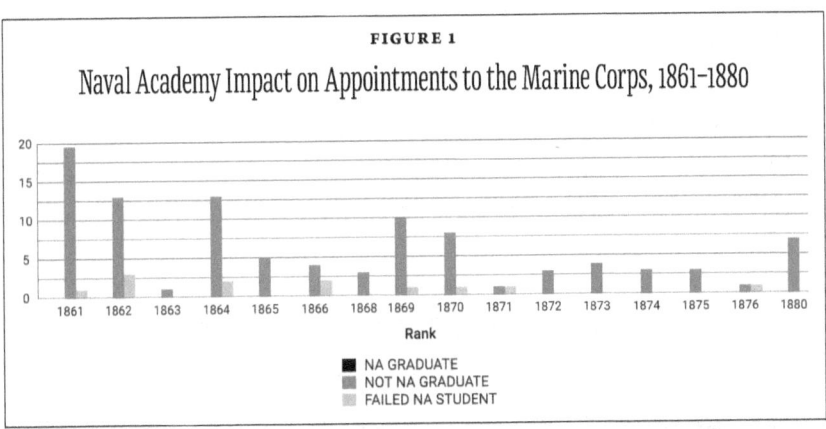

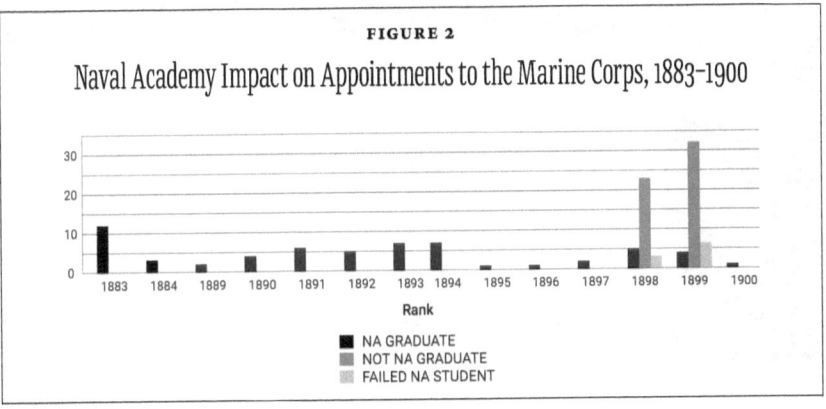

Academy, mostly sons of military officers or those with political influence. Waller's 1880 commission followed this pattern, but that practice would soon change, with profound implications for Waller's future.[9]

Beginning with 1883, shortly after the passage of the Naval Appropriation Act of August 5, 1882, twelve freshly minted graduates[10] of the Naval Academy received commissions as second lieutenants in the Marine Corps, and the new appointment pattern eliminated non–Academy graduates as Marine officers (Figure 2).

Later, however, the demands of the war with Spain and other American expansionist policies created additional shifts, and the Corps began to absorb large numbers of volunteer officers. "The Spanish-American War brought a number of volunteer or 'militia' officers into the [naval] Service for the duration, but their careers were extremely precarious—and brief,"[11] but this was not true in the Marine Corps.

A total of seventy-three officers received commissions from 1898–1900 (Figure 3). The two non–Naval Academy graduate groups totaled sixty-three, and 42.8 percent (twenty-seven officers) of these stayed in the Marine Corps and achieved the rank of colonel or above by the end of their career. Eleven officers of the non-Academy career track achieved general grade, six reaching

**FIGURE 3**

### Naval Academy Impact on Highest Rank Attained During Career in Marine Corps Officers Commissioned, 1989-1900

| | 2 LT | 1 LT | CAPT | MAJOR | LT COL | COL | BGEN | MGEN | OVERALL TOTALS |
|---|---|---|---|---|---|---|---|---|---|
| NA GRADUATE | 0 | 0 | 3 | 2 | 0 | 3 | 1 | 1 | 10 |
| NOT NA GRADUATE | 9 | 3 | 8 | 7 | 3 | 14 | 5 | 5 | 54 |
| FAILED NA STUDENT | 1 | 2 | 0 | 2 | 1 | 2 | 0 | 1 | 9 |
| TOTALS BY RANK | 10 | 5 | 11 | 11 | 4 | 19 | 6 | 7 | 73 |

the grade of major general. Naval Academy-based officers from this era, however, boasted only two general officers.

The Spanish-American War triggered a postwar expansion of the officer corps that once again reached beyond the Naval Academy. Expeditionary duty, colonial activity, expanded naval operations, and World War I increased opportunities for Marine veterans of the Spanish-American War, while expanded personnel authorizations made room for newcomers as well. During those years following the war with Spain, the advantage shifted from the Naval Academy graduates, at least for the next two decades, but these trends had no impact on Waller or his generation. His competition continued to be drawn from those entering the Corps before 1897.[12]

By the end of the nineteenth century, three categories of Marine officers, Academy graduates, non-Academy graduates, and failed Academy students, comprised two main groups in the officer corps. Of these three categories, Waller represented one group, whom we might call the Old Corps, comprised of those who did not attend the Academy or were failed Academy students who did not graduate. Opposing the Old Corps were the Academy graduates. Each group overlapped the other in service and each group competed for choice assignments and promotion to the four highest positions available—namely colonel, brigadier general, major general, and commandant of the Marine Corps.[13] This struggle triggered a class conflict between the two groups that gained intensity and fervor as the Naval Academy graduates assumed positions of leadership. In this instance, the term "class conflict" applies not to two groups where one is acknowledged as dominant with the subordinate group recognizing and contesting that dominance; rather both groups argued for supremacy, each viewing the opposing cadre as a threat to the survival of the Corps. Waller, a typical example, envisioned no scenario whereby the Academy graduates could assume any satisfactory role in the Corps. He rejected the Academy officer who could not point to years of development in the field mentored by seasoned officers or could not demonstrate a record of success and accomplishment leading men. The Academy officers, in turn, viewed the old warriors with disdain, judging men such as Waller as obsolete in the new technological, professional Marine Corps and thus having no role to play.

An examination of individual careers reveals patterns in promotion that reflect the growing power of the Academy graduates and explains the frustration and bitterness of officers like Waller, as the political war fought at headquarters in Washington eroded the long-established criteria for success. Field experience, enviable combat records, mission success rates, leadership by example, and loyalty to these precepts and to the Corps proved to be of little value when faced with a competitor equipped with an Academy education and a support network enlivened by Naval Academy ties and friends in high places.

The promotion patterns for all three categories commissioned during the four decades before 1900 reveals that the bulk of the non–Academy graduated officers left service as captains or lower (Figure 4).[14] Officers who served in the Civil War or in the Spanish-American War conflicts made up many these positions, however, and never seriously contemplated a career in the military. Most left service as soon as the national emergency dissipated. The inclusion of so many noncareer officers in the data renders it difficult to judge the relative status of the two groups. But by deleting all officers who received their commissions during the Civil War or Spanish-American War eras, it is possible to survey officers who likely made reasonable attempts to establish a career for themselves in the Marine Corps.

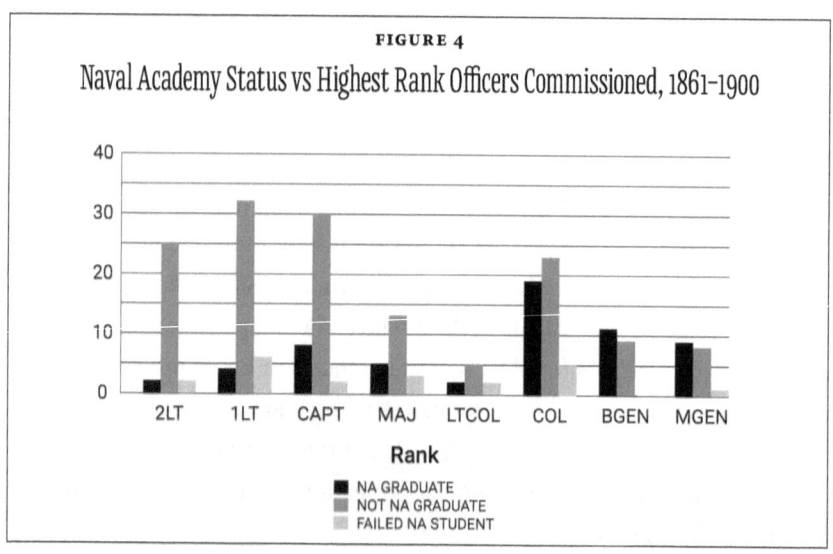

The officer group, when adjusted to eliminate the Civil War and Spanish conflict officers, includes only those commissioned during the period 1866 to 1897—the non–Naval Academy segment (1866–1882) and the Naval Academy portion (1883–1897). In this analysis, the overwhelming domination of the Academy graduates over Waller and his group becomes obvious. With the officers of the two war eras eliminated from the population, both remaining groups were relatively equal in size (Naval Academy fifty officers, non–Naval Academy fifty two officers)[15] and in appointment dominance—that is, the number of years each group dominated the appointment process[16] (Naval Academy fifteen years, non–Naval Academy eighteen years) (see Figure 5).[17]

In career outcomes of the modified group, the Naval Academy graduates excelled in every comparative category, including those reaching high rank cluster (colonel or higher).[18] In the general grade outcomes, eighteen Naval Academy graduates reached brigadier or major general as opposed to only four nongraduates.[19] Adding in colonels to the categories for general, the resulting totals maintain a ratio of about four to one (thirty-four to eight). Non-Academy officers like Waller who were commissioned after 1866 had only a slim probability of achieving promotion to the highest grades, although Waller proved an exception, reaching major general shortly before his retirement in 1920.

The bulk of the non-Academy officers finished significantly lower than their Academy counterparts in their quest for military achievement. During the years following the Civil War through 1897 on the eve of the Spanish American War, slightly over 73 percent ended their careers in the junior rank cluster; only 7.6 percent reached the middle rank cluster; fewer than 20 percent achieved high rank cluster (Figure 5); and only two officers received appointments as commandant.[20] After George Barnett's selection over Waller in 1914, no non-Academy officers from the 1866-1882 group attained the commandant's office; the next five commandants came from Naval Academy classes of 1883, 1890, 1891, 1892, and 1894.

As officers reached maturity within the ranks, other indications of Academy ascendancy threatened officers lacking an Academy background. Waller and other southerners were part of a shifting regional matrix wherein the North and the Midwest/West sections of the country began producing more

**FIGURE 5**

## Naval Academy Impact on Highest Rank Attained (War Era Officers Excluded), Officers Commissioned, 1866–1897

|  | 2 LT | 1 LT | CAPT | MAJOR | LT COL | COL | BGEN | MGEN | OVERALL TOTALS |
|---|---|---|---|---|---|---|---|---|---|
| NA GRADUATE | 2 | 4 | 5 | 3 | 2 | 16 | 10 | 8 | 50 |
| NOT NA GRADUATE | 11 | 17 | 7 | 1 | 2 | 4 | 1 | 3 | 46 |
| FAILED NA STUDENT | 0 | 2 | 1 | 0 | 1 | 2 | 0 | 0 | 6 |
| TOTALS BY RANK | 13 | 23 | 13 | 4 | 5 | 22 | 11 | 11 | 102 |

successful officers.[21] Figure 6 illustrates the regional breakdown by Naval Academy status.[22] Regardless of status, whether graduate, nongraduate, or a failed Naval Academy student, all three groups exhibit trends away from the South as the source for Marine officers. For Waller and other southerners aspiring to leadership positions within the Corps, a southern background provided little support in contrast to how it may have been in antebellum times.

Promotion to higher rank in the Marine Corps thus reflected both Naval Academy status and regional origins. These new regional patterns impacted officers achieving colonel as their highest rank (Figure 7),[23] as at no time did the South dominate at the colonel level. Certainly, the departure of southerners for service in the Confederacy[24] accounts for the low numbers in the period before 1883, yet that trend held up during the Naval Academy and the post-1898 war eras as well.

In the group achieving the greatest success in the Corps, those reaching general grade (this group includes those appointed commandant), a shift occurred away from northern dominance to the introduction of a strong western influence. Part of the explanation rests with the dramatic domestic expansion and westward movement taking place during the last decades of the

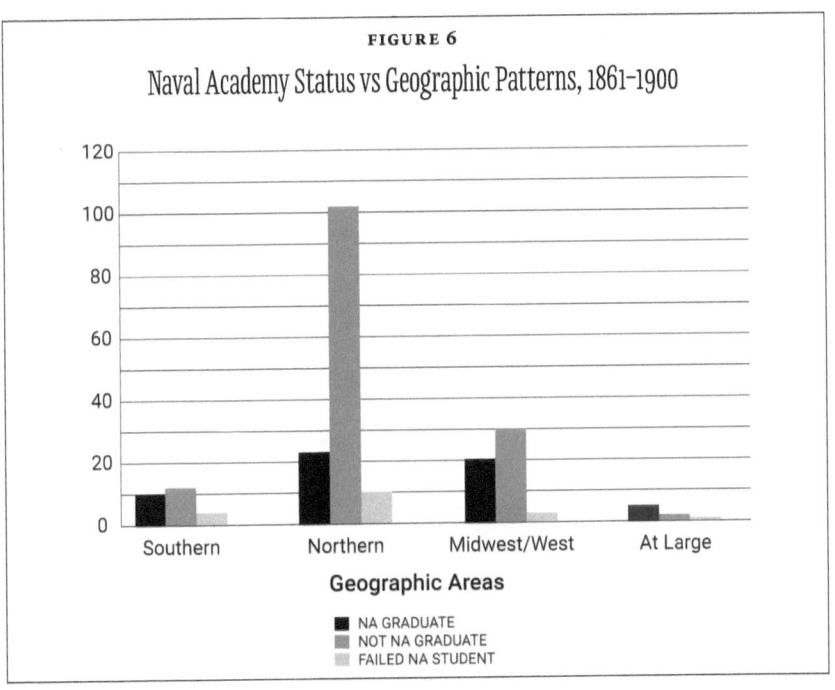

**FIGURE 6**
Naval Academy Status vs Geographic Patterns, 1861–1900

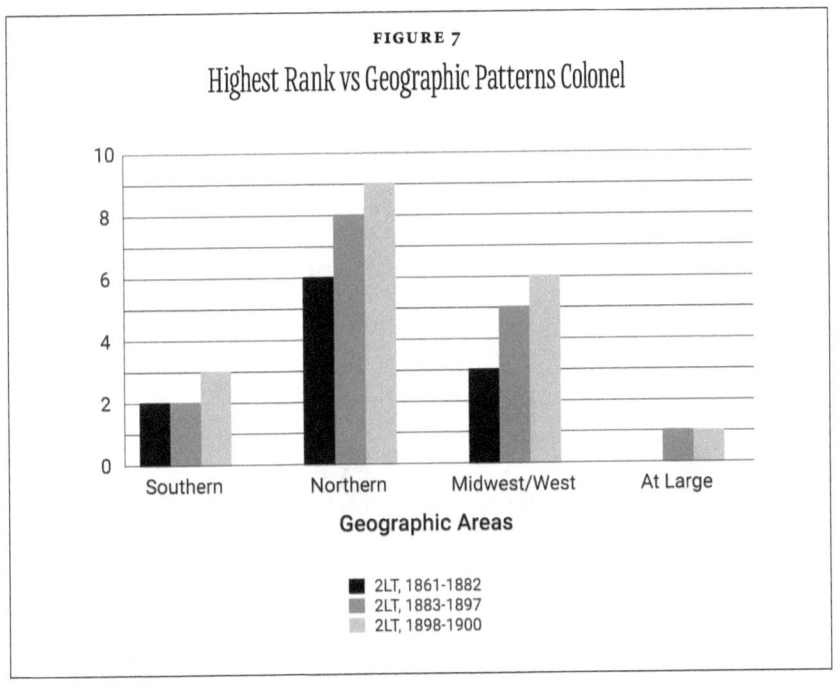

**FIGURE 7**
Highest Rank vs Geographic Patterns Colonel

nineteenth century. By 1890, the West was settled, with a population base concentrated in urban centers in the northeast, and in mining, cattle, and farming regions throughout the western states and territories. Economic incentives drew populations into the New West during the late nineteenth century and contributed to the availability of men from other than the eastern regions.

Western areas now competed with northern states for the most successful

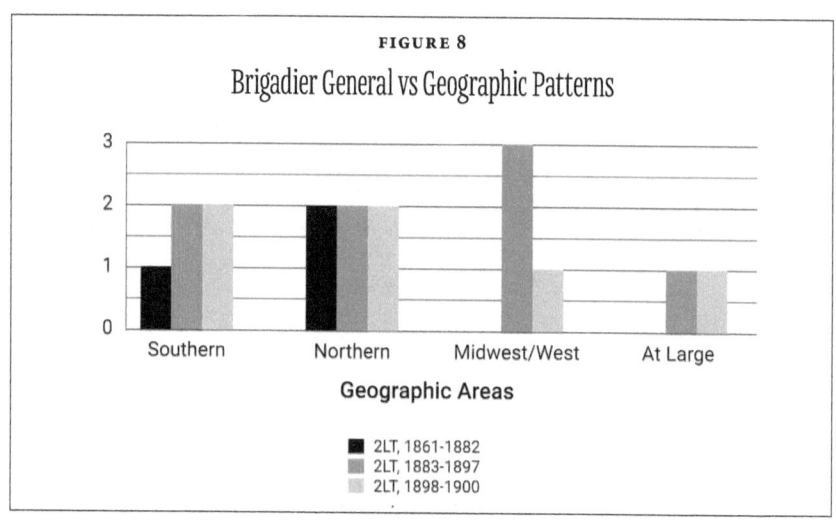

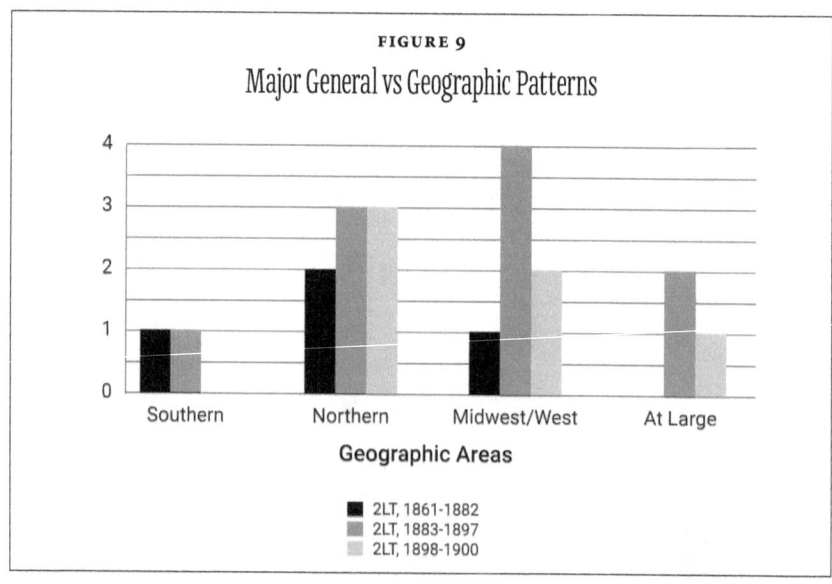

officers, particularly in the group of Naval Academy officers commissioned before 1898 (see Figures 8 and 9).[25] This sector influenced the Corps heavily for several decades into the twentieth century, as the first men began to emerge as generals before World War I.

Waller viewed these developments with deepening rancor. His frustration with the Naval Academy crowd surfaced throughout his career, but the resentment intensified after his service in Asia and his court-martial for murder in the Philippines in 1901. Despite his broad based success as an emerging officer, Waller understood the changing dynamics in the Corps but remained resolute in his quest for success in the field and recognition from Headquarters.

Against this backdrop of transition within the Marine officer corps, Waller reported to the Marine Barracks at Norfolk and settled into garrison duty routine for the next two years. He and Clara established their new home a few blocks from his mother, while Waller began to build upon the lessons learned from Cochrane during his European tour of duty. Serving under Colonel James Forney at Norfolk, Waller gained additional experience working with men, performing officer-of-the-day duties, conducting training in company and battalion drills, overseeing target practice, supervising signal class, and assuming various other garrison duties.

## BACK TO NORFOLK AND BEYOND

These Norfolk years proved productive for Waller as he established his reputation for efficient garrison work with yet another veteran Marine, while at the same time engaging in the pleasant Norfolk social life brought by his membership in the Tazewell family. With but one brief temporary assignment to Brooklyn in New York, Waller enjoyed his shore assignment at home in Norfolk with his new wife and surrounded by family. During his career he would frequently return to Norfolk, often for long assignments between sea duty, a common practice for Marines in that era.

On September 18, 1886, Waller's first son was born in Norfolk, and Waller carried on the family tradition by naming him Littleton Waller Tazewell Waller, Jr. That same September, Waller received orders promoting him to first lieutenant. Colonel James Forney, commanding the Marine Barracks

Clara Waller with son, Littleton W. T. Waller Jr., circa 1887–1888. *Courtesy of the Waller Family Archives.*

at Norfolk, rated Waller's professional ability as "excellent" as Waller continued to put into practice lessons learned under Cochrane, fine tuning his grasp of the fundamentals of field work and leadership.[26]

Later that fall, just a few days before Christmas, Waller's mother, Mary Waller, died "at her residence on Granby Street," surrounded by her children and family. The obituary eulogized her in simple terms, noting that as the daughter of Governor Tazewell of Virginia, Mary Waller "possessed the traits that mark the character of a truly Christian woman and many persons will miss the kind charities that she was always so willing to extend to those in need." The family gathered at the Granby Street mansion for the funeral, and for Waller, it proved a sad farewell to his mother who soon would be followed by his ever-attentive aunts. As one stage of his life came to an end, another began. Orders soon came ordering Waller to sea, a regular

Mary Waller shortly before her death, Norfolk, Virginia, circa early 1880s. *Courtesy of the Waller Family Archives.*

requirement for Marine officers of his day. While Clara dreaded the long separations, eventually she grew to accept them as a necessary part of their life in the Marines.[27]

On April 28, 1887, Waller wrote the commandant requesting to "be informed of my position on the roster for sea; also if there is any probability of my orders being sent next month." On May 14, Waller received orders to report on board the aging steam sloop of war *Iroquois*, a Civil War–era vessel patrolling Pacific waters, "protecting American interests and commerce." On May 20, Waller said his goodbyes to Clara and the family and left Norfolk for the journey to Panama, and the next day, sailed on the Pacific Mail Steamship passenger liner *Newport*. The voyage took him down the Atlantic Coast and through the Caribbean, arriving at Aspinwall, Panama (renamed Colón in 1890), on May 29. The next day, Waller crossed over to Panama Bay on the Pacific Coast and reported aboard the *Iroquois*, where he took command of the Marine Guard on May 31. The cruise on the *Iroquois* provided Waller an opportunity to demonstrate leadership skills and be judged by his performance.[28]

Reminiscent of his cruise on the *Lancaster* and the *Nipsic* on the Mediterranean under Cochrane, the patrol along South America's west coast brought Waller new opportunities for travel and discovery, this time in the Western Hemisphere. Although diplomacy and showing the flag were important missions for the *Iroquois*, Waller filled his days with routine drill, training, and work with his men. Lacking the importance and proximity to European centers of power, Waller's assignment took him into the backwaters of Latin America, expanding his experience to the Hispanic world where he would often find himself in the years ahead. Determined to put his mark on the ship's guard, Waller wasted no time in getting to work.

"I find that the Marine Guard . . . has been without Field Music since May 1885, and the men know nothing about skirmishes and other signals," wrote Waller in a letter to Commandant McCawley on his first full day on board the *Iroquois*. He requested that "the guard may be completed by the addition of a drummer and a trumpeter." Waller noted that the rifles then in use by the guard were "of obsolete pattern" and many were not serviceable. He immediately sent a requisition for new rifles to the quartermaster and included an explanation for the request in his letter to McCawley. "We are

The USS *Iroquois*, a sloop of war (1859–1910) at Mare Island, California, in 1890, two years after Waller left the ship. *Courtesy of U.S. Naval History and Heritage Command.*

very much in need both of Field Music and rifles" and indicated that the *Iroquois* would "probably remain here [Panama Bay] for several weeks." Two weeks later McCawley's reply reached Waller.²⁹

The commandant approved Waller's requests for musicians and new rifles for the guard but voiced his concern about the expense of making those changes at Panama Bay. McCawley informed Waller that the *Iroquois* would soon reach Mare Island Navy Yard and that "I can order two [musicians] from

1st Lt. Littleton W. T. Waller, circa late 1880s. *Courtesy of the Waller Family Archives.*

that post, and the arms can easily be exchanged without expense." Meanwhile, Waller set about molding the guard into an efficient unit, taking care to apply the tenets of Cochrane, who hammered home the lesson that an officer owed his primary responsibility to his men. From these beginnings, Waller established his reputation as a field commander adept in the training and equipping of men to accomplish a mission.³⁰

The *Iroquois* remained at Panama Bay until June 27 when the sloop cast away all lines and set sail for Peru. During the following months, Waller followed a pattern reminiscent of the *Lancaster* on the Mediterranean: the normal routine of drill and quarters while at sea, marked with social visits on board from diplomats and members of the American community at the ports of call. Ashore, Waller toured local venues, hunted, and played tennis. On board, Waller spent much of his free time writing letters to his wife and painting pictures of the local scenes and the *Iroquois* that he presented to friends.

On March 6, 1888, Waller transferred ashore at Mare Island in San Francisco, California, for a month before receiving new orders to return to the east coast. In evaluation of Waller's service on the *Iroquois*, the ship's captain Commander Richard P. Leary gave Waller high marks, describing Waller's professional ability during the cruise as of "very high order." He further appreciated Waller's "very efficient instruction and work with the guard."³¹

Waller waited at Mare Island for orders that soon came designating him for service on the *Pensacola*, a vintage three-masted screw steamer and veteran of the Civil War, then inbound for New York from a long stint on the European Station. Waller entrained for the Brooklyn Navy Yard, arriving there on March 31, 1888, and immediately began organizing the Marine Guard, requesting new personnel, and dealing with discipline problems. The USS *Pensacola*, scheduled to become the flagship for the Atlantic Squadron, required major repairs before it could take up its place in the fleet. To Waller's delight, the *Pensacola* moved to the Norfolk Navy Yard for the repairs, where he found himself once again at home. It soon became apparent that the repairs would take some months and "no men will be sent to her until she is fit for sea." Waller spent the remainder of the summer working with the guard and in late August "requested one month's leave of absence" beginning September

5. Waller transferred ashore, reporting for duty to Commodore George Brown, commanding the Norfolk Navy Yard, and a few days later, he began his leave.[32]

With the delay in repairs for the *Pensacola*, Waller knew that he would be reassigned, and soon after returning to duty, he wrote headquarters to "kindly inform me how I stand on the sea roster?" He noted that if his time was "near," he requested duty aboard the new USS *Yorktown*, a steel-hulled, twin-screw gunboat protected by an armored deck. Until that time, Waller had served all his sea duty on Civil War–era ships, obsolete vessels that by the end of the century were ready for retirement. Beginning in the 1880s, the United States initiated an aggressive ship building program that soon produced the New Steel Navy. The *Yorktown* was one of many new ships that would join the fleet during the next decade. Waller was anxious for a posting to one of these modern warships, but his next cruise would take him down the east coast of South America aboard two Civil War–era ships. Yet unknown to him, fate held still another opportunity to lead Marines into the midst of chaos and revolution. Argentina waited.[33]

On November 1, 1888, Waller joined the *Kearsarge* at Portsmouth, New Hampshire, where it had been commissioned over twenty-seven years earlier. Waller's orders called for him to organize a replacement guard for the *Tallapoosa*, a wooden-hulled, double-ended steamer, the flagship for the South Atlantic Squadron, then cruising along the South American east coast. The *Kearsarge* would deliver Waller and his replacement guard to their new station on the *Tallapoosa*. The old *Kearsarge* spent much of the 1880s in Europe and had returned to Portsmouth for decommissioning in 1886. During the following two years, the vessel received a much-needed overhaul and renovation. One day after Waller arrived in Portsmouth, the *Kearsarge* was recommissioned and spent its remaining years in Latin American waters. On board the *Kearsarge*, Waller assembled the replacement guard for the *Tallapoosa*. Three months later, on January 31, 1889, the *Kearsarge* appeared at Montevideo, Uruguay, where Waller transferred his men to the *Tallapoosa*, relieving the Marine guard on that vessel.[34]

Through the spring of 1889, Waller drilled the guard while the flagship cruised along the eastern coast of South America. Unfortunately, the ship's "rock shaft was broken on the 28th of May last and she was towed in to

The USS *Tallapoosa* (1864–1892), a 1173-ton Sassacus-class "double-ender" gunboat, at the Portsmouth Navy Yard, Kittery, Maine, circa 1886, following her final rebuilding. Waller joined the Tallapoosa with a replacement Marine guard at Montevideo, Uruguay, three years later. *Courtesy of U.S. Naval History and Heritage Command.*

USS *Kearsarge* in New York in 1890, just returned from Montevideo, Uruguay, after making rendezvous with the *Tallapoosa*. *Courtesy of U.S. Naval History and Heritage Command.*

Buenos Aires." While officials in Washington vacillated on what to do about repairs, Waller and his men took the opportunity to visit the capital city. During this respite, however, a number of the men deserted, leaving Waller to struggle with an understrength guard beset with low morale and a high rate of drunkenness and other petty offences for the rest of the cruise. Waller inherited the Marine guard and its problems when he joined the *Tallapoosa*. Many years later, Rear Admiral Caspar Frederick Goodrich, who served as executive officer of the *Lancaster* in 1882 with Waller, wrote about the rising problems of desertion and discipline aboard ships. Goodrich suggested that any increase in desertion rates suggests "that things are not quite right on board" the ship. He argued that in such cases there is usually one or more reasons for the breakdown in leadership. Goodrich reasoned "that discipline is slack or uneven," or that daily meals were substandard. Other contributing causes could be "that the men are subjected to unnecessary nagging; or that the administration of justice is harsh and arbitrary." Goodrich concluded that the ship's captain was ultimately responsible. Whatever the specific cause for the lapse in discipline on the *Tallapoosa*, Waller soon had an opportunity to put his leadership into action. While the *Tallapoosa* waited in Buenos Aires for repairs, tension onshore rose as revolutionary elements began to move against the Argentine government.[35]

"The revolution began on the 26 of July at 3 a.m. in the artillery barracks on Plaza Lavalle. The fighting in that neighborhood was fast and furious" throughout the rest of the day. Government regiments moved forward "to oppose the insurgents," but the insurgents "marched over to them and towards evening" many government forces had joined the rebellion. By the end of the day, the insurgents had incorporated "all the artillery, some cavalry, the engineers, and two or three regiments of the line" along with assorted groups of cadets and noncommissioned officers from a nearby training facility. Over the next two days the revolutionaries joined battle with loyalist troops and the police who "were hated by the troops and by the citizens." The uprising enjoyed broad public support, with the police and the army hard-pressed to defend themselves. Against this backdrop, captains from the *Tallapoosa* and several vessels from England, Spain, Italy, and Uruguay conferred and laid plans to protect their citizens and diplomats ashore.[36]

On July 27, the violence spread to the streets and insurgent vessels bombarded the city, triggering action from the foreign vessels anchored in the harbor. Waller landed his guard "for the protection of the American Consulate and the residence of the Minister, John R. G. Pitkin." Uncertain conditions, with fighting throughout the city and artillery raining down everywhere, created havoc and fires. Waller's thoughts must have returned to Alexandria as he positioned his Marines in much the same way Cochrane had done at Alexandria in 1882. The revolution was smaller and the danger less widespread, but Waller and his Marines were ashore protecting American interests as Marines had done before in Argentina's revolutionary past. A few days later on the twenty-ninth, a signal appeared on a government building "stating the 'Peace has been proclaimed.'" As insurgents saw the signal, "in a mysterious manner, the rebellion ceased." The next day Waller brought the Marines back on board the *Tallapoosa*, and the city slowly returned to normal. Waller recorded no attacks on his men, no looters captured, no graves dug in the lee of the consulate wall, but the Marines had their moments with wild artillery barrages and pitched street battles raging around them.[37]

For Waller it was an exciting conclusion to an otherwise uneventful cruise. In October, he made plans to join his wife and young son in Portugal, "I respectfully request permission to remain one month in Europe dating from the time of my arrival in Lisbon. Please forward reply to me at No. 69 Riva Nova de Francisco de Paula, Lisbon, Portugal." Waller's long sea duty had finally come to an end. In late November 1890, he sailed from Argentina for Lisbon where Clara and young Littleton waited. It was Waller's first visit to Clara's Lisbon home since his courting days. The leave passed quickly and soon Waller, Clara, son Littleton, and sister-in-law Lulu Wynne boarded the *Gallia* in January 1891 for the voyage to New York. For Clara, the voyage held special memories. Just six years earlier she had boarded the *Gallia* alone for the trip to America and a new life, but this time a growing family accompanied her.

## MILITARY LAW

For the Wallers, the return to Norfolk began a four-year period of transition. The next year a second son, John Beresford Wynne Waller, was born, and

Left to right, clockwise: Clara Waller, Littleton W. T. Waller, Jr., Littleton W. T. Waller, John Beresford Waller, Norfolk, Virginia, circa 1894. *Courtesy of the Waller Family Archives.*

Waller family photograph taken in front of their Norfolk home, circa 1894. Back row, Littleton W. T. Waller, Clara Wynne Waller. Front row, John Beresford Waller, age 2 and Littleton W. T. Waller Jr., age 8. *Courtesy of Waller Family Archives.*

surrounded by his growing family, Waller made an important career decision that would illuminate his talent for strategy and staff work. Aware of the growing competition from Naval Academy graduates, Waller decided to study law to enhance his professional prospects. The strategy bore fruit, even bringing him to the attention of the solicitor general in an appearance before the U.S. Supreme Court.[38]

After returning to Norfolk, Waller enrolled in a yearlong study of law at Norwood College in Nelson County, Virginia, some 160 miles away. Marine Corps records do not reveal leave or special assignments for Waller during this period, so it is probable that he read for the law under a prescribed program laid down by Norwood, a common practice in legal circles during those times. Although Waller received no degree or certificate of completion, in November 1895, both the federal District Court and Circuit Court in the Eastern District of Virginia admitted him to the bar and certified that Waller was "qualified as an Advocate and Proctor" in both jurisdictions.

In the years before 1895, Waller had served on court-martial panels during his tours of duty, but it is not known if such assignments prompted his interest in the law. It seems likely that he saw law as an avenue of enhancement for his professional development as an officer. By 1895, the numbers of Naval Academy graduates had reached significant levels, and expertise in law provided Waller another means of competing with the growing number of officers in the Marines who enjoyed not only the Naval Academy fraternity but also a university education—neither of which Waller possessed.[39]

Apart from service on court-martial boards, for a time in the early 1890s, it appeared that Waller was building a reputation for himself in law beyond the military. In June 1894, Legh R. Page, an attorney in Richmond and Waller's first cousin, employed Waller to assist in the "matter of one cotton claim" for cotton seized by the government. While Waller engaged in this sort of limited consultant work outside the Marine Corps, he continued to sit on general courts-martial as part of his assignment to Marine Barracks at Norfolk. After a month's leave in September 1894, Waller received orders for the most important case of his legal career.[40]

Irregularities in the pay department on the USS *Franklin*, an aging frigate, then the receiving ship for the Norfolk Station, prompted the Secretary of the Navy to order an official inquiry. The investigation centered on Pay Clerk David B. Sayre, who served under Paymaster James E. Cann, who "besides being paymaster of the *Franklin*, was paymaster at Port Royal, S.C. and for the monitors at Richmond, Virginia," leaving Sayre unsupervised a few days each month while Cann traveled to the other stations. Following Sayre's arrest on October 10, Cann took charge of the investigation, and three days later, Waller received orders to serve on the court of inquiry. He reported for duty as judge advocate (prosecutor) in the case on October 16, the day the inquiry convened.[41]

For the next three days Waller worked with Cann to present the investigation's findings and argued that there were sufficient grounds for a court-martial. Three days later, the court "recommended that he [Sayre] be tried by court-martial on the charge of embezzlement." Waller received orders the same day to report to the Navy's advocate general for duty in the court-martial scheduled for October 30. The accusation of embezzlement charged that Sayre had "knowingly and willfully misappropriate[d], and appl[ied] to his own use and benefit" funds issued to him by Cann in "the sum of $1,971.11, in violation of Article 14 of the articles for the government of the Navy." Waller presented the government's case, and the court found Sayre guilty, sentencing him to two years confinement, loss of $2,210 in pay, and "then to be dishonorably dismissed from the naval service of the United States." When the trial ended on November 3, Waller returned to duty at the Marine Barracks while the defense prepared to appeal to the Eastern District Circuit Court in an effort to remove the case from military jurisdiction. For Waller, the Sayre case had barely begun.[42]

Sayre's attorneys successfully argued in Circuit Court that he had been held and tried without the benefit of presentment or indictment by a grand jury, a situation allowed only in time of war. The court agreed and issued a writ of habeas corpus, ordering Sayre "discharged from custody." Such finding by the Circuit Court called into question the practices and jurisdiction of military law then in place. Secretary of the Navy Hilary A. Herbert warned of the consequences if the decision were not reversed: "If the principles enunciated in this opinion are correct, very material modification should at once be made in the methods of the administration of justice in the navy, and it would seem, in the army as well." Herbert urged the attorney general to appeal the case, suggesting that Waller "confer with and render such further assistance to the United States Attorney [Francis R. Lassiter]" as needed in the appeal. On December 14, Lassiter and Waller filed an assignment of error with the Circuit Court, seeking a reversal of the earlier decision. Judge Robert W. Hughes handed down the final finding confirming Sayre's appeal and ordering his release. The government immediately appealed the decision to the U.S. Supreme Court.[43]

The government's case shifted to the Department of Justice in Washington, and Lassiter recommended Waller to Solicitor General Lawrence Maxwell, Jr., who replied that "it would be agreeable to me personally to have Lieutenant Waller appear with me in the Supreme Court in the argument of the case." Still Maxwell harbored certain doubts. "I do not know how that can be accomplished in view of the rules of the court." He promised to submit a motion to the Supreme Court requesting that Waller be "allowed to appear as counsel before the court" in the Sayre case. Maxwell, however, left office before this could be done and his successor, Holmes Conrad, made the motion to admit Waller as counsel.[44]

During January 1895, Waller worked on the case, and Conrad soon submitted a motion in Waller's behalf to the Supreme Court. It would be Conrad who would oversee Waller's baptism of fire before the high court and who would give him unusual opportunities, a course of action based on Lassiter and Maxwell's confidence in Waller's talent. Conrad, a power in Virginia Democratic politics, who had recently served as assistant U.S. attorney general, took office in February and was content to delegate the writing of the brief to Waller, who knew the case better than anyone. The court granted the motion, and Waller soon began his work in Washington, crafting preliminary drafts of the brief soon to be argued before the nation's highest court.

The Supreme Court accepted Waller's arguments that Navy regulations were constitutional, and that Sayre's trial and detention were lawful, and directed that Sayre be remanded into custody to serve out his sentence.[45] What is remarkable about *Johnson v. Sayre* is not its final resolution, but Waller's role in the case before the Supreme Court. In May, Conrad wrote Secretary of the Navy Herbert, revealing Waller's contribution to the case:

> On the side of the appellant, which was represented by the United States, the responsibility and labor of maintaining it at the bar of the court, was borne by Lieut. L. W. T. Waller, U.S. Marine Corps who, on my motion, had been allowed to appear as counsel before the court in that case.
>
> I cannot allow the occasion to pass without expressing to you my sense of the value of the services rendered to the Government in this matter by Lieut. Waller.
>
> His printed brief, filed in the cause, so ably and adequately presented the entire argument, that I found it unnecessary to add anything to it.
>
> In the oral argument at the bar of the court, although opposed by two able and experienced lawyers, he met all the demands of the occasion with the readiness and skill of a trained advocate.[46]

What is notable about Conrad's letter is not the praise that may be routinely given on such occasions but the explicit description of what Waller contributed to the case.

With little formal legal education and less practical experience, Waller bore the responsibility for crafting the government's response to the Circuit Court's rulings and then stood before the Supreme Court justices and argued the case against attorneys who clearly should have overwhelmed him. Oddly enough, *Johnson v. Sayre* was both the first and last major case that Waller argued in civil court. Although the Sayre case continues to be used as an important precedent in cases involving military law and authority, Waller did not seek to build his reputation in court. Although he made application for the position of judge advocate general of the Navy, nothing came of it. He was too junior to be considered, and by the time Waller reached the rank of colonel, his value to the Corps lay in other areas. Despite routine court-martial assignments during the remainder of his career, Waller's future lay not in the courtroom, but in the field with his men.[47]

## WAR LOOMS AHEAD

With the Sayre case behind him, Waller returned to his duties at Marine Barracks at Norfolk. In August, he took a one-month leave but soon received notice to "hold yourself in readiness for orders to command the Marine guard of the USS *Lancaster*," then undergoing repairs in New York. At the end of August, headquarters ordered Waller to proceed to New York to serve as judge advocate for an upcoming general court-martial. While Waller was engaged in this work, he received sea orders to the old side-wheel steamer *Lancaster* scheduled to be recommissioned on September 12. Waller sailed from New York back to the South Atlantic on the first ship he had served on, but this time he commanded the Marines, the post that Cochrane had occupied in 1882.[48]

During the next two years, the *Lancaster* sailed along the eastern coast of South America, revisiting the ports of Waller's old *Tallapoosa* days. These were times of routine duty, fighting against the boredom of cruising foreign waters while showing the flag. Waller recorded little of interest as he commanded the Marine Guard on the South Atlantic Station. On March 20, 1896, Waller was detached from the *Lancaster* and joined the protected cruiser *Newark*, the first modern cruiser in the Navy. For Waller, it was his first assignment to a vessel other than the aging steam sailing vessels from earlier eras. The *Newark* had much that Waller's other ships lacked: armor, speed, and firepower. A few months later, shortly after his promotion to captain, Waller joined another new ship, the battleship *Indiana* at New York, where he remained until the end of the war with Spain.[49]

During his time onboard the *Indiana*, Waller trained the Marine guard and commanded his Marines on the secondary battery operations. Waller's work with the secondary battery represented a new phase of shipboard routine for him. Later the next year, during the war with Spain, Waller and his Marine Guard manned the secondary battery and engaged the enemy at San Juan in Puerto Rico and at Santiago, Cuba. During those first days of July 1898, the *Indiana*'s gun crews played a vital part in bringing to a close naval operations against the Spanish in the Caribbean. However, as he came on board the *Indiana* for the first time in September 1896, Waller had little clue what lay ahead for him, months of training and gunnery practice that would make a difference in the war for empire.

During training off the coast of New England, the *Indiana*, despite only just recently being commissioned, suffered from a number of defects with the

The USS *Indiana* (1893–1919), designated Battleship no. 1. *Courtesy of U.S. Naval History and Heritage Command.*

gun mounts, the boilers, and a myriad of other repair problems. In the year and a half before the war with Spain, the Navy addressed the maintenance issues at Brooklyn Navy Yard and in a special dry dock in Nova Scotia. Later in September 1897, the *Indiana* steamed south to Hampton Roads, Virginia, and on to Key West, Florida, as tensions with Spain began to escalate. Despite the maintenance efforts that yielded some success during the early months after commissioning, boiler problems and other issues continued to plague the *Indiana* as it steamed into enemy waters during the months leading up to the battle with the Spanish fleet at Santiago.[50]

The *Indiana* and the North Atlantic Squadron spent the early months of 1898 at Key West and the Dry Tortugas. On February 16, news of the sinking of the USS *Maine* reached the fleet anchored at Dry Tortugas, and Admiral Sicard[51] called "a council of his captains" and decided to "to proceed to Key West, leaving the remainder of his squadron in Tortugas." The *Indiana*, still having maintenance issues with its boilers and various equipment, remained at Dry Tortugas "until March 21, occupying the time in retubing and cleaning boilers, overhauling the machinery now in much need of repairs, and training the crew to a high point of efficiency for war." Captain Henry C.

Taylor reported that "patrol boats were used to guard the entrance through the reef, and a vigilance was observed which thoroughly trained officers and crew for war."[52]

The *Indiana* left Dry Tortugas on March 21 and "anchored outside the reef at Key West to eastward of Sand Key Light." There Taylor ordered the ship's company to finish "the retubing of the boilers on April 1st, and on April 2nd" moved the battleship to waters beyond the anchorage "for a few hours' trial of the engines and boilers," giving the gun crews some practice firing on targets. Taylor reported that "the boiler tubes proved to be in order, and no special defect was observed," but he complained that the engines suffered from "the loss of steam around pistons and through leaky valves." Taylor predicted that the loss of pressure was "so great that a speed of nine knots for cruising and of ten and a half for battle was the most we could expect to attain." Despite earlier problems in New England with the gun mounts, Taylor described that "the guns and mounts were very satisfactory in their workings." Taylor later wrote that "the drills and vigilant watchfulness continued during our stay here, and added their part to the efficiency manifested by the ship's company during the war." During the months aboard the *Indiana*, Waller and the Marines had ample opportunities to train and drill on the secondary battery, and the experience paved the way for their success at San Juan in Puerto Rico and in the battle with the Spanish fleet at Santiago. When hostilities against Spain erupted in May 1898, the Navy ordered its fleet from Florida to Cuban waters where Navy officials expected to find Admiral Pascual Cervera's Spanish fleet waiting for the expected American attack. For Waller and the battleship's Marines, the cruise into hostile waters would bring about the ultimate test under fire, one where they would not be found wanting.[53]

On April 20, Captain Taylor received orders to move the *Indiana* "to Dry Tortugas for coal, and having coaled, returned to Key West, arriving there at daylight," two days later. On the approach to Key West, Taylor received a signal that war had been declared "against Spain and that the fleet was under way for Havana" in search of the Spanish fleet, its whereabouts unknown at the time. Taylor joined "the column in obedience to signal without anchoring, and proceeded" to waters off Havana Harbor. The *Indiana* "patrolled

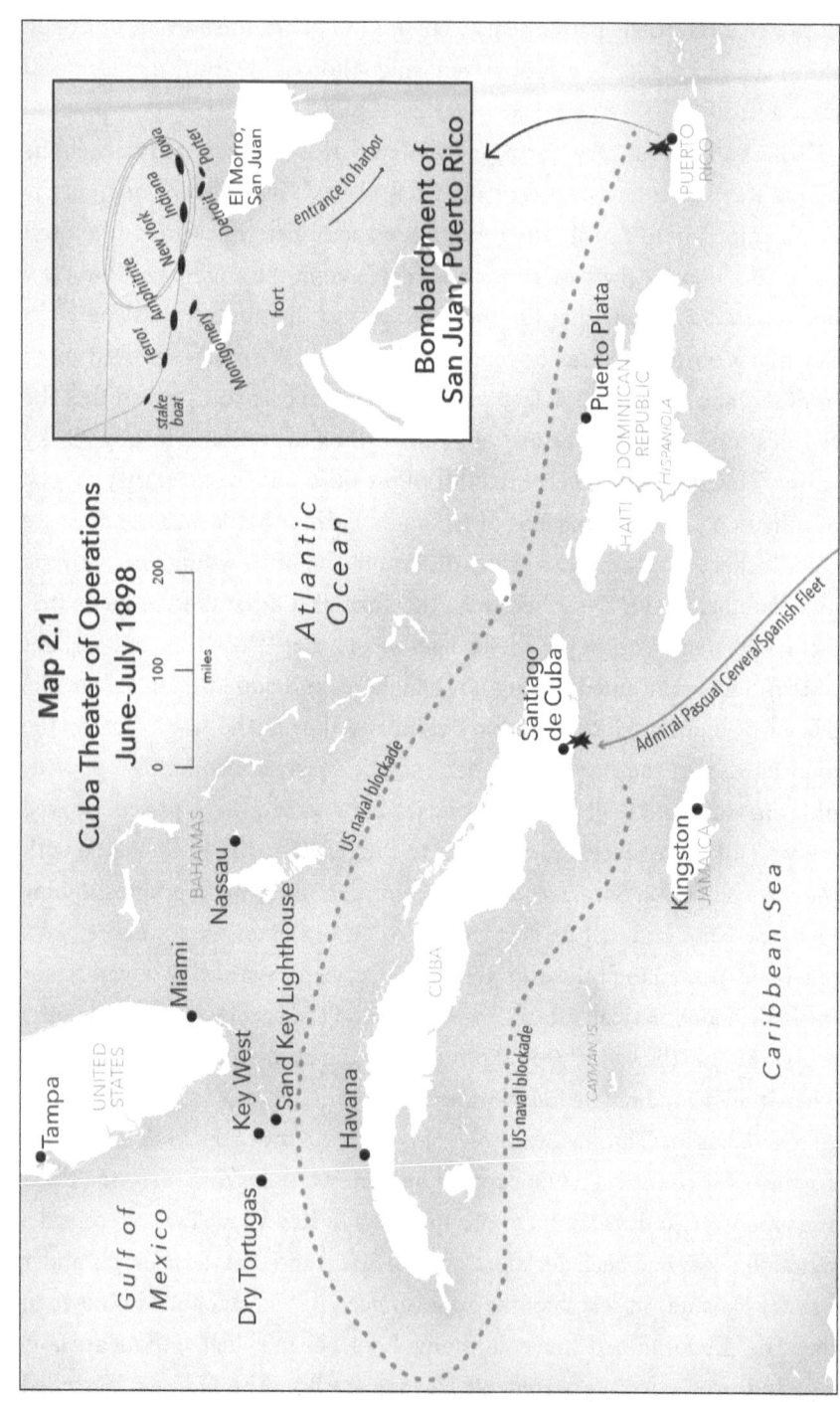

Map 2.1 Cuba Theater of Operations June–July 1898

with the fleet for several days and established the blockade of that port" (see Map 2.1).⁵⁴

On May 1, Navy officials in Washington learned that the Spanish fleet had departed the Cape Verde Islands on a course for the West Indies. "The *Indiana* proceeded to Key West and coaled ship, and on May 3, returned to the blockade, and the next day, proceeded with the Commander-in-Chief and squadron to the eastward." Expecting to find Cervera at Puerto Rico, "we arrived off San Juan de Puerto Rico before daybreak on May 12 and formed for attack." Using the unprotected cruisers *Detroit* and the *Montgomery* as markers on the eastern and western positions opposite the harbor entrance, the *Indiana*, second in line behind Sampson's flagship, the *Iowa*, began the attack on the fort and shore positions at the harbor entrance to San Juan (see Map 2.1). "We opened fire, following the movements of the flagship, at daylight, and continued the firing during the three passages made in front of the forts."⁵⁵

Low visibility in the misty early morning, together with the smoke from the ships' guns and shore batteries, did not prevent the gun crews from establishing range to targets during the first pass on the Spanish positions (see inset on Map 2.1). As the gun crews began their second pass with corrected ranges to the targets on shore, "the action now became brisk and vigorous on both sides. Our fire was very effective."⁵⁶

As the ships steamed past the harbor for the third pass, Admiral Sampson in the *Iowa* led the *Indiana* and the rest of the squadron "out of action to the northward and westward a few miles, and after a council with some of his captains, [Sampson] decided not to renew the action." It was clear that Cervera and his ships were not in the San Juan harbor, and Sampson intended to follow his orders to discover the location of Cervera's fleet and to "destroy his ships." Sampson gave orders to set a course to the west, and "when off Puerto Plata, San Domingo," the admiral learned that the Spanish fleet had put into Curaçao, off the coast of Venezuela, and that Cervera had departed that harbor, sailing "in a northwesterly direction."⁵⁷

Admiral Sampson predicted that Cervera "would proceed from Curaçao to one of four points—San Juan, Santiago de Cuba, Cienfuegos, or Havana." San Juan and Santiago were discounted as possibilities since Sampson and his squadron was in range of both places. The consensus reasoned that Cienfuegos or Havana would be the most likely destination for Cervera and his ships. Sampson ordered Commodore Schley and his Flying Squadron to Cienfuegos, while Sampson and the North Atlantic Squadron made for Key West for coaling in preparation for the impending battle with Cervera. Confident that the encounter was imminent, Sampson wanted to be ready. Unknown to Sampson, Cervera did not go to Havana or Cienfuegos but instead steamed into Santiago, Cuba, where he waited.[58]

On May 19, the *Indiana* arrived at Key West and quickly filled its coal bunkers and sailed for Havana, "where she remained until news was received by the Commander-in-Chief that the Spanish squadron had gone to Santiago de Cuba." Still worried that the Spanish fleet would attempt to reach Havana, Sampson and a large part of his squadron patrolled the northern Cuban coastline, keeping "a strict watch . . . day and night to intercept the Spanish ships if they came eastward." Once news came that Cervera's squadron had not left Santiago, Sampson ordered the *Indiana* to Key West for coal and "occupy a few days in working at boiler repairs with the help of a force of mechanics sent there by the Department from the North."

The mechanics could not repair the boilers, but they did clean and scale the boilers, "and a force of divers, sent to Key West from the North, cleaned the ship's bottom quite thoroughly."[59]

Meanwhile, General William R. Shafter assembled an invasion force at Tampa, Florida, and the Navy Department ordered Captain Taylor and the *Indiana* to take "charge of the convoy destined to take General Shafter's army from Tampa to Santiago de Cuba with the *Indiana* as senior ship." While the repairs were underway at Key West, Taylor used the time "organizing the expedition, drafting the regulations," and developing "precautions against attack from the small vessels of the enemy stationed in the bays and rivers along our route." Taylor in the *Indiana*, together with the *Detroit, Montgomery, Vesuvius,* and *Bancroft*, reconnoitered "the channels north of Cuba as far east as Cay Lobos and returned to Key West on June 12th, having developed the fact that none of the enemy's vessels were in that locality." On June 14, the transports loaded with Shafter's landing force left Tampa, and Taylor moved his escorting vessels from Key West to Dry Tortugas and waited for the convoy to arrive.[60]

On June 16, Taylor took command of the expedition, and the *Indiana* sailed from Dry Tortugas with thirty-five transports, "carrying about sixteen thousand men, under command of General Shafter, and were convoyed by a force of fifteen vessels." The voyage to the southern coast of Cuba was uneventful, and after some delays, the expedition reached the landing location at Daiquiri and Siboney. Determining that the area proved clear of the enemy, the *Indiana* left the convoy and proceeded to Santiago to join Sampson and the blockade (see Map 2.2).[61]

Up to this point in his career, Waller's experience on board ships had been on older vessels, without the armament and the modern equipment found on the *Indiana*. His principal duty in those early years focused on training the Marine guard for the traditional shipboard duties that included discipline, marksmanship, and support activities with the ship's crew. The Marines were important tools in landings in locales where American lives and property were at risk. Showing the flag and diplomatic activities provided breaks from the long and tedious routine of cruising in foreign waters. On the *Indiana*, Waller found additional duties and roles for the Marine guard. The modern battleship designs added new levels of gunnery and demands for ships' crews. Waller demonstrated the value of Marines working as part of the overall gunnery crew. In the months leading up to war footing, Captain Taylor recognized that value and later commented on Waller's contribution to the *Indiana*'s successes in the war, and on Waller's leadership during operations against Spain in the Puerto Rican and Cuban waters.

The *Indiana* arrived off Santiago "at 8.25 a.m.," and an hour later, Sampson signaled the *Indiana* "to go close in." Taylor had the *Indiana* at general quarters and ready for action. After their success at San Juan, Waller and the Marines confidently manned the secondary battery, ready on the approach to the coastal batteries protecting the harbor. With the Texas already engaged with the enemy fortifications on shore, Taylor gave the order to attack the batteries. "We went in and opened fire, first on the eastern battery" positioned at the Morro Castle, "and later, having silenced them, we steamed to the westward across the entrance, engaging the Socapa and Punta Gorda batteries, until signaled to withdraw." Taylor reported that "these batteries

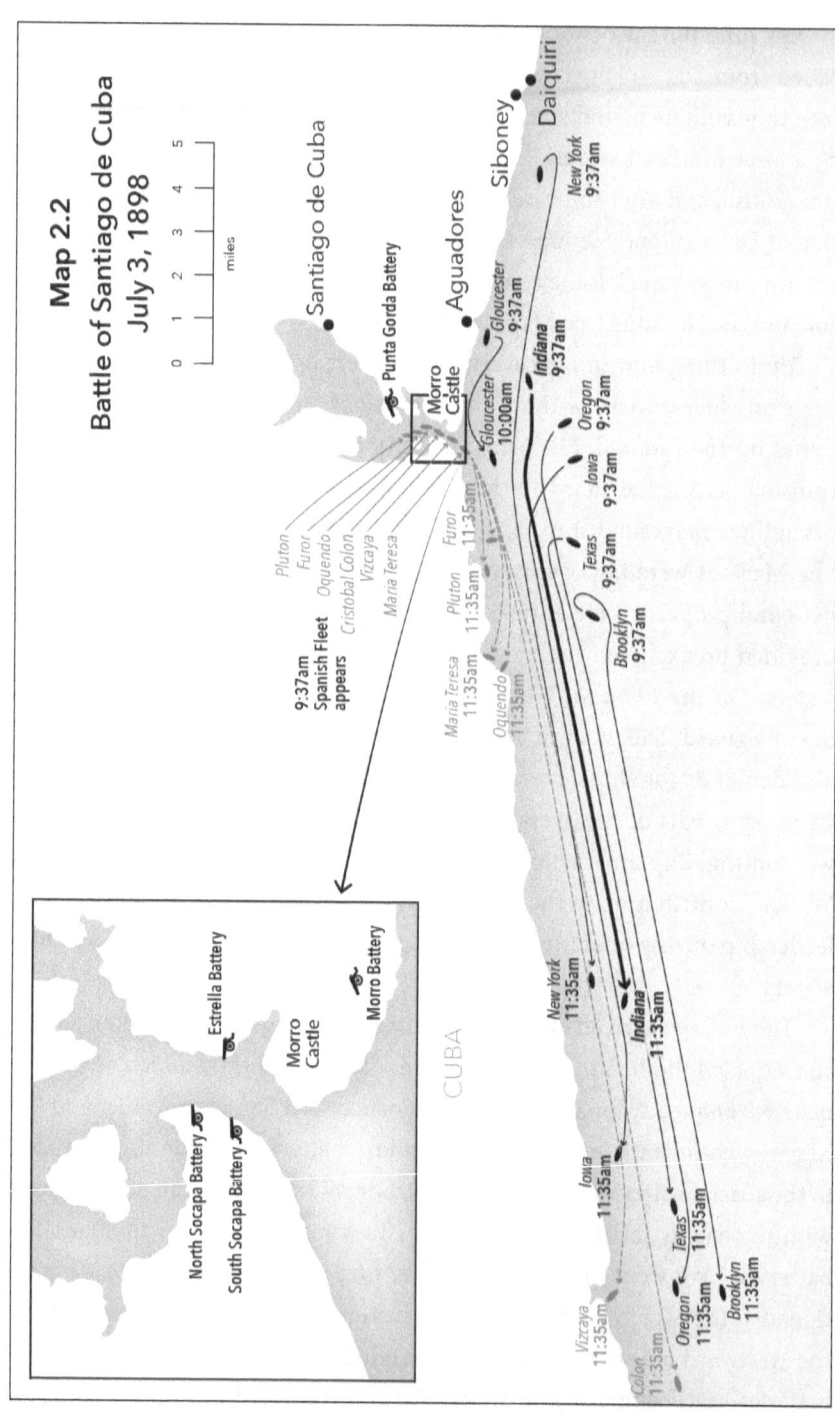

engaged us briskly, and their projectiles, though generally wild, fell at times quite near us, one of them exploding under water so near the ship's side as to dish one of the bow plates."

On June 30, low on coal, the *Indiana* left the blockade for Guantanamo to replenish its bunkers. While at the coaling depot, Taylor learned that Sampson planned to "attack the batteries at Santiago entrance on July 2, and keep them engaged while the army, then in position in front of the city, would advance upon the entrenchments which protected the city." Taylor stepped up the coaling work and got underway after midnight, reaching Santiago in the early morning hours on July 2.[62]

Arriving on station, Sampson "signaled the *Indiana*, take position between flagship and Oregon. We engage the batteries at daylight." Taylor maneuvered the *Indiana* into position off Morro Castle and "cleared for action, and at 5:25 a.m. beat to general quarters." Taylor opened fire on the eastern batteries with his port guns. Throughout the early morning, the *Indiana* bombarded first the eastern batteries, then moved back to the westward harbor approach to target the Punta Gorda guns ashore.

With occasional ceasefires, the *Indiana* maintained the bombardment and "at 7:32 ceased firing and secured in obedience to signal." Taylor reported that "many shots fell near us, but we were not struck." The blockade remained in place throughout the rest of the day and on into the night. The next day, Cervera and the Spanish decided to act.[63]

Early in the morning, Admiral Sampson and the flagship *New York* left the blockade for Siboney to confer with General Shafter on the next steps to take Santiago. "When the flagship was about 4 miles east of her blockading station, . . . , the Spanish squadron was seen steaming out of the harbor entrance." Taylor reported that the *Indiana* crew was "at quarters at 9:37 a.m. of July 3, preliminary to general muster, noted two guns fired from the *Iowa* and general signal, 'Enemy's ships escaping.'" Taylor noted that he "at once cleared ship for action, and the crew were at the guns in a remarkably short time." With Waller and the Marines at their station in the secondary battery, they did not have long to wait for action.[64]

The Spanish squadron steamed out of the harbor single file with Cervera and his flagship, the armored cruiser *Infanta Maria Teresa*, leading the way (see Map 2.2). Behind Cervera came the armored cruiser *Vizcaya*, the unprotected cruiser *Cristobal Colon*, and the armored *Almirante Oquendo*, trailed by the torpedo-boat destroyers *Furor* and *Pluton*. The Spanish ships turned to the west out of the harbor, hoping to outrun the American vessels. Hampered by a poor grade of coal and slower speeds, the Spanish ships proved to be no match for the better-equipped blockaders. As the Spanish ships emerged from the harbor, "the initial fire of all the Spanish ships was directed at this vessel [*Indiana*], and although falling very close," the Spanish shells "only struck the ship twice, without injury to ship or crew."[65]

The *Indiana*, positioned off the mouth of the harbor, fired on each Spanish vessel "as they came out one by one and continued the action later by firing principally at the *Maria Teresa*, *Oquendo*, *Furor*, and *Pluton*." Taylor reported that Waller and "our secondary battery guns were directed principally on the destroyers, as also were the six-inch guns." Both destroyers were sunk by the Marines in the secondary battery and by the guns on the "*Gloucester*, which . . . had come up and engaged them close aboard." The rest of the Spanish fleet fared little better as the American squadron maintained a parallel track westward along the coast, "keeping as nearly abreast of them as possible," firing in pursuit of fleeing vessels.[66]

By 1:20 p.m. early that afternoon, all the Spanish vessels were either sunk or beached and burning. The *Indiana*'s batteries "ceased firing" and Sampson, in the *New York*, ordered Taylor to "go back and guard entrance of harbor." The naval battle for Santiago had ended. General William Shafter concluded the war ashore two weeks later. In the interim, the *Indiana* maintained its station "off Santiago de Cuba until July 17, partaking in the long-range bombardment of that city on July 10 and 11."

On July 17, the *Indiana* departed its station at Santiago and steamed the short distance to Guantanamo for coaling and repairs. Later in August, the *Indiana*, along with the *New York* and other ships in the squadron, departed Cuba for New York harbor—arriving there on Saturday, August 20. The war was over for Waller and his Marines. At New York, Waller received orders to report to Marine Barracks, Norfolk. After a brief leave, Waller reported for duty at Norfolk on September 17, 1898, once again reunited with Clara and family in his Norfolk home.[67]

In a series of reports, the *Indiana*'s Captain Henry C. Taylor recorded his observations of Waller as Marine commander. From January 1897 through the eve of the war, Taylor submitted several fitness reports on Waller and each was complimentary as Taylor wrote the obligatory "excellent" ratings of an officer engaged in routine duty. But Taylor's report for the period ending September 1898 provides insight into Waller's actions during the engagements with the Spanish in Cuban waters.

Taylor wrote that Waller "possesses exceptional qualities. [Waller] has his guard in finest condition." Impressed with Waller's command presence and bearing, he wrote that he "has every professional qualification and appears to have in addition the natural ability for high commands." Taylor left no doubt that when the heat of battle reached critical mass, Waller was an officer he wanted on board his ship. Waller "is invaluable aboard ship. [He] showed with great credit in command of Marine guard and of secondary battery during the war and showed calm and bravery in all the actions including Cervera's defeat on July 3." When asked if Waller was fit to be entrusted with hazardous and important independent duties, Taylor penned simply "decidedly yes."[68]

After years of routine cruising and shore duty, the Spanish-American War gave Waller an intimate taste of fleet action. His command presence in this action suggested to Taylor that Waller possessed the natural talent for leadership in the field, and Santiago proved but a prelude for the Philippines and China actions that loomed ahead that would test Waller yet again.

With the war's end, Waller returned to Norfolk, after almost two decades of service in the Corps behind him. During that time, he had gained experience in volatile and chaotic troops landings in times of revolution and great danger. He had also spent years honing skills in the diplomacy of empire while, at the same time, developing expertise in the fundamentals of military leadership and the handling of men. Waller also demonstrated a distinctive talent for the law and for legal combat at the highest levels. All these skills would be brought to bear in Waller's coming assignments in Tientsin, Peking, and Samar; actions where he would be put to the ultimate test.

CHAPTER 3 **TO THE EAST: THE PHILIPPINES AND CHINA**

As the year 1900 unfolded, U.S. Marines in the Philippines grappled with Filipino resistance to American rule even as conditions in China worsened with the emergence of the "Society of Righteous and Harmonious Fists"—the Boxers. Dedicated to eliminating all foreign influence in China, the Boxers targeted Christian missionaries and their Chinese converts in Chilhli province. Encouraged covertly by the Dowager Empress Tzu Hsi and her court, the Boxers expanded their operations against the foreign missionaries in rural northern China. These environments of violence in the Philippines and China compelled the Marines to develop strategies of confrontation in both theaters of engagement.[1]

In rural Shansi, eighteen Protestant missionaries from Oberlin College had established a viable work among the Chinese in that area. Driven by their sense of mission, these foreigners were "repulsed by the native lifestyle" and determined to effect change. Ignoring the Chinese culture, these Oberlin brothers and sisters neither learned the Chinese language nor understood the traditions and customs of the people with whom they lived. Their letters home disdained and ridiculed the very peasants they purported to rescue. Arrogant and distant, these missionaries made themselves ideal targets for the Boxers. In their rampage through Shansi, the Boxers murdered six Oberlin men, seven women, and five children and displayed their heads on poles as a sinister declaration of Chinese sovereignty and nationalism. The Boxers spread their terror throughout the region, tracking down and murdering the foreign devils and their Chinese converts.[2]

By late spring 1900, the Boxers had reached Peking, openly demonstrating against the foreign concessions while targeting foreign homes and businesses in the city. They decapitated any foreigner they seized and those Chinese Christians who refused to reject the foreign religion and return to idol worship. They placed their heads on poles and in baskets hung from the south wall in full view of the Europeans in the legations. Turmoil rolled across the city as jeering Boxers increased their numbers and demonstrated openly against the foreigners. Meanwhile, surviving Chinese Christians slipped into Tientsin and Peking, spreading their disturbing news about the Boxer terror in the North.

As each day passed, the Boxers grew bolder, whipping up the anti-western fever in the city streets. The foreign ministers, confronted by the growing danger, realized that the empress could not be trusted with their safety. In the face of the burgeoning chaos, each legation sent frantic messages for reinforcements, urging the immediacy of relief. Against this backdrop, U.S. Marine Commandant Brigadier General Charles Heywood tapped Major Littleton W. T. Waller to command a new battalion of Marines organized for service in Guam, but fate decreed other plans for Waller and his men.[3]

Shortly after the close of the Spanish-American War and his service in Cuban waters, Waller assumed command of the Marine Barracks in Norfolk—thankful once again to be home among friends and family. During this respite, Waller recruited new men and did occasional special duties at League Island and in Norfolk.[4] Waller also drew his share of legal assignments, particularly because his earlier success before the Supreme Court in the Sayre case marked him as an able military lawyer.[5] During the summer of 1899, Captain Waller appeared before the promotion board and received recommendations for promotion to major.[6]

While working through these routine duties, Waller and Clara welcomed a third son into the family, Henry Tazewell Waller.[7] Waller enjoyed his Norfolk home on Pembroke Avenue with his three boys and wife Clara. Family events and social gatherings with his Marine Corps friends filled these blissful days, and his junior officers collected memories, filling their scrapbooks that frequently revealed a jovial Waller smiling out from across the years. Their off-duty relationships laid the groundwork for the strong loyalties later voiced by his officers and men in Waller's times of crisis.

It was a portrait of Waller that few of his Naval Academy competitors ever saw, but one that reveals much about Waller's personality and character.[8] While he never forgot a slight or forgave an enemy, Waller's loyalty

Colonel Littleton Waller, center top, with friends, Norfolk, Virginia, circa 1905. *Courtesy of George C. Reid Collection, Marine Corps Historical Center, Quantico, Virginia.*

and gratitude to his associates knew no limits. In the days that would soon follow, when Waller's character and his judgment would be put to the test, his enemies would be quick to attack and condemn, but his friends would be supporting and approving.

On September 23, 1899, Waller cabled the commandant requesting information about his next posting. He explained that if he was "to be detached from this post within the next month or two," he needed advance warning to take care of private business and arrange to rent his Norfolk home. Assuming that his next assignment would be stateside, Waller planned to move his family with him. He suggested to General Heywood that his preference would be the command of the Marine Barracks at Washington, D.C., and failing that, "Colonel Huntington [at New York] has expressed a desire to have me if a Major is sent to that post." The Marine Corps, however, had other plans for Waller, and arrangements for renting the Norfolk house were tabled for the time being. New orders came down from headquarters, not for New York or Washington, D.C. Ahead lay a journey to the East to the Philippines and China, places where Waller would make his mark on history.[9]

In October 1899, Major Waller received "preparatory orders to hold myself in readiness to command a battalion of Marines for service [on] the Island of Guam." Heywood wrote Waller at Norfolk that the Third Battalion would "be composed of seventeen officers and four companies, aggregating 324 enlisted men." The plan called for two companies organized at New York under Waller's supervision, while the other two companies assembled in Washington, D.C., with Captain H. L. Draper organizing the units until Waller arrived there by train and added Draper's Company A and Company B to the battalion for the trip to Mare Island in California (see Figure 10).[10]

On October 25, Waller arrived at League Island at Philadelphia and reported to Commodore Silas Casey and Colonel R. W. Huntington "for duty with the Marine Battalion." Although Waller did not officially join the Third Marine Battalion until November 1, he worked with Assistant Quartermaster R. P. Faunt Le Roy and headquarters personnel to secure equipment and

**FIGURE 10**

### Third Marine Battalion

| COMPLEMENT | ORGANIZING OFFICERS |
|---|---|
| **Company C and D:** | **At New York:** |
| 9 Marine Officers | Major L.W.T Waller, Commanding |
| 1 Naval Surgeon | First Lieutenant J.C. Breckinridge, Adjutant |
| 2 Gunnery Sergeants | Captain P.M. Bannon |
| 8 Sergeants | First Lieutenant L.M. Gulick |
| 10 Corporals | First Lieutenant H.T. Bearss |
| 2 Drummers | Second Lieutenant Wm. H. Parker |
| 2 Trumpeters | Second Lieutenant N.G. Burton |
| 136 Privates | Second Lieutenant L.M. Little |
|  | Second Lieutenant Wirt McCreary |
| **Company A and B:** | **At Washington, D.C.:** |
| 7 Marine Officers | Captain H.L. Draper |
| 1 Naval Surgeon | First Lieutenant E.A. Jonas |
| 2 Gunnery Sergeants | First Lieutenant Logan Feland |
| 8 Sergeants | First Lieutenant W.H. Clifford, Jr. |
| 10 Corporals | Second Lieutenant Wade L. Jolly |
| 2 Drummers | Second Lieutenant F.M. Wise |
| 2 Trumpeters | Second Lieutenant Stephan Elliot |
| 136 Privates | |

transportation facilities to move his battalion to the West Coast. It proved to be a complex logistical undertaking.[11]

Stores and personal issue items were assembled and packed at League Island for the expedition and included campaign hats, blue uniforms, leggings, knapsacks, campaign suits, and tropical helmets. This equipment would be "loaded in Philadelphia, and attached to the train when it passes through that city." Heywood also sent a freight car by barge to the Navy Yard at New York, ordering Waller to ship officers' baggage and the clothing and other stores for the New York companies aboard the car prior to departure. Two Colt automatic guns and forty thousand rounds of ammunition were also loaded onto the rail car at New York. Heywood cabled Huntington to "deliver the colors for the battalion to [Waller] in New York," telling Waller that "I feel sure that you will defend them with honor to the Corps." On November 1, Companies C and D left New York on the Chesapeake and Ohio Railroad with Waller commanding. The officers enjoyed Pullman car accommodations while the enlisted men traveled in "tourist cars." A dining car was added to the train to serve "three meals a day for the men en route" to

USS *Solace* (1898–1930) served as a hospital ship and as a transport during the time that Waller and the Marines were aboard en route to Guam and the Philippines. *Courtesy of U.S. Naval History and Heritage Command.*

California. Waller's contingent reached Washington at 2:30 in the afternoon and left for California an hour later. During the hour layover in Washington, the commandant handed Waller a new flag that the battalion would carry into the campaigns that soon would follow. Draper's Companies A and B followed a half an hour behind. The battalion reached Mares Island off San Francisco, California, on November 7, and three days later, the Marines boarded the USS *Solace* and sailed for the Philippines.[12]

Meanwhile, the request for an additional battalion of Marines for Guam had been canceled by the governor. He explained that "owing to the scarcity of food and lack of facilities for quartering the additional battalion asked for," the deployment should be delayed. At the same time, operations in the Philippines demanded more Marines, so the Third Battalion sailed on to Manila for service in the islands. En route from San Francisco, the *Solace* stopped for coal in the Hawaiian Islands and, on December 9, docked briefly in Guam to drop off four officers to replace those lost to the Guam garrison through death and illness. The *Solace* continued on to Cavite near Manila, where Waller landed on December 15 and deployed the Third Battalion for operations in the Philippines.[13]

The next month, Waller received orders to select five officers and join them in a move to Guam in the early summer, an assignment that Waller had been expecting since receiving his posting the previous October. Guam held no attraction for an aggressive commander, and no doubt Waller hoped for a change in his orders. As the summer approached, events in China set in motion plans that would indeed divert Waller and his officers to the rescue of the international concessions at Tientsin and Peking.[14]

## THE CHINA RELIEF EXPEDITION

In response to the fast-deteriorating conditions in Peking, the ministers had requested immediate assistance as the Boxers began to threaten their positions in the Legation Quarter. Responding to this May 28 appeal, the foreign governments quickly assembled an international force thought to be sufficient for the task. The Americans selected "50 Marines, five sailors, and a Navy doctor" from the *Oregon* and the *Newark*, commanded by Marine Captain John T. Myers.[15]

Myers acted quickly, even replacing the baggage with twenty thousand rounds of rifle ammunition and eight thousand rounds for the Colt machine gun. Myers and his Marines joined an international force that included British Royal Marines, German Marines, the Japanese Special Naval Landing Force, Russian sailors, Austrian Marines, and Italian sailors. On May 31, this relief expedition of 337 officers and men arrived by train in Peking. To Myers "the dense mass of Chinese which thronged either side of the roadway seemed more ominous than a demonstration of hostility would have been." In the Legation quarter, the troops found a much-relieved crowd of about a thousand foreign civilians and diplomats. For the next three weeks, Myers and his counterparts patrolled the Quarter, keeping the Boxers at bay, yet he recognized that the situation could prove untenable should the Boxers decide to mount an all-out attack. More help was needed in Peking.[16]

During early June, the Boxers accelerated their efforts to isolate Peking from the outside world. The "Fists" destroyed the rail line leading from the port at Taku to Tientsin, began to threaten the rail route from Tientsin to Peking, and sent thousands of Boxers swarming into Peking, burning and attacking any foreigners or Christian converts they found. By June 9, 1900, it was evident that Peking would need more armed assistance if the legations were to survive. At the same time, the dowager empress grew increasingly hostile to the growing foreign military presence in China, and imperial soldiers soon joined the Boxers in their attacks. China then declared war against all foreigners. While conditions grew increasingly desperate, Myers and his Marines patrolled the quarter, rescued occasional pockets of refugees outside the quarter, and skirmished against Boxers. Further south, officials at Tientsin debated what to do.[17]

On June 9, an international council convened in Tientsin to discuss the situation remained indecisive, unable to agree on the specifics of a rescue plan. The United States' contingent at Tientsin included just over a hundred men under the command of Navy Captain Bowman H. McCalla, which was too small to carry much influence. While the multinational force counted about twenty-five hundred officers and men, the senior officers and diplomats could reach no agreement. McCalla, impatient with the gathering, finally declared that "I don't care what the rest of you do. I have 112 men

Commandeering rolling stock in the Tientsin rail yard, the Seymour Expedition carried materials and supplies to repair damaged rails as they made their way north, June 10, 1900. *Courtesy of U.S. Naval History and Heritage Command.*

here and I'm going tomorrow morning to the rescue of my flesh and blood in Peking." He declared that "I'll be damned if I sit here 90 miles away, and just wait." The old sailor's boldness carried the day, and the next morning, a relief expedition commanded by Vice Admiral Edward Seymour of Britain's Royal Navy sallied from Tientsin with McCalla second in command.[18]

Commandeering locomotives and freight cars from the Tientsin rail yard,

Boxer soldier, somewhere in China, 1900. *Courtesy of National Archives.*

78 | CHAPTER 3

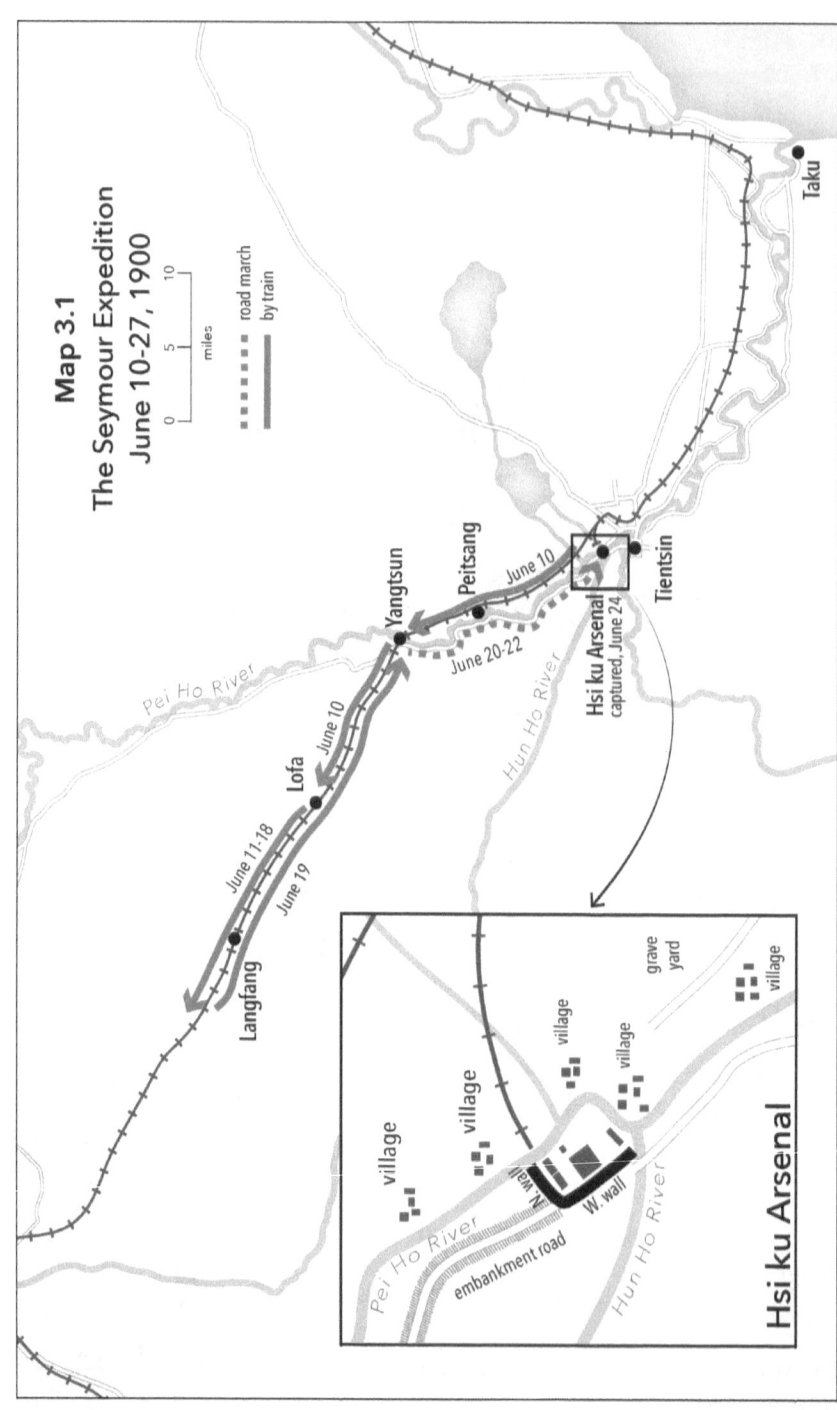

Map 3.1 The Seymour Expedition June 10-27, 1900

Seymour's expedition carried materials to repair the damaged rail line to Peking. Slowly, the expedition worked its way toward Peking, and within a week, Seymour had reached Langfang, just twenty-five miles from the objective (see Map 3.1). But at Langfang, the tide turned against the rescuers as the Boxers and Imperial troops swarmed down on them, forcing a retreat back toward Tientsin on foot. Pursued by their relentless foe, the hapless expedition retreated to the Hsi Ku Arsenal, just six miles outside Tientsin. With over 300 wounded and hounded by hordes of irregulars and imperial soldiers, the battered relief column seized the arsenal where they found temporary shelter. Now the Legation Quarter in Peking, the Seymour Expedition at Hsi Ku Arsenal, and the Tientsin legations were all subjected to increased attacks as the situation deteriorated rapidly. The only hope for relief lay with governments outside China, and time was running out.[19]

## FROM TAKU TO TIENTSIN

Meanwhile in the Philippines, Colonel Robert Meade, commanding all Marines ashore, prepared the First Regiment to sail to Taku, China. "At first the state of affairs [in China] not being considered as serious, [I sent] only thirty men under 1st Lieutenant Henry Leonard." The situation proved more desperate. "Later, a more earnest appeal for troops" reached the commander in chief and prompted the dispatch of Company A of the First Battalion under command of 1st Lieutenant Smedley D. Butler. "Knowing the need of a field officer in China," Meade decided to send Waller in command of all Marines ashore in China. Although already detailed for Guam, Waller persuaded Meade to send him to China first, delaying the Guam assignment and the major left for China shortly behind Leonard's detachment. Waller's small force of six officers and 101 men reached Taku, twenty-nine miles from Tientsin, on June 18 where he added Leonard's element to his own, assembling a total force of eight officers and 131 men. Waller's orders directed him "to land and cooperate with the powers to move forward with the first column of relief for the besieged city of Tientsin." On the nineteenth, Waller moved a short distance beyond Taku where he commandeered a train "and proceeded up the railway carrying a construction car" with him. The advance on Tientsin had begun (see Map 3.2).[20]

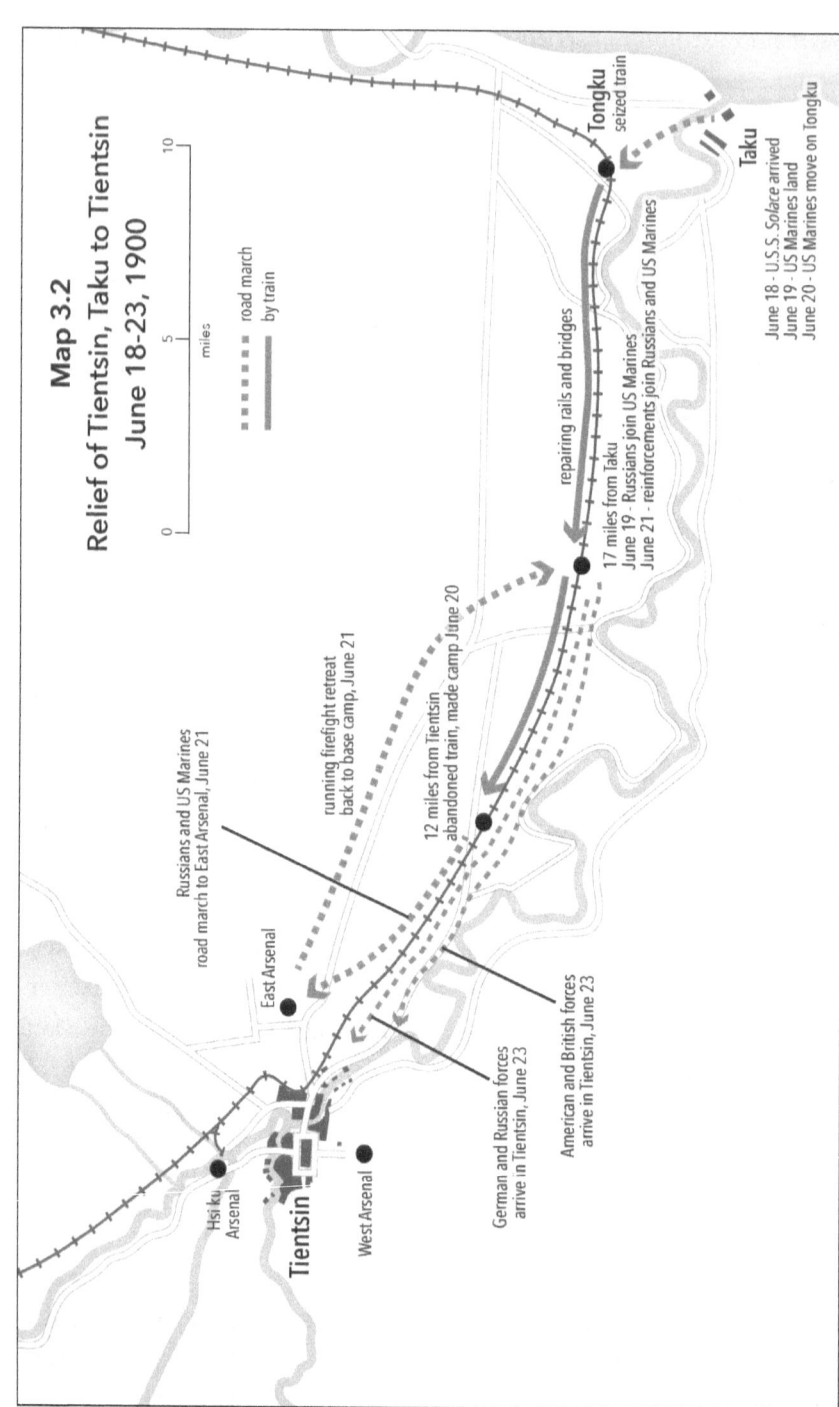

During the day, Waller's train repaired damaged rails and blown bridges, moving steadily closer to Tientsin. Twelve miles from Taku, Waller "picked up a battalion of Russians" and continued to roll toward Tientsin. Five miles later, Waller reported that he had "used all my material and finding the road impossible," decided to make camp for the night. The combined US-Russian force halted seventeen miles from Taku and twelve miles short of Tientsin, where Waller positioned the three-inch gun on the tracks and established a defensive perimeter as darkness closed in. Later that evening at eleven o'clock, Waller counseled with the Russian colonel, and the two decided that they would hold their position until relief could come up from Taku and allow the march to continue.[21]

Waller retired for the night but was awakened at 2 a.m. with the startling news that the Russian commander had decided to "push on with his four hundred men and attempt to get into Tientsin" by road march. He had unilaterally determined that the danger to the allied population at Tientsin warranted the risk of a night march to the besieged city with the men at hand. Waller faced a dilemma. No rules of command existed that governed the impasse, but Waller decided that the risk to his men was greater without the Russians, so he reluctantly agreed to be "overruled." Waller felt that there was only a "slim chance of passing the East Arsenal [on the approach to Tientsin] with a force of only 500 men and no [artillery]." The relief column soon had reason to regret the Russian's decision.[22]

Waller determined that his three-inch gun was defective so he "disabled it and rolled it into the river." The Russian battalion struck out for Tientsin with Waller's Colt gun crew under 1st Lieutenant David D. Porter in their van. Waller led the rest of the American Marines onto the line of march, bringing up the rear. Without further opposition, the force marched toward Tientsin through the night, reaching the East Arsenal at 7 a.m. "There we met a small flank fire which was quickly silenced by our sharpshooters," but minutes later the Marines "met a very heavy front and flank fire from 1500 or 2000" entrenched Boxers. Waller deployed his men, and "my line feeling the flank fire turned to the left and rear confronting the flank movement." The Marines held their position "for some time" until the Russians began "to fall back and form on our right at a distance of about one hundred yards." The Russian withdrawal drew enemy fire to Waller's left flank.[23]

The Colt gun crew supporting the Russian front took heavy fire and was soon reduced to two men. The gun had jammed several times so Lieutenant Porter disabled and abandoned it, retiring to Waller's main force. The major, informed that "the Russians would retreat to a point four miles beyond our rear," began his own withdrawal, fending off the Chinese for four hours as he pulled back. Finally, Waller "succeeded in fall[ing] back, bring[ing] our wounded [out] by hand. At 2 p.m., we had reached our camp having marched 30 miles and fought for five hours." Driven back to a defensive position some sixteen miles outside Tientsin, Waller waited for reinforcements, which arrived from Taku three hours later. He then "decided to act in cooperation with the British under Commander Christopher Craddock." One army general officer, who later wrote high praise for Waller's leadership under these harrowing conditions, suggested that "less stubborn and less skillfully handled soldiers would have been overwhelmed and massacred."[24]

Victoria Road area in the British Concession, Tientsin, China. The American Marines billeted in the China Merchants Steam Navigation Company building on this street. *Courtesy of University of Bristol Library, Special Collections.*

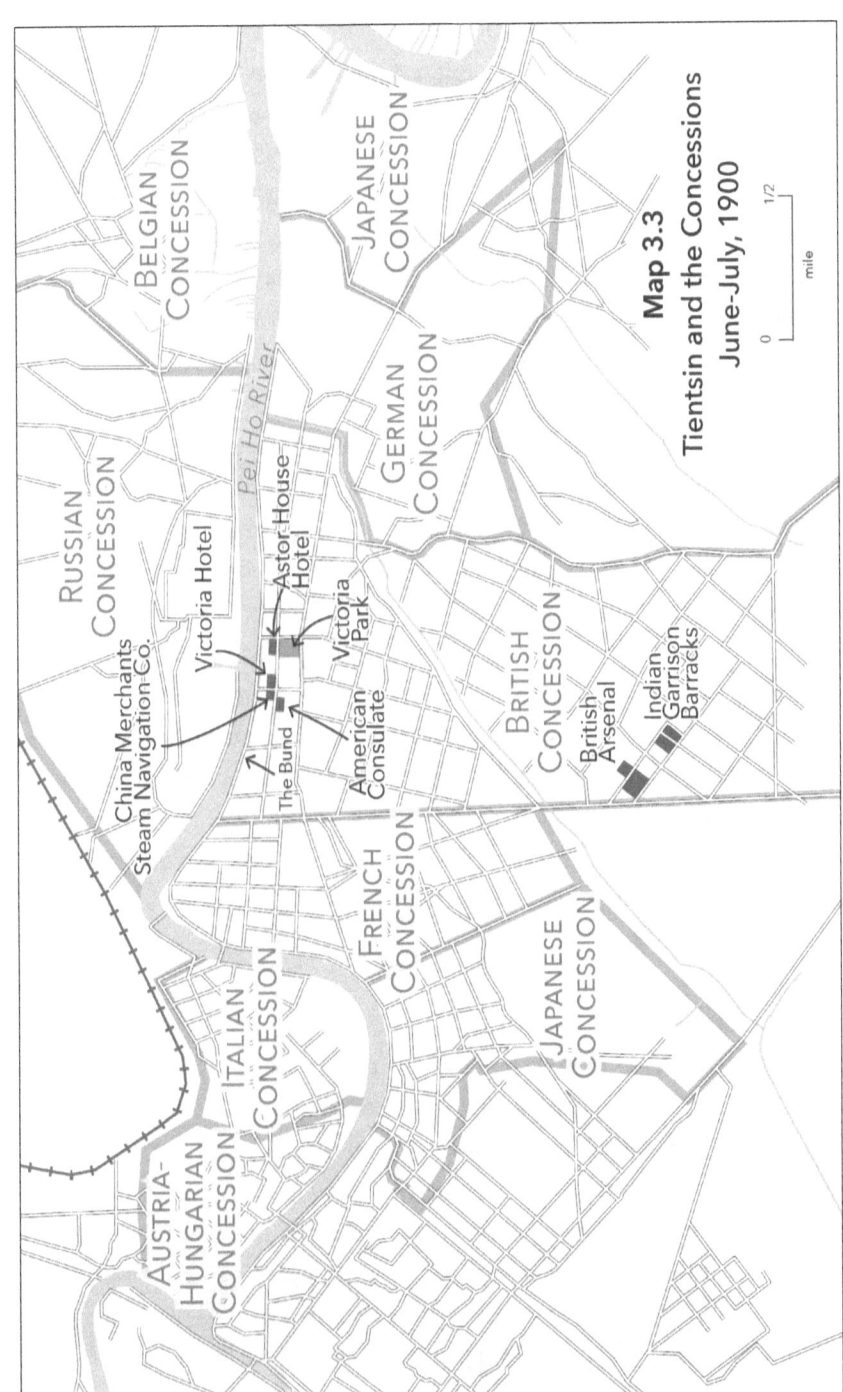

Map 3.3 Tientsin and the Concessions June–July, 1900

That night the multinational force camped outside the city and planned to march toward Tientsin in two columns the next day. The force comprised about two thousand men with contingents of English, German, American, Italian, Russian, and Japanese troops. The battle plan called for an early departure, allowing the detachment to reach the East Arsenal early in the morning and surprise the defenders. At 4 a.m., the troops formed up into two columns, with Waller's Marines leading the British column and "occupying the right of the firing line." At 7:30 a.m., the first elements "struck the enemy" and "drove them steadily until about 12:30 when we entered Tientsin relieving the besieged Europeans." During the fighting, on the approach to Tientsin, the Marines lost one killed and three wounded.[25]

Waller moved into a building owned by the China Merchants Steam Navigation Company on Victoria Road in the British Concession and rested his men for the remainder of the day while he conferred with the other commanders and wrote his report to the commandant (see Map 3.3). Growing Boxer infiltration into the Walled City at Tientsin posed an immediate threat to the legations and foreign population who sought protection there, but over seven thousand Boxers also occupied the Tientsin Arsenal and more flooded into the city every day, preventing any immediate attempt to relieve Peking using the limited forces at Tientsin. In addition, the Seymour Expedition remained trapped at the nearby Hsi Ku Arsenal, in danger of being overwhelmed by the more numerous Boxers. The foreign powers moved swiftly to resolve these difficulties.[26]

## OPERATIONS AT TIENTSIN

Shortly after midnight on June 25, a rescue team made up of Britons, Russians, and Waller's Marines left Tientsin under the cover of darkness and headed for the Hsi Ku Arsenal, just eight miles distant. "We met very little resistance and succeeded in relieving the besieged at 12 a.m. Our casualties being three wounded, two [by] shell and one bullet wound." Waller praised the efforts of Seymour and McCalla at the arsenal, saying that they had taken it "by a brilliant charge and without knowing what they had opposed," seizing a "plentiful supply of all sorts of munitions of war" (see Map 3.4).[27]

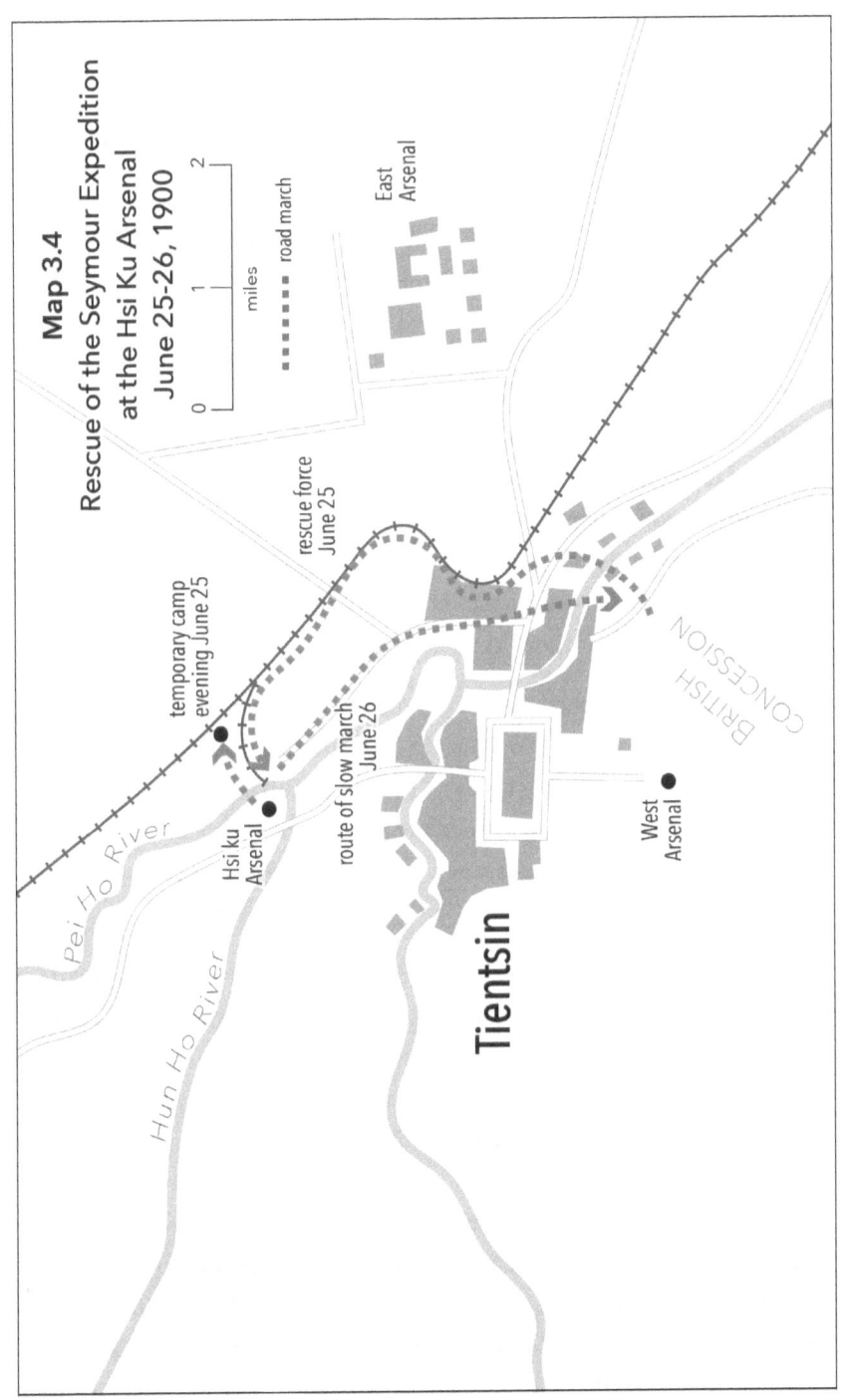

Map 3.4 Rescue of the Seymour Expedition at the Hsi Ku Arsenal June 25-26, 1900

After spending the night on the riverbank opposite the arsenal and tending to the wounded, the men turned back toward Tientsin at 4:30 a.m., "the march being very slow and toilsome on account of the large number of disabled men." By midmorning, Seymour's force reached the safety of Tientsin. McCalla, suffering from three wounds, turned over command of all American sailors and Marines to Waller. With the Seymour Expedition now safe, the foreign powers turned to the growing Boxer menace in Tientsin, knowing that Peking's situation grew more desperate.[28]

In his June 28 report to the commandant, recapping the events since his march from Taku, Waller recommended several of his junior officers "for such reward as you may deem proper." His remarks concerning his men left no room for misunderstanding, they had "made history, marked with blood." Waller expressed his hope for the future: "they were the first in the field, and please God, they will remain until the last man, woman and child is relieved from the toils of these barbarians." Waller summed up his assessment of his men who had marched from Taku:

> Our men have marched 97 miles in the five days, fighting all the way. They have lived on about one meal a day for about six days, but have been cheerful and willing always. They have gained the highest praise from all present, and have earned my love and confidence. They are like Falstaff's army in appearance, but with brave hearts and bright weapons.[29]

In these China operations, Waller earned his reputation as a soldier's soldier. Marines who served under Waller in the field championed him faithfully over the next twenty years, as he fought the coming political wars in the emerging new Corps. Waller never lacked support from those who recognized that he had suffered alongside his men in the heat of battle, and such experiences forged a bond that never weakened.

As for himself, Waller declared that "I can only [. . .] say that I did my best. I have carried the colors you surrendered to me through each fight. Today the Chinese Imperial colors are beneath them." In his endorsement to this report, Rear Admiral Louis Kempff strongly suggested that "a suitable medal for Major Waller and five percent additional pay for life in various grades he may reach" be awarded to the major for his service under fire in June. Kempff's remarks reflected the high regard Waller enjoyed for his abilities commanding men in the field. "I was delighted when the Marines arrived in the *Solace* to find that Major Waller was in command; feeling certain that the men would be well cared for and render creditable service." The admiral reported that "foreign officers have only the highest praise for their [Waller and McCalla] splendid fighting qualities."[30]

Back in the U.S., however, Waller's career was reported in a far different context. In June 1900, the *New York Journal* wrote that Waller had been captured by the Boxers and had been beheaded. The *Journal* claimed that the Boxers mounted Waller's head on a pole, flaunting it as a grisly warning to the western barbarians. The story was even accompanied by a sketch showing Waller's headless body lying on the ground next to a pole with his head exhibited on top. Having heard nothing from the Marine Corps officially, Waller's brother wrote the commandant on June 23, asking if the account was true. Heywood replied three days later that nothing was known about Waller other than what "has been published in the newspapers." The account was of course false, but it caused the family great distress. Waller had suffered no wounds from the Boxers and would die an old man in 1926.[31]

Meanwhile in China, Waller reported that Peking had sent word on June 23 that everyone had moved into the British legation, but that the defenders there had little ammunition left. A concentrated artillery barrage on the legation would, he predicted, inflict unacceptable civilian suffering. Waller, anticipating the worst, wrote that "there seems small chance of any movement [from Tientsin] toward Pekin[g] for three weeks." It would be, in fact, almost five weeks before the relief column could sally north. In the meantime, the foreign powers evacuated noncombatants from Tientsin while engaging the growing numbers of Boxers and imperial soldiers who threatened to overwhelm the concessions at Tientsin. The situation demanded swift and determined action.[32]

On June 27, the Russians moved on the East Arsenal, which posed the greatest immediate threat to the powers at Tientsin, but they were "driven back" by the more than seven thousand Boxers who occupied the fortress. The stymied Russians called for help, and Waller dispatched Second Lieutenant

Drawing—*Major Waller Praising His Men's Bravery.* The American troops under Major Waller helped to capture the East Arsenal at Tientsin, swimming the Pei-ho River and wading deep water under a hot fire. The British, Japanese, and Russian commanders sent letters to Major Waller, praising his skill and bravery. He lined up the American Marines, wet, muddy, and hungry, and read them the letters but gave the men all the credit. He reported later that his Marines looked like Falstaff's army, ragged, but with light hearts. *Courtesy of the National Archives.*

W. L. Jolly with forty Marines, along with his adjutant First Lieutenant A. E. Harding, to join the British under Commander Craddock for a second assault on the arsenal. With a command of eighteen hundred men, the westerners finally breeched the parapets and drove the Chinese from their fortifications. "Our men charged over the parapet with a British company" as Jolly led the British and American Marines in routing the arsenal's defenders. With the East Arsenal in allied hands, Waller and the other foreign commanders began drawing up plans to pacify the rest of Tientsin. The Americans had little to contribute since Waller's "effective strength" was down to eighty-nine men (see Map 3.5).[33]

As June turned to July, Waller grew increasingly frustrated with the delays in moving against the rest of the belligerents. The Chinese had failed to prevent the foreign landings at Taku, the rescue of Seymour, and the

# TO THE EAST: THE PHILIPPINES AND CHINA | 89

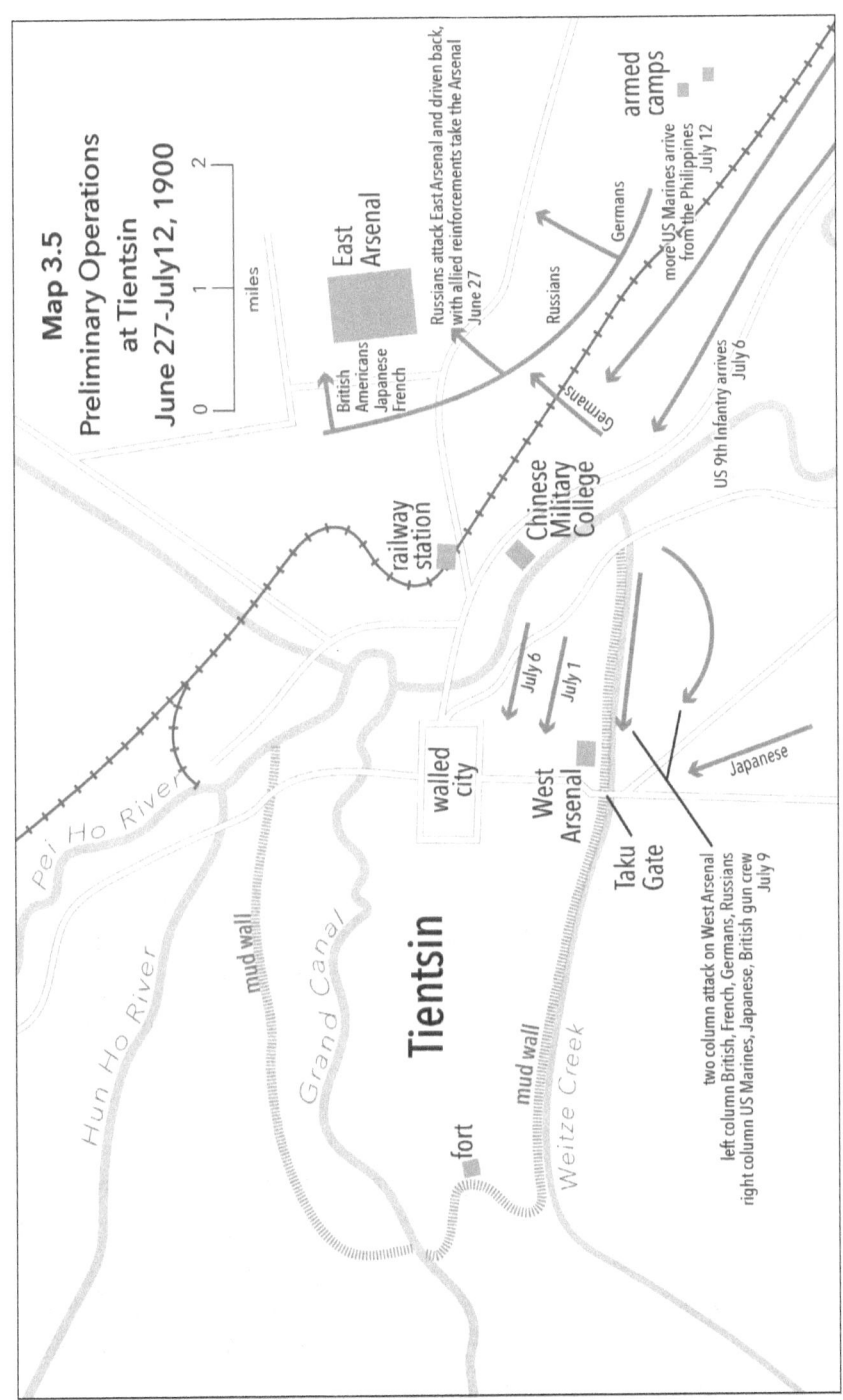

foreign buildup at Tientsin. Now was the right time to move against them, Waller argued, since any further delays would only allow the Chinese to regroup with the large numbers of Boxers flooding into Tientsin each day. But Waller's most significant problem proved to be the small size of his own force. Although respectful and willing to listen to his ideas, the other commanders reasoned that a nation contributing less than one hundred men should have little voice in determining how the combined expedition should be used. A frustrated Waller could only wait for reinforcements and prod the other leaders to action.[34]

While Waller fumed in China, the request for more Marines reached Asiatic Station commander Rear Admiral George C. Remey on board the flagship *Brooklyn* in the Philippines. At the time, Colonel Meade, who commanded the First Regiment remaining at Cavite, had been placed on the sick list, and Major Kidder White assumed temporary command. White told the admiral that "no Marines could be spared from the fighting then going on around Cavite with Aguinaldo's roving band." Meade exploded when he heard the news, immediately ordering White's arrest. Lieutenant Louis M. Little remembered Meade's anger. "The old gentleman who was laid up with rheumatism sprang six feet from his bed of pain, and the air was blue with his imprecations." Meade lost no time in warning Remey of White's error, and three days later the admiral asked Meade if the First Regiment, minus one company, could be ready to embark the next morning with "stores for three months." Meade replied that "I could and would." Through the night, the ailing colonel readied his command for sea, and leaving one company behind to maintain conditions on Luzon, the rest of the regiment sailed for Taku "via Hong Kong, Nagasaki, and Chifu."[35]

Meanwhile Waller joined in the preparations for an assault on the positions in Tientsin's Walled City where the Chinese had established formidable defenses. "I have ordered the American women and children out of this place and will try to get some off in the morning." Even as the urgently needed reinforcements steamed toward Taku, the Chinese artillery pounded the foreign positions at Tientsin continually. "We were shelled each day," Waller cabled, "the Chinese fire being very accurate; our barracks were struck three times and the adjoining houses five or six times each."

On July 3, Waller assigned Smedley Butler and eighty men to join a British battalion "to capture a gun that had been annoying us considerably." The Chinese moved the gun across the Pei Ho River preventing the Allies from taking it, but in vicious hand-to-hand fighting, the British-American force succeeded in taking two villages that had "given us much trouble, forming cover for 'snipers.'" Although successful in routing the Boxers from the villages, the enemy escaped with the gun in hand. When the order to retire came, part of the British force, the Wei hei wei (British Chinese), came under heavy fire and was in danger of being overwhelmed. Butler "deployed the Marines, advanced at the double to the position, opened fire by volleys, and permitted the [British] Chinese regiment to fall back in comfort." Butler then ordered his men to fall back "by section" and suffered no casualties. The episode revealed the significant forces that the Chinese had brought to bear on the foreign concessions. The day before, Waller had reported that reinforcements were needed to take the Tientsin fort. "It is a great menace to us at present." Waller and his Marines waited for the reinforcements while conditions deteriorated all around them. They did not have long to wait.[36]

The Ninth Infantry Regiment finally reached Taku on July 6, loaded immediately onto a train, and moved swiftly to Tientsin. With these fresh soldiers, on July 9 Waller and the allied forces mounted a two-column attack toward Tientsin's West Arsenal where the Chinese were threatening the concessions' western flank along the river. Waller commanded the right column of American Marines, Japanese sailors, and a British gun crew (see Map 3.5). "We were shelled heavily by the Chinese, but fortunately without casualty, although frequently covered with dust and stung by stones and gravel thrown up by bursting shell." The left column, led by the British, "hotly engaged the enemy and had them on the run in about thirty minutes." As the Chinese scattered, many retreated to the west of the arsenal while some took shelter in the arsenal itself. British and Japanese artillery units "silenced" Chinese guns firing from the distant mud forts while Japanese cavalry pursued the retreating Chinese to the west. Waller and the Japanese sailors "rushed" the arsenal under heavy fire as they "cleared the plain between the arsenal and the city."[37]

To Waller's delight, just after midnight in the early morning hours on July 12, Colonel Robert L. Meade arrived with the remainder of the First Marine

Colonel Robert L. Meade in his undress uniform, circa 1900. *Courtesy of U.S. Naval History and Heritage Command.*

Brigade, building the American strength to 348 Marines and 673 infantries, just over one thousand officers and men. Waller handed over command to Meade, who would last just two weeks before being invalided home amid a career-damaging scandal.

Meade's Marines "joined Waller's command at the China Merchants' Compound at the corner of Victoria and Canton Roads." The officers billeted in nearby houses close to officers from the British Marines and the Royal Welsh Fusiliers. Many of the Americans formed close bonds with their British counterparts, living and fighting together as danger and tension linked the two officer corps. The British knew of Waller's service in Egypt, and his continued goodwill and cooperation in China strengthened the camaraderie. In the years following the China Relief Expedition, the U.S. Marines and the Royal Welsh Fusiliers would exchange annual well wishes commemorating their service together in China.[38]

Meade had little time to get settled. He arrived in the darkness of night and found Tientsin "under shell fire of the enemy." The international forces controlled only the legation area outside the Walled City gate. Recognizing the situation's urgency, Meade noted that "the Walled City, strongly fortified, and all other portions of Tientsin, also strongly fortified, were held by the Chinese imperial troops and the 'Boxers.'" Through the streets, Chinese sharpshooters leveled a constant fire, beginning "about 10 o'clock and lasting until about daylight." After sunrise, British headquarters summoned Meade for a conference to plan an attack on the city for the next day. Meade "was called upon to furnish a quota of 1,000 men" for an attack scheme of two columns, with the Japanese forces on the right and the British and Americans on the left. The left column included "two companies of the Royal Welsh Fusiliers leading, followed by the Marines . . . , the English naval brigade, and finally the Ninth United States Infantry." The final battle for Tientsin was about to begin.[39]

At 3 a.m. on July 13, Meade led the American Marines from their quarters and joined the international force under the command of British General A.R.F. Dorward in the assault on the Walled City. Under Meade, Major Waller commanded the First Battalion with Captain C. G. Long heading the Second Battalion. Meade wrote later that "we marched through the Taku gate of the [mud wall] in two columns, the Japanese forces . . . to the right and the English and American forces on the left" (see Map 3.6). The attacking left column included two companies of Royal Welsh Fusiliers in front followed by the American Marines and the English sailors with the Ninth U.S. Infantry in the rear. The columns moved under cover of darkness parallel to the mud wall in a generally northwesterly direction until reaching a point just south of the West Arsenal where both columns turned north toward the Walled City. During the advance, the British artillery positioned itself halfway between the Taku gate and the West Arsenal and commenced firing on the Chinese "just before our arrival . . . at the south gate at 5 o'clock a.m." The Chinese guns replied "vigorously," but the British gunners proved "so accurate . . . that every shell landed" on target and "at about 5:45 o'clock a.m., the Chinese magazine" blew up "with a shock which was almost like an earthquake."[40]

Shortly after, Meade was ordered "to support the Royal Welsh Fusiliers in an attack on the extreme left, and we crossed the [mud] wall in skirmish line." As the attackers struck north toward the Walled City, Waller and his battalion protected the left as the Chinese attempted a flanking movement from the west. Long's Second Battalion "was about a thousand yards in our right rear protecting our flank and rear from a considerable body of the enemy." The van met heavy fire from Chinese artillery and from snipers positioned in the Walled City and on the approach to the south gate. The push proved tough going as the allied troops crossed a swampy, flat terrain littered with trenches and grave mounds. "The fire of the Chinese, both in artillery and infantry, was fearfully accurate . . . and I thank God for the mounds and dikes."[41]

Using the mounds and trenches to shield their advance "by rushes," the Marines worked their way forward in a ragged line and dug in some

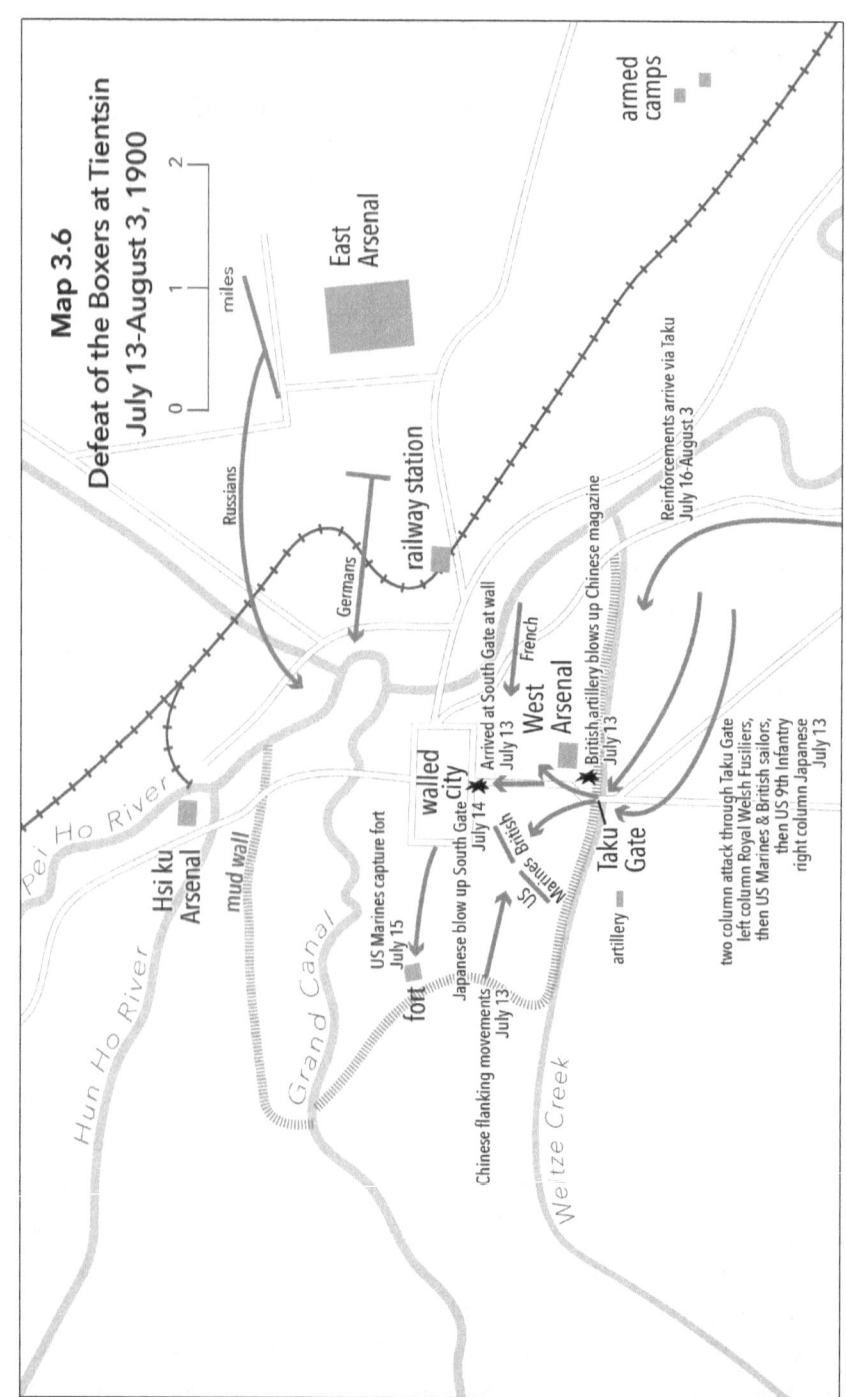

eight hundred yards from the Chinese. The Royal Fusiliers extended the skirmish line on the right. "On the firing line the action was especially hot and the enemy's fire especially rapid and accurate." At 8:30 a.m., the Chinese launched a flanking movement in large numbers along Waller's left. Under heavy fire, Waller turned his line on the left to confront the oncoming threat and successfully repelled the Chinese. Later, the Chinese feinted to the left flank, but the Marines, with Long's artillery company in the Second Battalion, had reached the mud wall and laid down a withering crossfire that carried the day. Meade reported that "the effort of the enemy proved a failure, and we drove them in." Throughout the rest of the day, the Chinese fired sporadically on the allied positions but launched no further efforts to flank the tenuous positions in the swampy graveyard. By nightfall, it seemed apparent that no breach of the city's gate would come that day so General Dorward ordered a pullback to the safety of the mud wall in the rear. For the Marines and the Fusiliers on the line, the withdrawal proved to be "the most difficult action of the day."[42]

With Chinese fire infiltrating their positions, Meade "ordered the withdrawal in small parties of eight or ten men, to rush from mound to mound or trench to trench." Despite the heavy fire, the skirmish line retreated to the southern side of the mud wall. They spent the night there with guns at the ready as Dorward sent food and water to the beleaguered troops resting during the night. Word reached the weary men that the Japanese complement would blow the south gate to the Walled City early in the morning whereupon the combined forces would rush the gate. At 6 a.m., true to plan, the Japanese blew the gate and the Marines rushed into the Walled City only to find it "filled with dead Chinamen and animals."[43]

The enemy had retreated to the suburbs with the Japanese in hot pursuit, driving the Chinese from the city. With the close of action on the fourteenth, all of Tientsin belonged to the foreign powers, and Dorward immediately made plans to consolidate his control of Tientsin and the surrounding countryside. On July 15, Dorward served notice to each of the commanders that he "contemplated moving on Pekin[g] in about a fortnight." With Chinese officials in flight, city residents together with allied soldiers looted the city in an eruption of anarchy.[44]

One Marine wrote that Tientsin "was looted by the [allied] forces and almost all have more loot than they can take care of." One of Waller's officers commented that no city had been "more thoroughly looted" in history than Tientsin, and Peking would "afford a richer harvest than Tientsin." Lieutenants Robert H. Dunlap and Little "found a trunk fairly filled with silks, satins, and priceless brocades." To save them from the fires burning all around them, Little explained, "we were about to put them in the trunk, when a harsh voice said 'Good morning, young gentlemen, what are you doing here[?]'" The voice belonged to Colonel Meade, who listened to the young lieutenants describing their efforts to save the precious textiles. Meade replied that "he too wanted to save a few things from the flames and that if we would allow him to put them in with ours[,] he would see that the trunk" was moved safely to storage in the legations area. Little complained that "of course that was the last that Dunlap or I ever saw of that trunk or its contents."[45]

Complaints about the looting reached Washington, prompting an immediate demand for an investigation. The official inquiry included testimony from Waller and other army officers that no looting had occurred in the American quarter during the brief occupation. Other than military stores seized from Chinese army warehouses and Chinese swords and arms kept by the officers and men, Waller explained that all looting had been done by Chinese prior to occupation. While Waller's report became the official position in Tientsin, unofficially, it was understood that looting had indeed taken place during the transition to American control, and individual Marine accounts confirm that reality. In the meantime, Waller and the First Battalion had one more operation at Tientsin before moving in relief of Peking.[46]

On July 15, Dorward ordered Waller to organize a small force of American Marines and Royal Welsh Fusiliers and scout "to the west" in search of a reported enemy fort. The major and his men found the fort and "rushed it without opposition, securing eight guns, many standards, arms, carts, ammunition, etc." The enemy simply melted away, leaving the allied forces in control of Tientsin and its environs. Later that same day, Waller and part of his First Battalion entered the city and took up guard duties there. They seized a large stock of gold bullion, securing it in a bank vault while Washington decided what to do with the treasure. While the Marines waited for the inevitable campaign for Peking, command of the regiment shifted once more to Waller.⁴⁷

Along with many of the officers in the Marine Corps of that era, Colonel Meade had a reputation as a drinker. Waller enjoyed the same celebrity, but for Meade, years of alcohol abuse had taken a serious toll, and in China, it impaired his judgment and contributed to his increasing physical disabilities. Henry Clay Cochrane, Waller's mentor and friend, recorded in his diary that Waller reported that Meade had been drunk and "offensive to Butler and other officers at mess at Cavite" earlier that year, and later at Tientsin, Meade, in a drunken fury, removed Waller from command due to a remark that Meade found distressing. Meade's erratic actions prompted his removal from command for medical reasons shortly after the battle for Tientsin, and he was invalided home.⁴⁸

The surgeon's report included a detailed description of Meade's physical infirmities and concluded that the "patient has been drinking considerably since his arrival in Tientsin. His drinking seems to affect him mentally, causing loss of memory. He is quite feeble." Admiral George C. Remey, commander in chief, directed Meade to send any "statement he may wish to have filed with this report direct[ly] to the Navy Department." Meade's subsequent response to the drinking charges was a rambling and desperate argument that only proved the surgeon's findings.⁴⁹

In the early morning hours of July 28, the distressed Meade slipped out of Tientsin while Waller approached the wharf. Meade had secretly changed his departure time to avoid seeing Waller that morning, and Waller wrote Meade later in the day saying he was "very much disappointed and considerably chagrined" to arrive at the dock "only

William F. Biddle, who later was appointed commandant of the Marine Corps. *Courtesy of the Library of Congress.*

to find you going down the river." He was "hurt at not being able to see you off at the last." Waller added that "I think, Colonel, that in spite of your desire to remain[,] it is far better for you to go home now." He argued that the campaign for Peking would be "severe" and intimated that Meade could not survive such a test of strength and will.[50] Once again Waller commanded the Marines in China, but it would not be for long.

Major William P. Biddle, who outranked Waller, sent word ahead that he had landed at Taku and would be in Tientsin soon. "While I am glad to see Major Biddle, I am sorry to lose command of the men. I have led them always until now. I suppose I must bow to the fortunes of war and a complication unforeseen by anyone." This statement, placed in an official report to the commandant, suggests a veiled confirmation that Waller actually commanded the Marines, at least tactically, in the battle for Tientsin, not the ailing Meade. There was no official response to Waller's missive to Washington. The growing allied response to the crisis in China and the resulting buildup left Waller too junior to retain command of either the American forces ashore or the Marine regiment. Despite his ambitions, the size of the force necessary to relieve Peking would require a general officer in command. The Marines had but one general officer, the commandant back in the United States, so from the beginning, it was clear that command must go to an Army officer.[51]

## THE RELIEF OF PEKING

On July 30, Major General Adna R. Chaffee arrived in Tientsin with additional reinforcements and assumed command of all United States forces in China. A few days later on August 4, the relief expedition left Tientsin and began a "succession of marches which are said to be as hard as any ever made," although they were "short,

Major General Adna R. Chaffee, U.S. Army. *Courtesy of the Library of Congress.*

from ten to twelve miles a day." For about ten days, the columns lumbered toward Peking through corn fields where the heat of the day and "the dust of the wagon trains and light batteries ahead combined with the heat and alkali water and the treeless country made" the trek brutal for everyone. Suffering men discarded their gear along the road, and many died where they stopped to rest. "Both sides [of the road were] lined with men from every foreign regiment 'mixed up together' in convulsions and foaming at the mouth." Waller's earlier prediction about the difficulties of the campaign ahead proved true. Meade would have suffered terribly on the march to Peking, but Chaffee wrote later complimenting Waller and Captain F. J. Moses, the two Marine battalion commanders, "whose energy, good judgment, and capacity to command their battalions in battle I noted with pleasure" (see Map 3.7).[52]

As the relief expedition moved toward Peking, the First Marine Regiment under Biddle included Waller's First Battalion with three companies of Marines and Moses's Second, also with three companies. The rest of the regiment remained at Tientsin. Columns of Russian, French, and German troops headed north along the left bank of the Pei Ho River while the British, Americans, and the Japanese paralleled their course to the stream's right. The allied expedition reached their first objective at Hsi Ku at 4:30 p.m. that same afternoon and bivouacked for the night. The march had proved uneventful thus far, but scouts located the enemy dug in on both sides of the Pei Ho River at Peitsung, and plans were made to attack early the next morning.[53]

From the beginning, the weather and terrain proved as much of an obstacle for the allies as did the Chinese opposition. Oppressive heat and choking dust, stirred up by the marching columns, dogged the expedition as it moved through high corn fields and villages along the way. During the first night at Hsi Ku, the rain fell unrelentingly, and the dust turned to mud. Waller and his Marines got little sleep during the turbulent night and at 2 a.m., the order went out to prepare for a 3 a.m. march.[54]

The Japanese led the column into Peitsung and bore the brunt of the fighting. At "3:30 heard heavy infantry fire to our front and left," and the firing grew heavy throughout the early morning hours as the Americans held back until about 7 a.m. Later, Waller wrote that "the Japanese troops engaged and defeated the enemy at [Peitsung], but our troops were not engaged." In reserve,

100 | CHAPTER 3

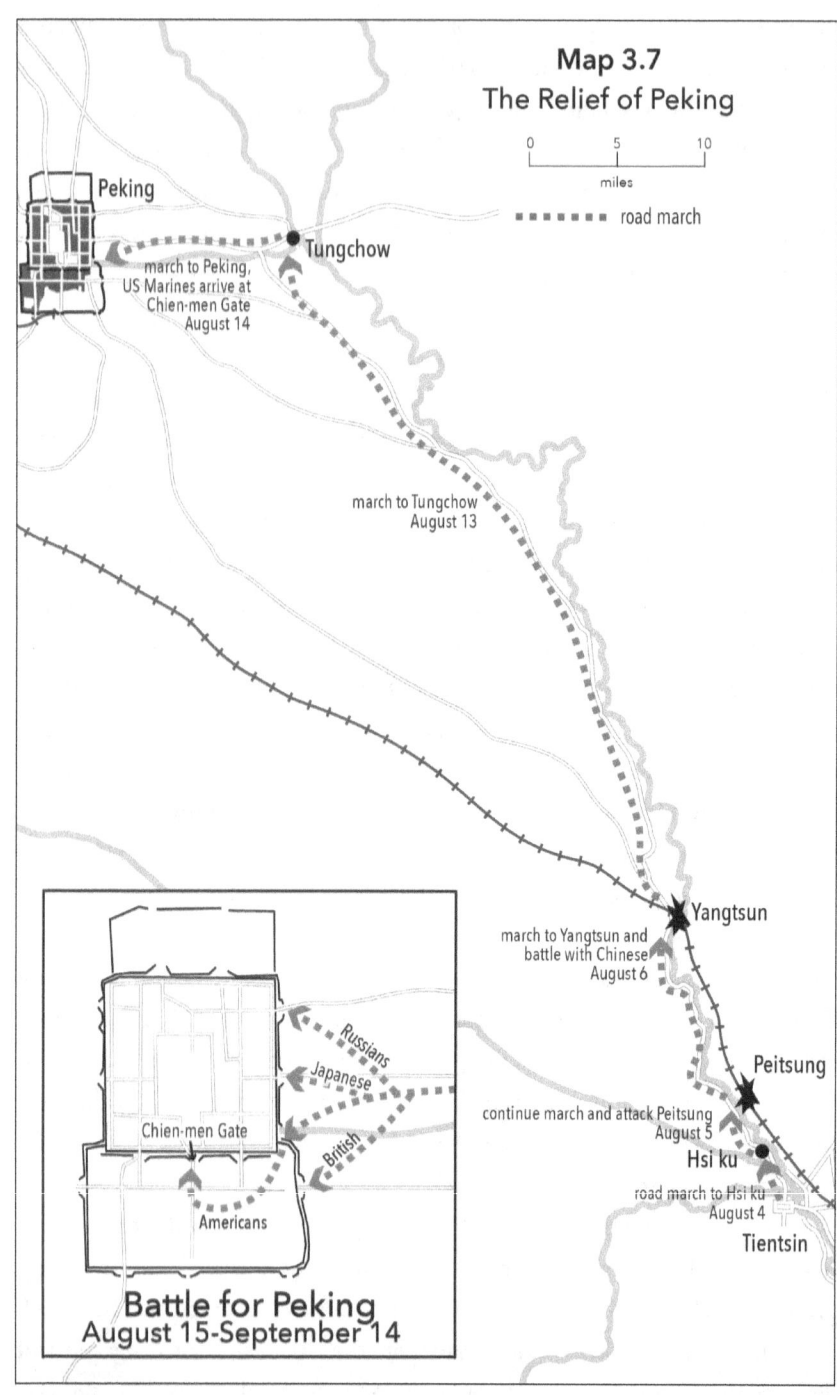

Map 3.7
The Relief of Peking

Waller and the Marines moved into camp at 2 p.m., while the Japanese and Russians mopped up the fleeing Chinese. During the day, the Japanese infantry pressured the Chinese and "charged [an artillery] battery and captured ten guns [while losing] 300 men[.] The [Japanese] are splendid soldiers and seem tireless. Everyone here considers that they have no superiors in the world." The Japanese continued their push throughout the day, and when the Chinese fled across "the river they fell into the hands of the Russians."[55]

The camp at Peitsung "was the first and last camp where there was any resemblance to military order as far as shelter tents were concerned." As the relief columns approached Yangtsun, fearful that any delay would bring them to Peking too late to save their countrymen, the pace of march accelerated even as the heat and dust brought a wearing fatigue down upon the allied infantry. At 7 a.m. on August 6, the main body left camp "in three separate columns, Russo-French, English and Americans." At Yangtsun, the Chinese defended the town with lines "developed . . . in concave form." The U.S. Fourteenth Infantry, along with the British, attacked the Chinese on "the right [of the enemy's position] and on the left side of the road embankment." The U.S. Ninth Infantry moved in on the left with Waller's First Battalion "on the line" supporting the artillery battery and Moses and the Second Battalion in reserve. Waller described the struggle's intensity: "numerous changes

Major William Biddle (left) and Major Littleton Waller (right) during a rest stop en route to Peking. *Courtesy of Marine Corps Historical Center, Quantico, Virginia.*

Major Littleton Waller sleeping on the field after the battle at Peitsung, August 5, 1900. *Courtesy of Marine Corps Historical Center, Quantico, Virginia.*

of direction and objective tired the men, and the great heat and the steady movement through high corn began to tell, the men dropping out of the line, overcome by heat." It would get no better. The heat and exhaustion proved to be Waller's greatest adversary. By the time Biddle's Marines reached Peking, over half his men had dropped out due to fatigue and heat-related illness. Both Waller and Moses were forced to assign able-bodied men to guard the sick and wounded left behind, leaving precious few for the attack at Peking.[56]

The Chinese had stood their ground at Peitsung and Yangtsun as the Japanese and Russian troops carried the fight to them. The Marines encountered the butchered bodies of the Chinese in both places, where "some were beheaded and their heads suspended from corn stalks by their pigtails." Both the Japanese and the Russians used the bayonet liberally, killing all Chinese stragglers and taking no prisoners; "the Russians chopped their heads off." The Chinese were particularly brutal in their retaliation upon Russian prisoners. In spite of such carnage, the primary enemy on the march continued to be the heat, and most of Waller's casualties on the march were heat-related.[57]

"On the thirteenth we reached Tungchow," about twelve miles from Peking, "the Japs ahead had already captured it and heaped up the dead in

Captain Henry J. Reilly commanded a battery of the 5th U.S. Artillery, which blasted open the gates at Peking. He was killed by hostile enemy fire on August 15, 1900, during the action to rescue the international legations from the Boxers. *Courtesy of Arlington National Cemetery.*

piles, and looted the city." During the night, rain fell again, bringing some respite to the beleaguered troops. The next day, the Marines led the advance against the Imperial City. "We took position on the Chien-men gate and cleared away the barricades, in order that the artillery might take position." Waller placed two companies in the "second story of the pagoda," while the Second Battalion under Moses "took position along the wall." The Marines "fired volleys" at heavily fortified enemy emplacements at the first gate; under heavy fire throughout the morning, the Marines drove the Chinese from their positions, gaining command of the Chien-men gate. During the fight, one of the infantry officers, Captain H. J. Reilly, received a mortal wound as he stood by his old friend Waller. Captain

Painting—Storming the gate to Peking, China, August 1900. Major Littleton W. T. Waller, USMC, in center (without hat). *Courtesy of the National Archives.*

The body of Captain Reilly, of the 5th U.S. Artillery, lying in the Chien-men (Front Gate) building, surrounded by his men. *Courtesy of National Archives.*

Smedley Butler later recalled that "I had been there only a moment when a bullet struck Captain Reilly in the mouth and killed him. That fine officer fell back into the arms of his life-long comrade, Major Waller."[58]

Until the end, Waller led his Marines, risking his life with theirs, confident of his place among men. The major endured the rigors of the campaign trail at a time when many of his men, younger and in better physical condition, fell aside. Waller demonstrated that through discipline and sheer will, he could command troops in the worst of times. His fellow officers in the allied command recognized this quality in his leadership, as did his superior officers. In China, Waller was put to the test and emerged with the reputation as a fighter and an effective commander. It would not be the last test, for Samar waited in the wings.

As the battle for Peking came to a close on September 14, General Chaffee appointed Waller provost marshall of the city. With growing public scrutiny and rising outrage over the looting in Tientsin and along the campaign trail, Chaffee ordered that Waller put a stop to the looting and cautioned all commanders to get control of their men. Chaffee was determined to stop the raping and killing of innocents in the American sector. Years later, Waller occasionally encountered charges that under his watch, looting and attacks on Chinese civilians were carried out with his blessing. But while the American soldiers and Marines did commit atrocities during the heat of battle, Waller aggressively executed an occupation policy of enforcement, securing the American zone of occupation and assisting the Chinese who found themselves under duress.[59]

In the end, the foreign settlements at Tientsin and Peking held off the Boxers until rescued by their countrymen, but it was a close thing. The relief operations in China illustrated, at least for the United States, that new responsibilities of empire demanded significantly new military and naval resources. The campaigns in the Philippines and China represented an expanding mission for the Marine Corps, one that competed with the Army and the Navy for resources and budgets, and one that grew as the twentieth century unfolded.

Waller and his Marines found that their training and equipment served them well in severe and unforgiving combat conditions. These qualities emerged during the battles for Tientsin and Peking, where overwhelming odds, heavy losses, a hostile indigenous population, and long communication lines demanded exceptional leadership from Waller and his officers and unquestioned discipline and loyalty from the men. This daunting combination ensured the relief of Peking.

CHAPTER 4 **SAMAR**

On September 28, 1901, Company C of the Army's Ninth Regiment at Balangiga, Samar, suffered overwhelming losses in a sudden attack. Filipino insurgents dressed as women in a funeral procession struck in a surprise attack, catching most of the soldiers at breakfast and without their weapons. The guerillas pursued the Americans in a frenzied wave of terror, giving no quarter and making quick work of the defenseless soldiers. Only a few escaped by plunging into the nearby river. Of the seventy-four-man garrison, only twenty-six survived to tell the story.[1]

News of the Samar massacre convinced stunned military authorities that resistance in the southern Philippines demanded increased action. American commanders responded by adopting a policy designed to generate "wholesome fear" among the Filipinos where "every hostile motion of any inhabitant . . . will be quickly and severely punished."[2]

While the situation clearly called for renewed pacification efforts, efforts which had proved successful in the northern islands, an untimely appointment shaped different results in the south. Seniority placed General Jacob Smith in charge on Samar, and although generally inexperienced in large commands, Smith would now direct American efforts to subdue the region. Hardly suited for such a volatile environment, Smith's mental faculties, one observer suggested, were so seriously flawed that he was prone to "outbursts in which he urged the most violent and irresponsible actions."[3] The events in Balangiga and the response in the councils of American power set in motion a new phase of military operations on Samar, one that would soon ignite a fiery debate at home where the Republican administration proved hard pressed to defend itself. At the heart of this political firestorm stood Colonel Littleton W. T. Waller, who soon became a symbol for imperialists and anti-imperialists alike. Fresh from China's campaign trails that led from

Taku and Tientsin to Peking, Waller found in Samar a new enemy, one that would lay a lasting claim on his future.[4]

During the summer months of 1901, military government had come to an end in the Philippines as Governor General William Howard Taft established civil authority over the islands. Insurgent activity declined but did not end, and Taft and General Adna Chaffee, Army commander in the islands, disagreed over the status of the insurrection and the appropriate policy for dealing with it. Taft, convinced that the military situation was stable, argued that diplomacy would engender democratic institutions and Filipino participation in the American colonial administration. But to Chaffee the situation was a "volcano" on the verge of eruption, and only swift military action could forestall catastrophic consequences for the new empire.

The heated struggle between Taft and Chaffee reached critical levels during the fall, and the question finally reached President Theodore Roosevelt in Washington. The ex–Rough Rider uncharacteristically avoided decisive action, simply urging his quarreling appointees to resolve their differences. After a few months in office, Roosevelt recognized the political danger for himself as imperialists and anti-imperialists clashed over the Philippine situation. There was real political division in the country over a foreign policy of

Major General Adna R. Chaffee commanded the Army in the Philippines. *Courtesy of the Library of Congress.*

William Howard Taft, governor general in the Philippines. *Courtesy of the Library of Congress.*

interventionism and empire building. Roosevelt's political foes were looking for Republican failures and misadventures that would give them leverage in the political battles underway and in the future. Wary of the potential for failures in the Philippines, Roosevelt chose not to weigh in on the Taft/Chaffee conflict. He cabled both men to work out their issues, offering no imperatives and leaving Taft and Chaffee to continue to pursue policy in their different fashions. For the troops in the field, this ambivalence led to a "year of guerrilla war" where the "Marine Corps met victory and disaster."[5]

The Balangiga massacre gave Chaffee the entrée he needed to argue the situation's urgency to the War Department in Washington. On October 16, he cabled Secretary of War Elihu Root that insurgents had launched a new uprising in Samar:

> Forty-six men, Company E, Ninth Regiment, US Infantry, under First Lieutenant George W. Wallace, in field, Lower Gandara, Samar, were attacked by four hundred bolomen today. Our loss, ten killed, six wounded, names not received; eighty-one enemy left dead on field; enemy beaten off.[6]

The next day Chaffee again cabled Root, detailing that the garrison at Weyler on Samar had been attacked by bolomen,[7] "some with rifles."[8] This report provoked an immediate response from Root, who recognized that the insurgents equipped with rifles represented a change in Samar resistance. The rifles, Root reasoned, "must have come from Balangiga," and he ordered Chaffee to "take appropriate action immediately to quell new insurgent uprisings [on] Samar."[9] Balangiga thereby became the tool by which Chaffee checked Taft's civil prerogatives and regained the authority to apply renewed military pressure on the "volcano" in Samar. This set the stage for Waller's Marines to enter the affair, and soon they would be at the center of the storm, one which would focus the world's attention on Samar.

In October 1900, the First Marine Regiment had returned to the Philippines from China on board the "the *Brooklyn, Zafiro,* and the transport *Indiana.*" With the Marines organized into a brigade of two regiments, the First Regiment moved to Olongapo on Subic Bay while the Second took up station at Cavite. Gradually, the number of posts assigned to Marine responsibility increased as the level of operations rose. Marine Commandant Charles Heywood reported that his men occupied fourteen stations, including six new posts established in the Cavite district during the previous calendar year. Waller and the Marines at Cavite protected American property, guarded the lighthouse, coal stores, and supply depot against a continuing security threat from Filipinos engaged in thievery or guerilla operations. It was to Admiral Fred Rodgers, commanding all naval forces in the islands, that Chaffee turned to for assistance in responding to the Balangiga disaster on Samar.[10]

## SAMAR OPERATIONS BEGIN

With new orders to put down the independence movement on Samar, Chaffee moved with dispatch. He established the Sixth Separate Brigade, a new command to be headquartered at Tacloban on nearby Leyte and charged with suppressing the violence on Samar swiftly and completely. Chaffee named Brigadier General Jacob H. Smith to command the brigade, a soldier he knew from Indian campaign days in the American West. Confident that Smith would act quickly and decisively, Chaffee's assessment proved distressingly correct.[11]

Brigadier General Jacob H. Smith commanded the Sixth Separate Brigade. Waller and the Marines on Samar served under Smith's headquarters. *Vernon Williams Archives.*

In early October, Smith cabled Chaffee that he would need at least a thousand men for the job and asked for a battalion of Marines from Admiral Rodgers. On October 19, Chaffee notified Smith that Marines would be assigned to his command and requested his suggestions for their placement. Smith decided to use the Marines at "Basey and east including Balangiga" in relief of Army troops then posted there.[12] Two days later, Waller received the first of two orders from Admiral Rodgers, placing him in command of the proposed Marine battalion under Smith. The mission proved to be the beginning of Waller's travail as well as the final large-scale action in the Philippine campaign.

> You are hereby detached from duty with the First Brigade U.S. Marines, Cavite, and from such other duty as may have been assigned you, and you will report immediately to the Senior Squadron Commander, Commanding Southern Squadron, for duty as Commanding Officer of the Marine Battalion destined for service in the Island of Samar, P.I.[13]

The next day Waller received a second order clarifying his status within the Navy chain of command during his detached duty in Samar:

> Your orders of October 21, detaching you from duty with the First Brigade, Marines, and directing you to report to the Commanding Officer of the Marine Battalion destined for service in Samar, are so far modified that you will not regard yourself detached from the First Brigade Marines.[14]

Joseph Schott, in his study of the Samar campaign, suggested that this second order's reference to Waller reporting *"to"* the commanding officer of the Marine Battalion was a typographical error since Rodgers intended that Waller be the commanding officer.[15] The more important issue in the second order, however, is the question of the authority under which Waller's command would serve on Samar. Although there would be great confusion later about Waller's detached status, Rodgers made it clear on October 22 that Waller was not detached from the Navy for temporary service with the Army but should operate in concert with the Army under General Smith's local control.

On October 22, 1901, at 8:30 in the morning, Waller's Marines (319 officers and men) began boarding Admiral Rodgers' Asiatic Fleet flagship, the armored cruiser *New York* tied up at the dock at Cavite. Toughened by the rigors of the Boxer campaign, Waller made certain that his command came aboard well equipped for the field work ahead. The night before embarkation, work parties loaded the battalion's artillery pieces, automatic guns, "an armorer's wagon and five pack mules." The next morning the men loaded over "40,000 rounds of rifle ammunition and 10,000 food rations in heavy wooden boxes" into the ship's spaces below decks. The battalion, carrying "full field packs and weapons," assembled on deck where the ship's company welcomed the Marines on board. Captain Morris MacKenzie formally greeted the Marines, then the chaplain delivered "a short inspirational talk which ended in a brief prayer." The crew then turned to and at 10 a.m., tugs eased the *New York* away from the wharf and the vessel maneuvered into Manila Bay where she picked up a pilot and rendezvoused with the gunboat *Zafiro*. Leaving Manila behind, the *New York*, trailed by the *Zafiro*, slipped through the cool and rainy morning, passing the old Spanish fortifications at Corregidor and sailing "through the south channel" into the South China Sea. Beyond the southern horizon lay the Marines' fateful destination, the island of Samar (see Map 4.1).[16]

Waller wrote that Admiral Rodgers "insisted on my being in his cabin with him. It was very pleasant indeed and he was exceedingly kind in every regard." Rodgers afterward maintained a personal correspondence with Waller that demonstrated the admiral's intention of holding to the Navy's line of authority throughout Waller's assignment on Samar. "I will be glad to

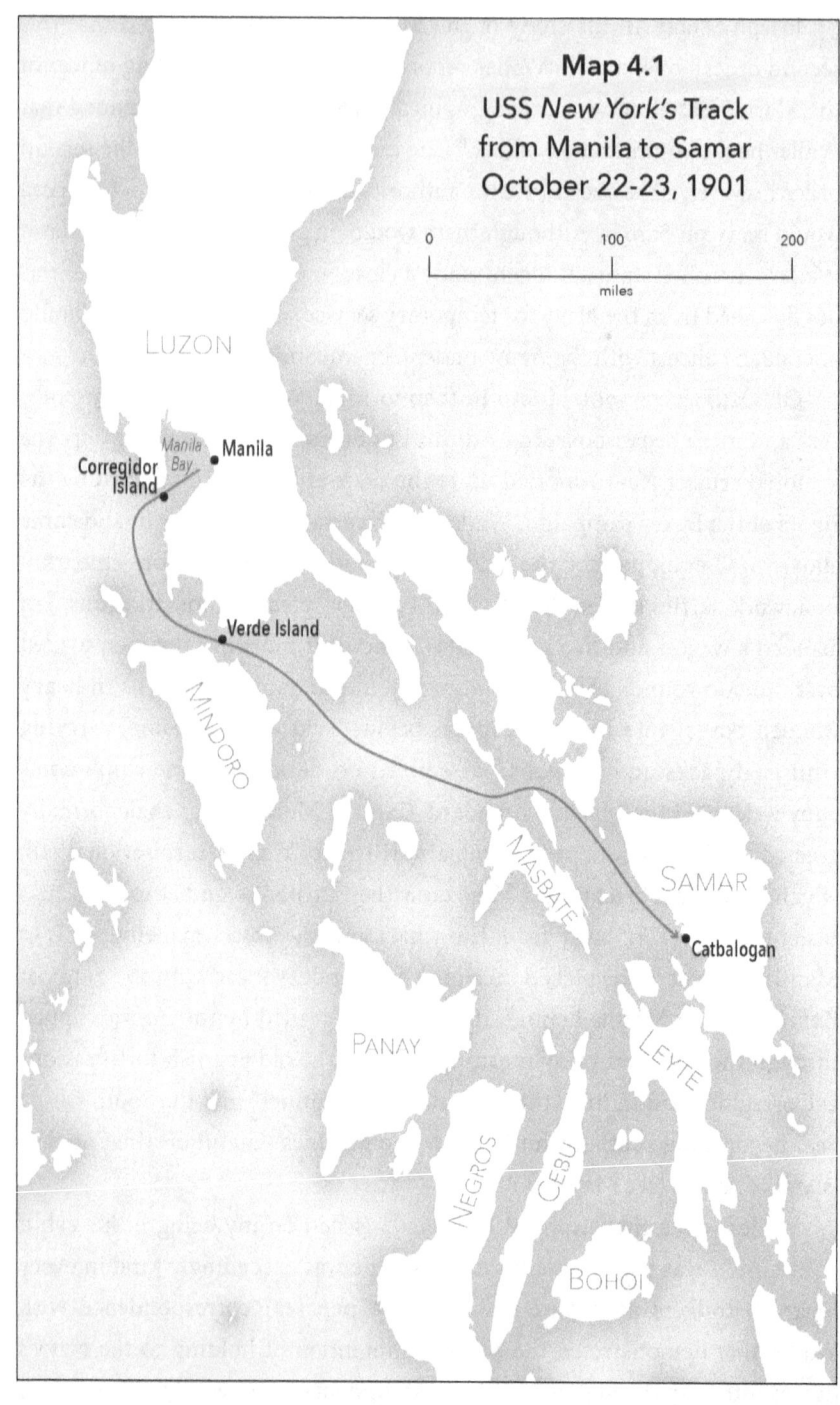

Map 4.1 USS *New York's* Track from Manila to Samar October 22-23, 1901

Rear Admiral Frederick Rodgers, a turn of the century photograph. *Courtesy of U.S. Naval History and Heritage Command.*

hear from you <u>personally</u> in regard to affairs in your part of Samar."[17]

Just before dark, the two ships passed through the Verde Island passage just south of Luzon where out of the darkening mist, the former Spanish cruiser *Don Juan De Austria* steamed toward them. As they passed, the *New York* "exchanged numbers" and sailed on south as the old warship disappeared off the stern into the rainy gloom. The rest of the evening proved uneventful as the *New York* passed the halfway point, steaming on into the night.[18]

The USS *New York* (CA-2), armored cruiser no. 2, underway, circa the 1890s. *Courtesy of U.S. Naval History and Heritage Command.*

The two vessels arrived off Catbalogan, Samar, on October 23 at about 11:30 a.m. General Smith waited as the two ships maneuvered alongside the dock, and as the engines fell silent, he boarded the *New York* to confer with Admiral Rodgers and Waller. In that meeting, Smith gave Waller clear indication of what he expected of his subordinate. Smith "told me that he had heard of me and my work in China" and promised, "Colonel, I give you free hand and if you do well here in cleaning up your district, I will see that you get two brevets for every one [that] you have rec[eived] already."[19] Waller confided to his wife a few days later "that would make me a general darling and [I] would assuredly pass the terrible office hunters in Washington."[20]

Over the years, Smith's conversations at Catbalogan have been confused with his documented remarks a few days later at Balangiga. Although many accounts suggest that Smith presented Waller with his "kill and burn" verbal orders in this first meeting, no evidence survives that details the conversation on board the *New York* between Smith, Rodgers, and Waller. Since Rodgers never testified in court on the issue, and Waller did not describe Smith's October 23 instructions explicitly in his testimony or in any private correspondence, only Waller's own orders that he dictated soon after his meeting with Smith provide clues to instructions given him by Smith aboard the *New York*.[21]

Facing an irregular campaign against an indigenous population where the enemy merged unidentifiably with the local people, Waller issued orders designed to isolate the insurgency. Reminding his officers of the treachery of the recent Balangiga massacre, Waller counseled them to "place no confidence in the natives and punish treachery immediately with death." He set October 25 as the deadline for all male Filipinos to come before Marine authorities to register and declare allegiance to American representatives. After that date, all remaining adult men must be considered enemy combatants. Waller warned his officers that the Filipino insurgent was "treacherous, brave, and savage," not to be trusted or relied upon regardless of appearance or situation. "The men must be informed of the courage, skill, size and strength of the enemy." Waller counseled that "we must do our part of the work, and with the knowledge that we are not to expect quarter." With these stringent instructions, Waller gave Samar's populace an opportunity to escape General

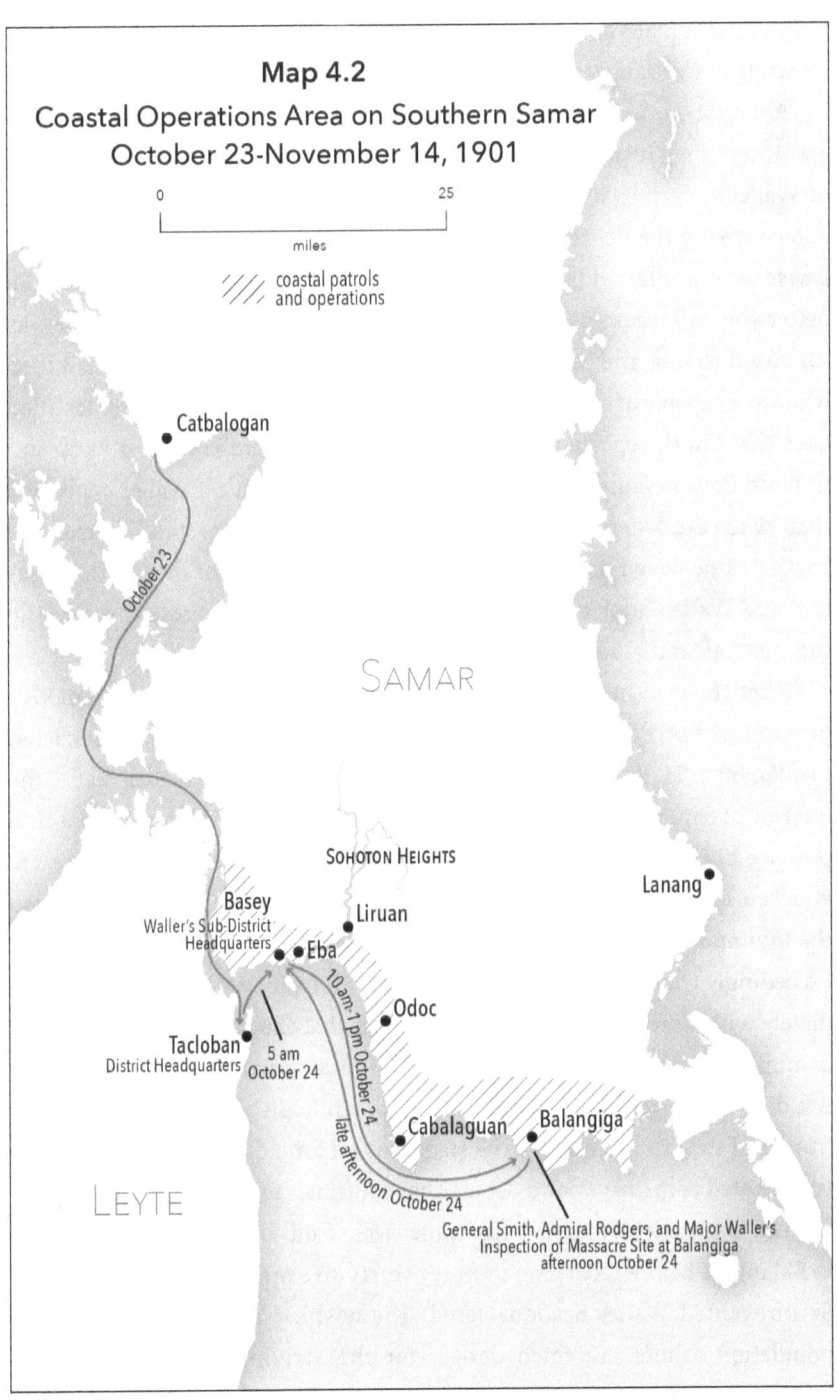

Smith's harsh plans and provided the Marines under him with a clear understanding of the danger they faced on Samar.[22]

A few days later found Smith, Rodgers, and Waller at Balangiga (see Map 4.2) where they inspected the massacre site and arranged for a detachment of Waller's Marines under Captain David D. Porter to garrison the village. After viewing the devastation, Smith told Waller that "I want no prisoners. I wish you to kill and burn. The more you kill and the more you burn, the better you will please me." Waller requested clarification on just who he was supposed to kill, and Smith emphasized that "he wanted all persons killed who were capable of bearing arms," anyone ten years or older. Waller testified later that Smith repeated this several times in the presence of others, and Captain Porter confirmed Waller's testimony under oath.[23] Waller explained that "when the orders were given by the General[,] we were standing over the partially uncovered bodies of the cruelly murdered men of the Ninth Infantry" and Waller "took into account the emotion felt by all present, especially the General, and modified the orders to suit the laws of war."[24]

After the meeting, Waller quietly told his officers that "we were not sent here to make war on women and children and old men." Yet some time later, Lieutenant J. H. A. Day brought Waller a note from Smith that read, "the interior of Samar must be made a howling wilderness." Waller soon put into practice his operational plan for Samar. "We have orders that where we are attacked to destroy everything, kill all the men, and drive the people into the mountains."[25] Waller wrote Clara that "these people are very brave, but exceedingly treacherous." He confided that "all treachery is punished immediately with death" and recognized early on that the authority vested in his command demanded circumspection. "This is a tremendous power for me to wield and I try hard not to abuse it, but it is difficult to forget my murdered friends of the 9th Infantry."[26] The stage was set for a disaster that would provoke heated controversy and debate that continues to the present day.

The first order of business for Waller was to off-load Porter's detachment at Balangiga before returning to Basey thirty-five miles away where General Smith wanted Waller headquartered. The hostility evident in the Filipino population ashore presented danger for the arriving Marines who "had lots of trouble in getting the stores landed at Balangiga."[27] Admiral Rodgers wrote Waller a few days later that "I did not like the looks of the place where Porter's detachment was left, and [I] sent another gunboat down with orders to keep one there all the time."²⁸ According to Waller, Rodgers had just cause for concern, for "we shelled the enemy beaches which was a great surprise to them and caused them to take to their heels and run." As soon as Porter got safely ashore and established the perimeter, Waller sailed back to Basey where he moved immediately against the local strongholds.²⁹

"I sent an expedition out against a town a little distance from here and captured 48 prisoners and burned the town." Waller ordered Porter to mount a similar patrol, keeping the pressure on the insurgents along the coastline. Translating the urgency of Smith's orders into action, Waller lost no time in denying the enemy the support from along the coastline. "Last night I shot a shell at a signal fire and it exploded beautifully and the fire went out immediately." During the first few weeks, Waller sent out numerous patrols along the coast and into areas further into the interior. The insurgents were operating from villages, towns, and small settlements located all through the inner coastal region from Basey down to Balangiga (see Map 4.2). His orders to the patrols were "to drive the people into the mountains and [to] destroy" the houses, crops, settlements, and anything found that could be of value to the insurgents. Samar was Waller's kind of soldiering: "You see I don't have much time to rest my feet, but I like it immensely."³⁰

Until the middle of November, Waller's Marines on Samar concentrated on coastal areas, burning huts, food supplies, livestock, and shipping—as the Marines put pressure on the insurgents and forced them deeper into the interior. Almost daily, Waller sent patrols out from Basey and Balangiga sweeping along the coastal areas around the two bases. Waller reported a constant pattern of destruction of houses, boats, and food, making the area inhospitable for the insurgents and driving them into the interior where they would not have access to communications and supplies from their supporters along the coastal waterways. "On the 8th [of November, I] sent a party to Eba to destroy it and kill or capture all men." The expedition enjoyed typical success, destroying "forty houses, three carabaos, and about one-half ton of hemp, killed nine men, captured eleven, all armed with bolos."³¹ In carrying out Smith's draconian policy on Samar, Waller summed up the first ten days of November: "two hundred and fifty-five houses burned, thirty-nine men killed, eighteen men captured, seventeen bolos captured, one ton hemp and one-half ton rice destroyed. Approximately thirty bancas destroyed. Thirteen carabaos killed."[32]

Waller's strategy cleared points of supply and support along the southern coast of Samar, and early on he began pursuing the fleeing insurgents inland toward the Sojoton region in the northeastern mountains. "My reports show that the people driven from the towns are falling back on the Sojoton district." He planned to "attack this country as soon as I can get a good platform made for my three-inch gun," which he needed to shell "the enemy out of the overhanging cliffs" there. Convinced that the insurgents would never be stopped without control of the island's heart, Waller readied for the march to the interior.[33]

## SOJOTON RIVER EXPEDITION

The Sojoton Heights, rugged volcanic cliffs on the Sojoton River in the Sojoton Mountains where the insurgents had been building defensive positions for years, were considered impenetrable; no Spanish or American force had ever attempted an operation against this redoubt. Determined to deprive the enemy of the protection that the Sojoton district afforded, on November 5, Waller sortied from Basey aboard two boats from the gunboat *Vicksburg* and "went to the Sojoton this morning, drove the enemy from his trenches, and captured lantakahs [bamboo cannons]." The gun platform used to protect the landing men and the three-inch rifle both worked well in the approach to shore, but after the fight the platform floundered in a cross sea and sank from sight. "The men were saved," the gun retrieved, and the party returned to the *Vicksburg* none the worse for wear. Waller reported that the platform had been "a great success" in the landing and attack and promised that he could make it "absolutely seaworthy." The Vicksburg boats returned to Basey with the Marines, and Waller pledged "to try again."[34]

During the next week, Waller continued his coastal clearing operations while he prepared for another expedition to the interior's Sojoton district. On November 13, he telegraphed Smith's headquarters at Tacloban and asked permission to "employ, uniform, and arm twenty natives as scouts." He needed the extra scouts for the expedition, explaining that he had "about ten [scouts] that have done excellent service without arms or pay." At the same time, Waller assured Smith that he would "always have them with white officers." The next day, Waller briefed Admiral Rodgers by wire that he planned not simply to clear but to "garrison the Sojoton," rendering it useless to the insurgents.[35]

Waller notified Rodgers on the fourteenth that he would "start [the] general round-up tomorrow," advising the admiral directly of the impending operation against the Sojoton cliffs target. He had one column under Porter already on the trail, moving toward Sojoton, killing "eight bolomen and eight carabaos" on the eve of the combined expedition (see Map 4.3). The next day Waller dispatched Captain Hiram Bearss with a second column of fifty men with orders to go by boat to Odoc and take the trail from there on foot, rendezvousing with Porter at Liruan that evening. Waller instructed Bearss to destroy all "villages and houses" along his route, and the captain complied, "burning in all 165" structures. Waller left Basey on the morning of November 16 while Porter and Bearss struck camp at Liruan and "proceeded to the neighborhood of the enemy's stronghold in the Sojoton." Waller, with boats and stores on the river, followed the land columns, arriving in the vicinity of "the overhanging cliffs in the Sojoton" the same evening. "We were able to communicate with the flanking column at that time about 200 feet directly above us, although not in sight." Waller received word from Porter warning that if he continued the river approach to the cliffs, Waller's men would suffer great "destruction." Waller then ordered the men from the boats and camped for the night while Porter and Bearss remained under cover with the Filipinos unaware of their presence on their flank.[36]

As morning broke on November 17, Porter and "the shore column struck the enemy's trail on the left bank[37] of the river" and encountered booby traps placed along the trail leading to an insurgent camp ahead. Porter followed the trail and "came upon a number of bamboo guns" with one aimed at them with its fuse burning. One of his men, Corporal Harry Glenn, "rushed forward and pulled out the fuse." The column continued up the trail and found "the enemy's cuartels" abandoned with food still on the cooking fires. Porter sent men ahead to a high overlook where they reported from their

120 | CHAPTER 4

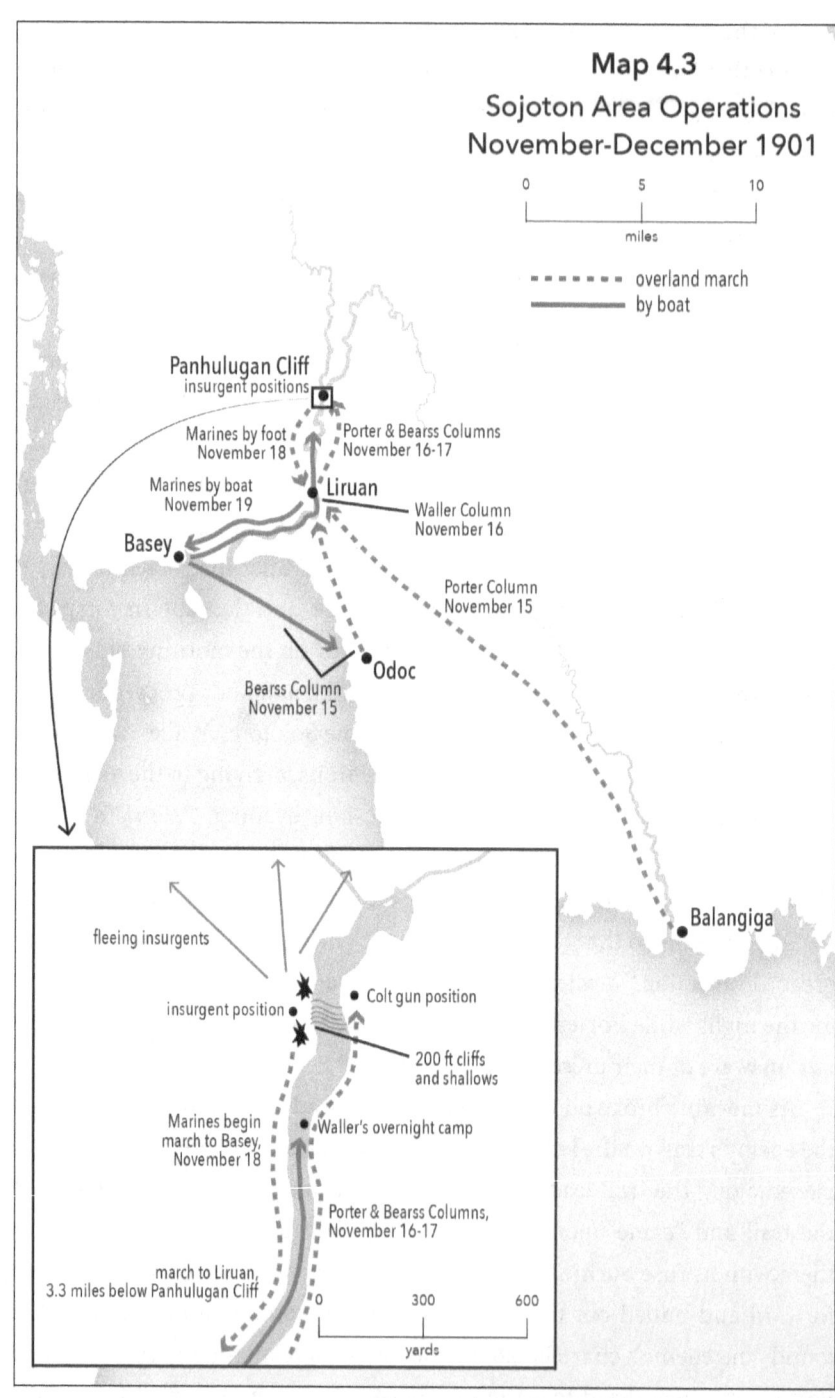

vantage point that two other camps could be seen on the cliffs across the river. Undercover, the Marines watched insurgents at work "preparing food, cutting bamboo, and variously employed," unaware of the Marines across the river from them. Porter wasted no time taking advantage of the situation.[38]

Meanwhile, unknown to Porter and Bearss up on the cliffs, Waller's column moved slowly up the river in the boats, just out of range of the insurgents. The enemy watched Waller's small flotilla approach, ready to fire when the boats came into range. The insurgents, unaware of the flanking column on the cliffs across the river, faced the oncoming boats with guns trained on the Marines on the river below, with "tons of volcanic rock" bundled up in "cages held in position by vines" ready to be released on Waller's approaching boats. But the attack came not from Waller's riverine force but from the flanking forces on the cliffs across the river and from below, via the guerillas' own bamboo ladder and handrail network.[39]

"Porter brought up his men and a Colt gun which was carried by native carriers." Ten minutes later, the gun crew opened fire on the surprised insurgent camp across the river, killing thirty of the enemy with the rest "completely routed." Before continuing the advance, Porter destroyed the "cuartel" and the food supplies left behind by the fleeing insurgents. Porter's column then "went down the cliffs" to the river below and "by means of two very small bancas and a raft, crossed the river." Using two-hundred-foot bamboo ladders "which the enemy had not taken time to destroy," the Marines scaled the cliffs and destroyed the rest of the camps. In pursuit of new targets, the Marines scaled "other cliffs on the right side," locating and destroying an additional camp as the "enemy fired two volleys and then fled."

As the smoke drifted off the cliffs, Waller landed his men and took stock of the victory just won.[40] The enemy camps had been protected by volcanic cliffs and reachable only by way of the Sojoton River, but Waller's attack and devastation had ended over three years of construction and planning for a "final rallying point." Although surprised by the Marines' flanking action, most insurgents escaped into the jungle, leaving behind their arms, equipment, and food supplies. "In addition to the spears and traps, there were innumerable rifle pits and many bamboo guns. The cliffs over the river are honeycombed with caves." Waller was convinced that his original plan to have both the land and water columns attack simultaneously would have spelled disaster for the boats on the river approach. "Instant destruction would have been the fate of the boats had they attempted the passage of the river before the cliffs had been taken." While the Marines' assault proved disastrous for the Filipinos, Waller mistakenly concluded that the action marked the end of the insurgency on Samar. Although dispirited and badly organized, the rebels continued threatening American outposts into the next year.[41]

A week after the initial Sojoton River attack, Waller revisited the area and for the rest of the month continued his combined operations on the river in conjunction with elements landed along the river banks. His expeditions overran other camps, found American equipment probably taken from Ninth Infantry victims at Balangiga, and "destroyed the powder mills, powder, twenty-seven bamboo cannon, bolos, spear heads, and tools." The columns discovered and "destroyed large cuartels near Sojoton Mountain," and Waller reported that "insurgent forces here reported to have been disorganized by defeat." With the Sojoton and eastern coastal operations leaving the insurgents "without organization" and "seeking food and shelter in the swamps and jungles of the surrounding country," Waller turned to his next assignment, one that would mar the history of the war and dog Waller for the rest of his life.[42]

## THE MARCH ACROSS THE SAMAR WILDERNESS

Waller planned an inland expedition to map the southern end of Samar, seeking a suitable route for a telegraph line connecting the east and west outposts. The Army had previously discounted the possibility of establishing such a communications link due to the geographical difficulty, but Waller's plans had other problems. "Not only would the Marines be marching at the height of the monsoon season, but most of their journey would be over narrow, jungle-covered valleys."[43] In spite of such obstacles, Smith wanted Waller to establish communications across Samar and measure insurgent strength in the interior. Recently involved in difficult operations in China where the Boxers controlled much of the countryside and enjoyed the sympathy of the Chinese people, Waller and his men found themselves once again facing an insurgency opposing them on difficult terrain with irregular tactics designed to thwart American firepower and training.

Local Army garrison commanders urged Waller not to move into the interior of Samar, suggesting it would be impossible to establish a telegraph line through the jungle. At the same time, they were appalled that Waller planned to take so few rations on the expedition. But for Waller it was a simple matter of mission: Smith ordered him to establish the communications line and to clear his subdistrict of insurgents. The Sojoton expeditions had uncovered trails that proved useful and Porter had also collected intelligence on older and less used trails in the surrounding jungle. Waller reasoned that with logistical assistance from native bearers and guides, he could discover other paths across the island, quickly establish the telegraph line, and in doing so clear the interior of insurgents at the same time. But weather and Filipino determination proved his undoing. The trail into the Samar interior was fraught with danger as the enemy marched among them when the Marines struck out from Basey.[44]

On December 8, 1901, Waller departed Basey with two columns of Marines southward along the coastline with the gunboat USS *Panay*,[45] loaded with supplies and equipment that shadowed the shore columns to their first destination at Balangiga. Captain David D. Porter waited at Balangiga with the rest of the Marines who would join Waller's operations into the interior of Samar. Over the next twenty days preceding his march across Samar from Lanang, Waller planned to work his way down the southwestern coast and across to the eastern coast. As he worked his way to Balangiga and points leading to the eastern coastline, he searched for insurgents and their strongholds along his route of march. Waller's patrols combed the terrain for hostile garrisons and positions and destroyed villages, houses, insurgent supply stockpiles, and booby traps along the way. Waller led one column on the beaches, skirting the coastal waters within sight of the *Panay* offshore. He positioned the second column about two miles inland under Captain H. I. Bearss (see Map 4.4). During that first day, the two columns worked their way towards Nipa Nipa and camped for the night just north of the village. Waller decided to stop there, "as the men had been fording streams all day and were wet up to their necks, also badly chafed."[46]

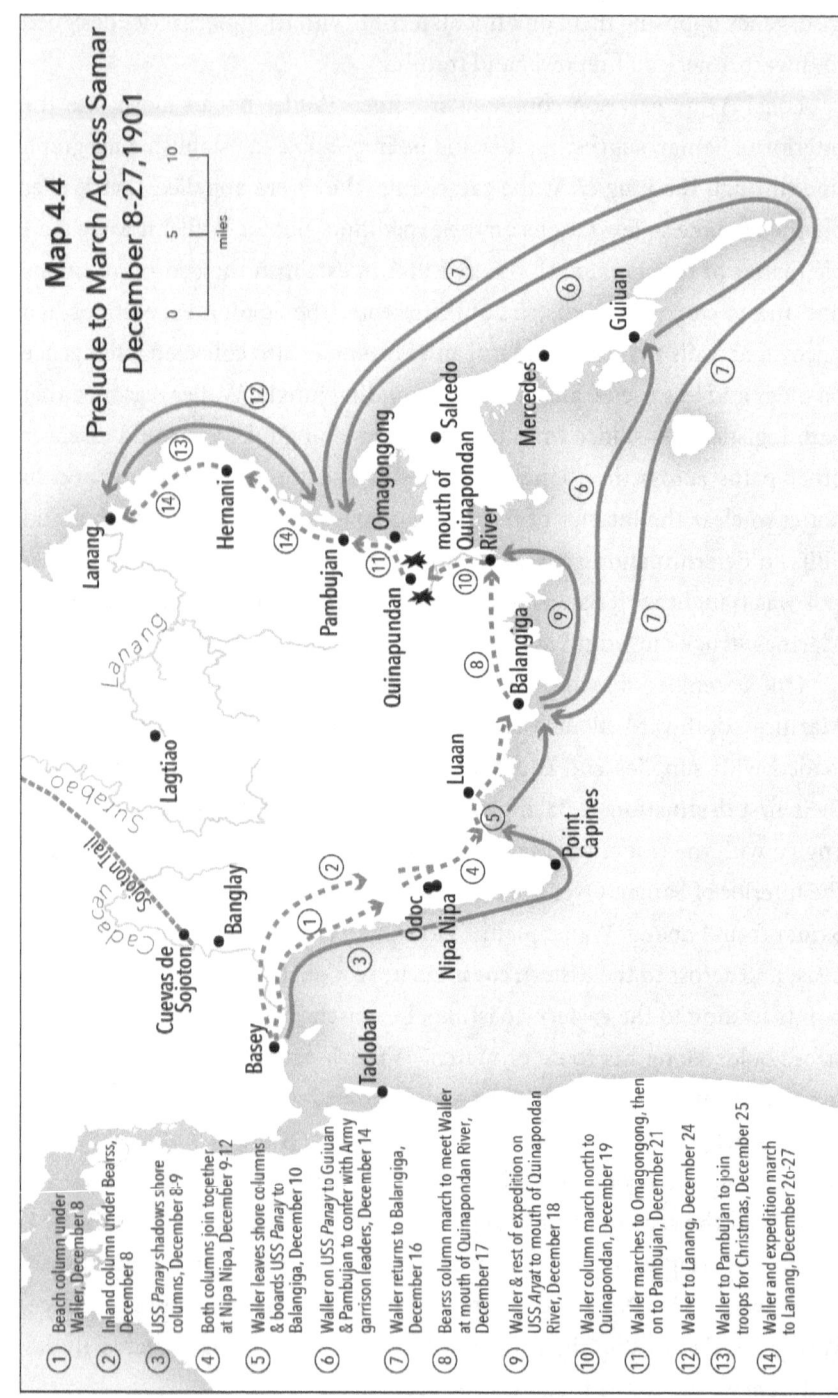

The next morning, as Waller started the march from Nipa Nipa, Bearss's inland column joined Waller's beach column, and the march continued southward. Along the way, several local men were captured, and they confirmed that the coastal settlements surrounding Nipa Nipa were used by the enemy in the interior to receive supplies from Leyte. As the expedition moved further southward, Waller continued to send out patrols to interdict rebel activity, kill or capture insurgents, destroy houses and structures, and burn food and other supplies.[47]

On the third day, just short of Luaan, Waller left the unified column under Bearss's command with orders to continue on to Balangiga, while maintaining patrols disrupted insurgent activities along the coastal areas. Waller boarded a cutter and made his way to Balangiga, expecting Bearss to arrive via the trail soon afterward. During the day, however, the column lost the trail, and heavy storms slowed their progress. At Balangiga, Waller grew "uneasy at the nonappearance of the column" and boarded the *Panay* to take him back to where he had left the column. Waller took a small boat ashore and fired a shot to signal Bearss. He "got an answer from a point between Luaan and Balangiga." Confident that all was well, Waller later reported that "the wind was blowing hard and rain coming down in torrents," so "I deemed it advisable to return with the small boat to the *Panay* and to Balangiga." The Bearss column arrived at Balangiga on December 12, two days later than their expected arrival.[48]

Waller decided to "let the men rest here for a few days while I proceed by gunboat to Guinan and Pambujan." On December 14, Waller boarded the *Panay* and traveled to Guinan where he hoped to draw rations from the Army garrison for his expedition, but he found that Captain Campbell King did not have enough rations for his own command for more than three days (see Map 4.4). Waller "made an emergency requisition" to Captain James K. Cogswell, commanding the *Isla de Cuba* and the senior naval officer on station. Cogswell "directed the *Panay* to take [the requisition] to Tacloban immediately and bring back the rations."

Meanwhile Waller arranged "a plan . . . with Captain King to act in concert with [Waller's column of Marines] and a column of infantry from Pambujan." Waller's plan included movement of a column of infantry from

Guinan under King, a second column of infantry from Pambujan, and the third column of Waller's Marines all moving "in the direction of Omagongong." The plan called for all three columns "to meet on the twentieth instant in the early morning, destroy the trenches and kill or capture the garrison." With the plan organized for King and with the rations on their way from Tacloban, Waller next "proceeded to Pambujan and explained the plan to Captain [Dwight W.] Ryther, directing him to meet me at Quinapundan on the nineteenth." With the arrangements complete at Guinan and Pambujan, Waller returned to Balangiga to set the plan into motion.[49]

On December 17, Waller ordered Bearss to take one column and march by trail to the mouth of the Quinapundan River. The next morning, Waller loaded the rest of his Marines and supplies on the USS *Aryat* and sailed the short distance to the mouth of the Quinapundan River where he rendezvoused with Bearss, unloaded barotos[50] and supplies for the trek up the river, and camped for the night. Waller sent the *Aryat* to King at Guiuan with supplies to stockpile at that garrison for King's command and for Waller to draw from in the days ahead.

On the morning of December 19, the Marines loaded the barotos with "tents, commissary stores and ammunition." Fighting a swift current, the Marines paddled "heavily loaded barotos" up a very narrow channel with "dense jungle" on either side (see Map 4.4). "They were fired on frequently from the undergrowth" and returned fire from "their own rifles . . . and the automatic fire of the Colt gun mounted in the bow of the leading boat." Waller's force had to abandon the boats short of Quinapundan, and "march four miles to the town, carrying their equipment, cutting their way through the undergrowth." Waller moved into the town, finding that the insurgents had faded into the jungle, leaving everything behind. The Marines camped for the night, receiving sporadic fire from snipers throughout the night. The next morning, on December 20, Waller sent two patrols led by Sergeant Quick and Captain Matthews into the nearby hills and clearings, drawing intense fire, "steady and continuous." During the resulting fights, the Marines "killed eight and wounded two, burned twelve shacks and captured the insurgent flag." Waller remained in Quinapundan one more night, but the next morning, Captain Ryther still had not arrived from Pambujan so

Waller decided that the expedition would wait no longer and gave the order to march toward Omagongong. Throughout the march to Omagongong, the Marines received fire from the enemy, but Waller concentrated on destroying "the trenches and earthworks" along the way, stopping to return the fire only once. Waller wrote in his report later that "the trail between Quinapundan and Omagongong and Omagongong and Pambujan is excellent. We made the march to Pambujan in three-and-a-half hours—nine miles." At Pambujan, Waller rested his men for two days while he waited for the USS *Aryat* to bring fresh stores to Pambujan from Guiuan. While he waited, he made final preparations for the march across Samar.[51]

Soon the USS *Aryat* arrived with stores from Guiuan that would be needed for the upcoming march across Samar. As Christmas Eve morning dawned, Waller boarded the *Aryat* for a quick trip up to Lanang. He outlined his plans for crossing Samar with Captain James N. Pickering, commanding Company K, Seventh Infantry at Lanang. While there, Army Lieutenant Kenneth Williams arrived in camp from "a twelve days' trip looking for the Sojoton Trail. He did not believe that the trail existed." Williams described "the hardships of the mountain climbing, even when he had a supply camp and shelters for his men." Both Pickering and Williams reasoned with Waller not to make the attempt across to Basey. They were convinced that the mission was impossible, and the effort would end in disaster, but Waller was not persuaded. Waller boarded the *Aryat* for the trip back to Pambujan to spend Christmas day with his command, making final preparations for the two-day march to Lanang that would begin the following day. At Lanang, on December 28, Waller planned to begin the march across Samar.[52]

Meanwhile at Pambujan, Waller organized his expedition for the march across Samar. From the large group of Marines, native scouts, and Filipino carriers, he selected a smaller force that would make the march across Samar to Basey. The rest would return to Balangiga. His select force included four Marine officers, one Army officer, fifty Marines, two native scouts, and thirty-three Filipino carriers. Waller ordered Captain A. J. Matthews to take command of all the remaining "officers and men, native scouts and carriers" and march back "to Balangiga via Omagongong and Quinapundan, with special instructions" to use all his resources and deception necessary "to kill the hidden riflemen at Omagongong." The next morning, on December 26, Matthews departed Pambujan, leading his force south to Omagongong, while Waller "turned our faces north for Hermani, Lanang, and the unknown interior from east to west between Lanang and Basey" (see Map 4.5).[53]

Waller marched up the coastline throughout the day, seeing "numerous signs of insurrectos," but they did not encounter any large groups or threats to the column. Waller reached Hermani at 4 p.m. and made camp for the night. After an uneventful night, the Marines broke camp at 6 a.m. and moved north toward Lanang. On the approach to Lanang, Waller had difficulty finding a place to cross the river and finally signaled Captain Pickering who "sent a banca hauled by a carabao and got the men over without casualty."

That evening Waller arranged with Captain Pickering to take some men from the Twelfth Infantry who would accompany the expedition for the first two days on the river and return to Lanang with the boats, leaving the force afoot. Waller issued orders that the march to the west would begin the next morning, despite the rain and storms that had battered the eastern coastal area for several days. As morning on December 28 dawned, "the clouds broke and the sun came out, giving us a promise of bright weather to come." The expedition "set out in bancas, going up the Lanang River" from Lanang and covered seventeen miles the first day. The weather then turned sour as Waller led his men up the river by boat. "The river was much swollen and much time was spent getting the boats through the rapids." At Lagtiao, Waller ordered the men ashore and sent the boats back with the Twelfth Infantry troopers. With the river rising and fraught with "dangerous rapids and rocky spots," the march slowed as Waller negotiated the difficult terrain, crossing and recrossing the river, making his way further into the interior.[54]

Throughout the next several days, Waller's column found a few insurgents and destroyed some supplies as the weather worsened and rain poured "down in torrential bursts." Slowed by the weather, nagging water sores, injured feet, and a growing fatigue among the men, the force proved poorly equipped and supplied for such a journey as it fell victim to the elements. Rapid currents in the Lanang River forced the Marines to struggle by land through the jungle-clad mountainous terrain. On January 3, low on rations and plagued by incessant rain, Waller decided that many of the men would

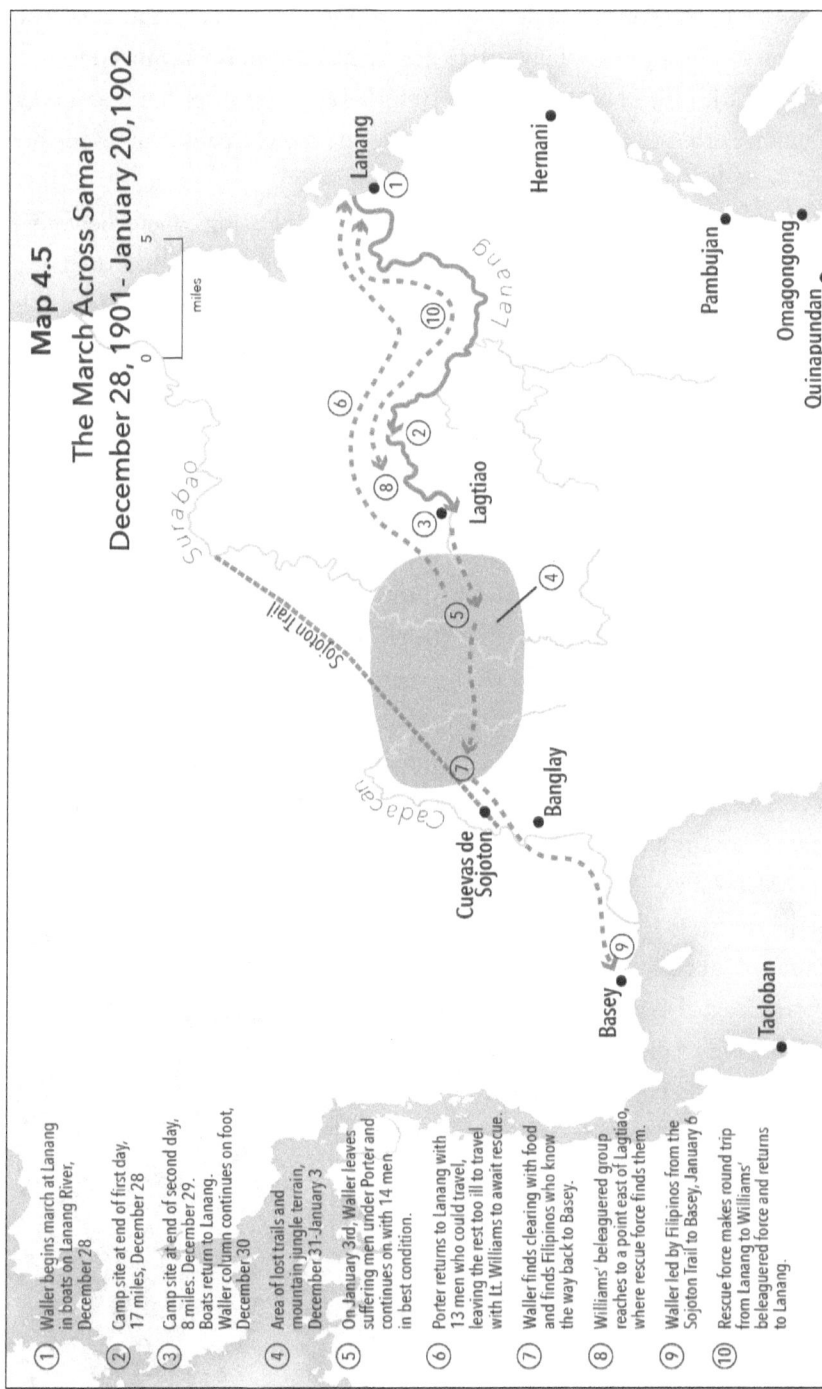

Map 4.5 The March Across Samar December 28, 1901 - January 20, 1902

not survive the trip. He took the thirteen fittest troopers and marched on in hopes of meeting a supply patrol that he had previously arranged to rendezvous with his party on the trail from Basey. The rest of the men under Captain Porter, all suffering from exposure and hunger, paused to rest before following Waller's well-marked trail.[55]

Waller pressed forward until he reached a clearing where he found bananas, young coconut palms, and sweet potatoes. The rain abated and "the sun came out" and using the glass elements from his binoculars, "we got a fire and cooked potatoes, not only enough for a meal, but to last us two days."[56] After feeding his men and resting, Waller decided to return to the main party. He sent word back to Captain Porter to build rafts so the entire party could float down the river. Porter attempted to do so but finally sent word to Waller that no suitable timber could be found. Upon hearing this report, Waller decided to resume his march across the hills. Waller later reported that he sent a native back to Captain Porter, "directing him to follow the advance column to a clearing where" Waller had found "a quantity of sweet potatoes, bananas, and young coconut palms." The message ordered Portor to bring his force to the clearing "until his men were in [a] condition to proceed." A few hours later the Filipino returned, reporting that "the insurrectos were so numerous that he was afraid." Waller decided to continue his march, leaving a message for Porter in the clearing.[57]

Meanwhile, Porter dispatched a native runner to track Waller, but the Filipino was unable to locate the Marines. Porter decided that the desperate condition of his men dictated that they return to Lanang and obtain help for the men who could not continue. Porter set out for Lanang with thirteen Marines and Filipinos, leaving the most serious cases

Captain David D. Porter, shown here later in his career. *Courtesy of the National Archives.*

Lt. Alexander S. Williams as he appeared five years after leaving the Philippines. *Courtesy of the National Archives.*

behind under the command of Lieutenant Alexander S. Williams. Porter directed the lieutenant to follow Porter back to Lanang if Waller did not appear soon. Porter hoped to reach help and return to Williams before the sick had to travel too far.

In the meantime, Waller had found some Filipinos who guided him back to Basey from where he immediately mounted a rescue expedition. For nine days, he searched for Porter and Williams but could locate neither group. Porter had by then made it to Lanang, and on January 17, an Army rescue force found Williams's party, which had been forced to abandon a number of the men, leaving them to die along the trail. By the time the Marines found their way back to Basey, Waller counted twelve dead from exposure and malnutrition, fully a fourth of the expedition.[58]

The survivors recounted tales of treachery and attack by the guides who survived the ordeal in better condition than the Americans. After Porter had left Lieutenant Williams's party behind, three natives attacked Williams with a bolo. Although wounded in the attack, Williams successfully fought off the attackers while other natives watched, making no attempt to aid him. These incidents of betrayal and a general "mutinous demeanor" throughout the latter stages of the march, Williams later testified, "caused me daily fear of massacre."[59]

Victor, who accompanied Waller and later was identified as an insurgent leader who had participated in the Balangiga massacre, approached Waller one night while he was sleeping and stole his bolo but "before the native could turn on him, Waller awoke" and disarmed him. Waller and others testified later at the courts-martial that the natives found sufficient food to sustain themselves but hid food from the Marines who suffered from starvation and exhaustion.[60]

One of the *New York Journal*'s most notorious political cartoons, depicting Philippine-American War General Jacob H. Smith's order "Kill Everyone over Ten," published on the front page, May 5, 1902. *Vernon Williams Archives*

Confined to a sickbed because of fever and physical exhaustion, Waller received word about the loss of the Marines and the natives' perfidy as Porter and later Williams reported in. Waller immediately ordered eleven Filipinos shot for treachery, and the command was carried out summarily without further investigation or trial. Unfortunately for Waller, word of American atrocities in the islands had already touched off a firestorm in the United States, where the Democratic minority in Congress sought an issue with which to attack Roosevelt. The execution of the native bearers prompted cries of outrage in Congress and the American press.[61]

## COURTS-MARTIAL FOR MURDER

When Waller and his command returned to Cavite on February 29, they were met with an enthusiastic welcome. Waller later gave an impassioned description of the reception as the Samar Marines arrived at the wharf:

Waller and some of his officers at Manila after his return from Samar. Left to right: Captain Samuel A. W. Patterson, Major Littleton W. T. Waller, Major Wendell C. Neville, and Captain James C. Breckinridge, circa 1902. *Courtesy of the Waller Family Archives.*

Leaving Samar without the faintest suspicion of anything wrong we reached Cavite. We looked forward to the meeting of our old chums and friends—we expected a warm welcome home. This welcome we received from the Flagship "New York"—the ship's sides were lined and cheer after cheer went up for us. Then with that, to us, sweetest of all compassion, the memory of brave, true men, held in reverence and honor by brave men, the flag was placed at half-staff and the band played "Home Sweet Home" for those of us slumbering the last sleep in Samar.[62]

Waller then reported to General Chaffee and learned that he and his adjutant, John H. A. Day were ordered to stand trial for the murder of the eleven Filipinos. Chaffee's news came as no surprise to Waller. Waller faulted his adjutant for these developments. In a letter to General Smith nine days before the Marines were relieved in Samar, Waller wrote that "only one thing

Captain John H. A. Day with outpost personnel at Dalachican on the causeway near Cavite before his departure with Waller for Samar. Left to right: 1st Lt. Ben H. Fuller, Capt. Henry O. Bisset, Capt. John H. A. Day, 2nd Lt. Robert F. Wynne, Dr. (Assistant Surgeon) Barton L. Wright, November 1899. *Courtesy of the National Archives.*

is to be regretted in our service here and that is, that through idle talk and a breach of hospitality an investigation has been necessary."[63] After the trial, Waller alluded to Day's behavior in Samar: "This charge was largely instigated by the vain boastfulness of one of the officers of my battalion."[64] While he never registered official complaints against Day, Waller did make a subtle comment through omission when in his recommendations list for awards for conspicuous service on Samar, only Day's name is listed without any recommendation. But regardless of their origins, the judicial wheels moved inexorably forward.[65]

Waller's court-martial convened and provided the American public with volatile testimony relating to Smith's orders and Waller's deeds, generating new cries to convict Waller as the "Butcher of Samar."[66] Waller testified, however, that he ordered the eleven natives shot because he had legal authority to act summarily in the case. His defense centered on the position that his orders to execute the Filipino guides sprang from General Order 100, dated July 1863. Waller argued that his assignment as a district commander on southern Samar endowed him with authority to apply General Order 100 to irregulars who "without commission and "commit acts of hostility."[67] Article 82 of General Order 100 states that:

> such men or squads of men are not public enemies, and therefore if captured, are not entitled to the privileges of prisoners of war, but shall be treated summarily as highway robbers and pirates.[68]

The prosecutor argued that Waller did not receive an appointment as a district commander and, as a consequence, had no authority under General Order 100 to act summarily, without due process. But the defense pointed out that General Smith in his testimony referred to Waller as a territorial commander and that Waller's reports were all submitted as from the commander of Sub-District, South Samar, a position never refuted or changed by authorities above Waller. In his testimony, General Smith referred to Waller's command numerous times as a district, strengthening Waller's contention that he had authority under General Order 100.[69] Experienced in the practice of both civilian and military law,[70] Waller conducted most of the questioning of witnesses and no doubt played a significant role in developing the defense strategy. The trial clarified both Smith's connection with the affair as well as the legal justification of Waller's actions.

The trial, which began on March 17, lasted for eighteen days, drawing great attention from the American press, which circulated lurid atrocity stories. A jury of seven Army and six Marine officers heard Waller assert, but General Smith deny, that Smith had sent him a handwritten note ordering him to turn "the interior of Samar (into) a howling wilderness." There were charges that racism was involved in the summary execution of the Filipinos, but Waller "defended his action . . . upon the ground that as commanding officer he was justified by the laws of war," and that Filipinos on Samar were savages. On the last day of the trial Waller summed up his defense by declaring, "as the representative officer responsible for the safety and welfare of my men, after investigation and from the investigation I had, considering the situation from all points, I ordered the eleven men shot. I honestly thought I was right then and I believe now that I was right."[71]

The court agreed with Waller's arguments, acquitting him by a vote of eleven to two. The same panel later cleared his subordinate, Lieutenant John H. A. Day. Brigadier General Smith, however, was later tried for his part in the affair, convicted, and retired from the Army.[72] Yet Waller's adjudicated innocence did not ensure for him the career success that he sought. Several years later, in 1910 and again in 1914, when his seniority placed him into consideration for elevation to the post of commandant of the Marine Corps, Waller was passed over, and many believed the Samar episode undercut this uniquely experienced officer who at the time was the most senior colonel serving in the Corps.[73]

The disastrous expedition across Samar did not, in the end, prove a complete failure. In his report upon his return and during recuperation in the Army hospital, Waller noted that:

> the hike had been valuable in proving there were no insurrectos in force in the mountains of the interior, that in good weather the hike could be made from Basey to Lanang in five days by using boats part of the way, and that a telephone wire could be strung through the mountains and not be disturbed by anything but falling trees.[74]

According to Marine Corps historian Allan R. Millett, "the insurgents were bound by their food needs and families to the coastal barrios,"[75] so as the Army and Marines forced most of the civilian population into American-controlled towns, the rebellion began to decline. By March 1902, all Marines had returned to Cavite, their task completed.

The trial and others like it caused considerable uneasiness for even the most ardent imperialists. While Roosevelt reacted to the atrocities in a political context, much of his response was personal. The press produced a mass of print supporting both the vanquished and the conquerors, and the correspondence and clippings supporting and attacking his actions filled Waller's papers. Marcus Howell composed a poem assailing the "carpers" and extolling Waller's actions; this work appeared in the *New York Sun*, on Sunday, July 6, 1902. The author sent a copy inscribed to the beleaguered Waller.

**SOLDIER AND CARPER**

A soldier a soldier's deeds must do,
Nor falter in the martial doing.
If savage foe wreaks savage hate,
His crime must bring him savage ruing.
Though deed for deed,
In blood for blood,
Revolts the non-combatant mind,
'Tis deed for deed,
In blood for blood,
Alone that awes the savage kind.

But let no soldier tell his tale
Of aught of treachery and killing:
How comrades died, on march or field—
War stories, pitiful and thrilling.
Let Truth sit dumb,
By muffled drum,
While Lies, their blaring trumpets blowing,
The brave defame,
Invoking blame,
And brute ingratitude bestowing.

Though fighters, midst the jungle starving,
Fever racked, and ev'ry danger spurning,
But strive for Country's flag and glory,
Let them, victorious home returning,
Court-martials face,
In vile disgrace,
The spite of petty malice learning,
And silence keep,
Though air may reek,
With lies that set their cheeks a-burning.

> But give the gew-gaw carper way,
> In halls of law and public press,
> To prate of lies and truths half told,
> To damn the hero, the savage bless,
> For lies to quote,
> He has by rote,
> And facts he promptly amends or smothers,
> While the brave and humane
> Are his evil refrain,
> And torturing foes his guileless brothers.[76]

Regardless of friend's praise or foe's attack, in the end Waller's fundamental mistake lay in his failure to understand the insurgent force he faced or the allegiance the ordinary Samarian had to the idea of independence. No pacification campaign as then practiced on Samar could generate conversion or tangible loyalty to the Americans. Waller reasoned that with loyal guides and bearers, equipped with the knowledge of trails and wild food supplies, he could expect to defeat the weather in a systematic expedition through the interior of Samar. His experience with guides who were at first unarmed and later armed and equipped formed the basis for his expectations. Pre-expedition intelligence from these loyal scouts and guides provided Waller perhaps with the assurance of a successful outcome, but his Filipino force would furnish him no such support or assistance on the trail.

Waller placed his confidence in the "quarter" he gave to the indigenous population when natives and prisoners "came in" voluntarily and "gave themselves up" and "were not killed—not slaughtered." But the process of pacifying with voluntary declarations and oaths of loyalty provided an avenue by which insurgent leaders could place operatives within the American infrastructure. Yet the practice of loyalty oaths failed to stabilize the coastal area; rather, it ensured the opposite result as the insurgency extended to every village and American garrison, making it impossible to know from where the enemy might come.[77]

Waller's court-martial did not address the question of what went wrong on the Samar expedition, but rather Waller's order to execute the prisoners:

Was it a lawful command under the circumstances that transpired on the trail? In the end the court agreed with Waller, that under the applicable rules of warfare, his decision to execute the eleven remained consistent with the rule of law.[78]

Waller, although acquitted of all charges in his court-martial, remained under a cloud for the rest of his career. His detractors were always quick to use the episode against him at every opportunity, and Waller spent the remainder of his life defending his decisions on Samar. In the end, it was all the ammunition his enemies needed to keep the Marine Corps commandancy from Waller's grasp.

CHAPTER 5   **INTERVENING YEARS**

While Waller faced the court-martial proceedings in Manila, and as the political firestorm rose to a fever pitch with the daily headlines dripping with venomous invective, Clara Waller turned to Commandant Charles Heywood with a remarkable personal appeal. Distressed by Waller's treatment and physical condition, Clara asked the commandant to expedite Waller's return home to recover. Pleading ignorance of regulations and inquiring whether "Major Waller would have to remain in Cavit[e] until the Record of the Court-Martial reaches the Department, and be acted upon," she argued that "in his case, and in consideration of his prolonged and arduous duties in China and the Philippines, I do feel that his health should be considered." Clara requested that Heywood issue orders "to the effect and so arranged, that [Waller] could leave on the first transport after the conclusion of the Court." She explained that "I have never before asked for anything, but this time I do feel that I am excused, as my husband's future health is a matter of deep anxiety to me."[1]

Clara's efforts to wrestle him from the quagmire in the Philippines may have had some effect. Waller remained in the islands until the verdict came in, finally releasing him for the voyage home in April 1902. Still frail and suffering from the effects of the jungle fevers, he packed his trunks with a few tokens for Clara and his meager possessions carried with him in China and the Philippines. Waller boarded the aging Army transport *Warren* for the trip home. Nearly two years had passed since he and the Third Marine Battalion had sailed to the East on the *Solace*. The trunks that he carried home included the flag given him by the commandant on Waller's brief stopover in the Washington rail yard on November 1, 1899. His men had "carried [the flag] through all the fights and battles in north China in 1900" and back to the Philippines where the standard led the assault on the

Sojoton cliffs on Samar. The flag did not accompany Waller on the march across Samar and was thus saved and remained with Waller for the rest of his life.[2]

Now suffering from the rigors of the Boxer campaign and the hardships of the march across the Samar wilderness, Waller looked forward to rest and the tranquility of home. The courts-martial had taken its toll on him, more than he admitted to those around him. "I freely confess to you that I am a wreck," he confided to Clara. "I showed a bold front, but the thought of you and my children, your anxiety and anguish came near unnerving me." Two days after learning of his acquittal, Waller sailed from Manila on the Army transport *Warren*, bound for San Francisco and the road to his Virginia home, determined to find respite with family and friends and healing in the hot mineral waters at Warm Springs, Virginia. His journey to the East was over. He would never return.[3]

The *Warren* put into San Francisco, where Waller traveled to Mare Island for a medical examination and respite before Navy physicians released him for the long train journey to New York. There his brother, R. Page Waller, met him at the station and ushered him aboard a steamer bound for Norfolk and home. By the time Waller reached New York, his voice was almost gone, and he "could hardly speak above a whisper and his words were unintelligible." One reporter observed that "aside from his eyes and throat," Waller "is suffering from a number of tropical ulcers, and his arms and limbs are covered with scabs of those which have healed."

During the desperate journey across Samar, "his right foot had been broken in two places," but by the time he reached Norfolk, it had healed sufficiently that "it gave him little trouble." Despite his determined efforts to appear as he always did—erect, firm, and with a military bearing, those who saw him step from the steamer onto the dock could see the evidence of his suffering in the Samar wilderness. He was quickly ushered into a carriage for the short ride to his brother's house for breakfast, before taking the short train ride to Virginia Beach where his wife and family and "a large number of friends waited for him as the train arrived in the station." It was a joyous reunion, not at all subdued by his inability to speak. He was vigorous in his handshakes and hand gestures, clearly overjoyed to be home.[4]

On June 23, Waller wrote the commandant that he had arrived home, and the next day Waller filed a request for three months leave, to begin July 10, which was granted three days later. The first order of business was a trip to the clothiers for some civilian clothing that fit, and a physical examination with Navy physicians at the nearby Norfolk Naval Base. It was during this time of rest and recuperation with his family that word came that citizens of Norfolk and throughout Virginia planned to present him with a ceremonial sword at a special dinner scheduled for the occasion on July 15. His doctors recommended that he go to Warm Springs in Bath County, Virginia, as soon as he could. The hot mineral springs there were thought to have recuperative value, and Waller made plans to move his family there as soon as the sword presentation took place.[5]

On a Tuesday evening on July 15, twenty-two years after Waller resigned from the Norfolk Light Artillery Blues to accept his commission in the Marine Corps, members and guests of the Blues gathered at the Armory Hall for dinner and a time of celebration. With his family and friends looking on, Waller accepted the sword and the accolades presented to him there. It was the beginning of a pleasant summer of relaxation and recovery. Three days later, he reported to headquarters by letter from Warm Springs, indicating that he would remain in Bath County for the foreseeable future.[6]

Warm Springs Hotel, Warm Springs, Virginia. *Vernon Williams Archives*

As the weeks unfolded, old colleagues from China and elsewhere sent missives of congratulations on his courts-martial victory, words that must have brought Waller vindication and redemption as he sought to put the episode in Samar behind him and move on. The first half of his military career was over, and the final two decades were about to begin.[7] The three months of leave soon ended, and Waller received orders on October 9 to "proceed to Philadelphia, Pa. and take charge of recruiting in that district." Two days later, Waller reported that he had arrived in Philadelphia and assumed command of the recruiting station there. On March 23, 1903, Waller received permanent promotion to lieutenant colonel, effective March 3, 1903.[8] During the rest of the year, Waller worked on recruiting in Philadelphia and various substations throughout the district. Waller expanded recruiting in the district in November and December, opening new recruiting offices in several cities in Pennsylvania and Ohio. The light duty allowed him to further recuperate and build up his strength. The assignment proved but a brief respite before he would take up his expeditionary duties once again.[9]

Meanwhile President Theodore Roosevelt's policies in the Caribbean revolved around the expanding American empire. The Spanish-American War, the Boxer Relief Expedition, and operations in the Philippines demonstrated the growing imperial opportunities for Waller and the Marine Corps. By 1902, lingering European encroachment in the Western Hemisphere, together with an American commitment to a variety of imperial motives, led to three decades of American involvement in Latin America, punctuated by military interventions and occupation. While Waller assumed his new post in Philadelphia, events were moving rapidly in Panama where he would command a regiment whose mission would be facilitating the construction of the Panama Canal and consolidating American power in the region. Panama would be the first of a series of missions where Waller and the Marines would enforce American prerogatives in Latin America. Expeditionary work in Panama, Cuba, Mexico, and Haiti all remained on the horizon where Waller's final two decades of service would be played out.

Waller's recruiting assignment reflected an attempt to deal with a growing manpower problem, as the Marine Corps encountered difficulty in attracting adequate recruits to fill its training program and address the increasing calls for Marines as expeditionary infantry in the ever-expanding colonial footprint. Following the Boxer Rebellion and operations in the Philippines, the War Department was reluctant to become involved in new colonial missions for the Army. The Marines, serving on ships in the fleet, were the first to land when required to protect American lives and property, hence it made more sense to reinforce landings with more Marines than transport Army units to distant trouble spots. This developing pattern placed increased demands on the Marines at a time when they were faced with a growing shortfall in manpower. In 1902, the Secretary of the Navy ordered the commandant to form a permanent expeditionary battalion available to respond swiftly to a call for infantry ashore. This led to an emphasis on battalion-sized training, where the Corps could land battalions that could link with other battalions on the ground and provide regimental or brigade forces equipped with greater flexibility, mobility, and maneuverability in expeditionary operations.

During 1903, Waller continued his recruiting work and opened new recruiting stations, expanded recruiting operations in established stations, and used his notoriety to attract young men who would staff the colonial battalions. Panama would be the first test for the new expeditionary battalions, and Waller would command a regiment there, charged with the responsibility to protect the new American canal being built across the Isthmus and insure American supremacy in the area.[10]

## THE PANAMA CANAL

Panama was not a new mission for Marines on ships. In recent years, Marines had landed from time to time to protect Americans there or to respond to various threats to American property. A civil war in 1901 in Colombia brought renewed threats to American interests in Panama, and by 1902, it was apparent that the violence had spread to Panama where the United States hoped to negotiate rights for the construction of a canal across the Isthmus. The United States failed to convince the Colombian legislature to accept the provisions of the Hay-Herran Treaty calling for U.S. payments in exchange for canal rights and the original holdings of the bankrupt French canal company in Panama. The impasse led to a period of instability as Colombian ploys and delays designed to increase the agreed-upon price produced a breakdown in negotiations and eventually led to Colombian efforts to tighten control over Panama.

On November 3, 1903, Panamanian rebels took control of Panama City and declared independence. The United States wasted no time in recognizing the new government and landing Marines from the *Nashville*. The arrival of the *Dixie* with a battalion of Marines on November 5 escalated American involvement beyond the role of protecting lives and property. Thirteen days later, the U.S. and Panama signed the Hay-Bunau-Varilla Pact, confirming American recognition and transferring a ten-mile strip of land for the canal to the United States.[11] Fearful that Colombia would send reinforcements to Panama to put down the revolution, Washington made plans to send additional military forces to Panama. President Theodore Roosevelt was determined to take and hold what would become the Canal Zone. More Marine battalions would soon follow.[12]

With the collapse of talks with Colombia, and Panama's success in breaking away, growing tensions between the Panamanian rebels and Colombian forces in the region, and the possibility of reinforcements from Colombia convinced officials in Washington that a more significant American presence was required in Panama. During the previous year in Panama, Marines had found themselves using the threat of force to maintain peace, with reports of encounters with Colombian forces becoming more frequent and delicate. Adding to the concerns on the ground in Panama were the tropical risks to the well-being of the Marines. The men "suffered considerably from remittent and intermittent fever," along with cases of dysentery and other tropical maladies appearing in camp, especially with those troops whose assignments placed them far from their main encampments and in locales where the Marines could not control the sanitary conditions at the outposts. As 1903 came to a close, these conditions prompted Washington to send a brigade of Marines to the Isthmus, with the Commandant of the Marine Corps in personal command.[13]

With the secession of Panama from Colombia and Roosevelt's immediate diplomatic recognition of Panama, pressure quickly mounted on Washington to prevent any Colombian efforts to recover the lost province or interfere with the ongoing transfer of the Panama Canal to the United States. There was

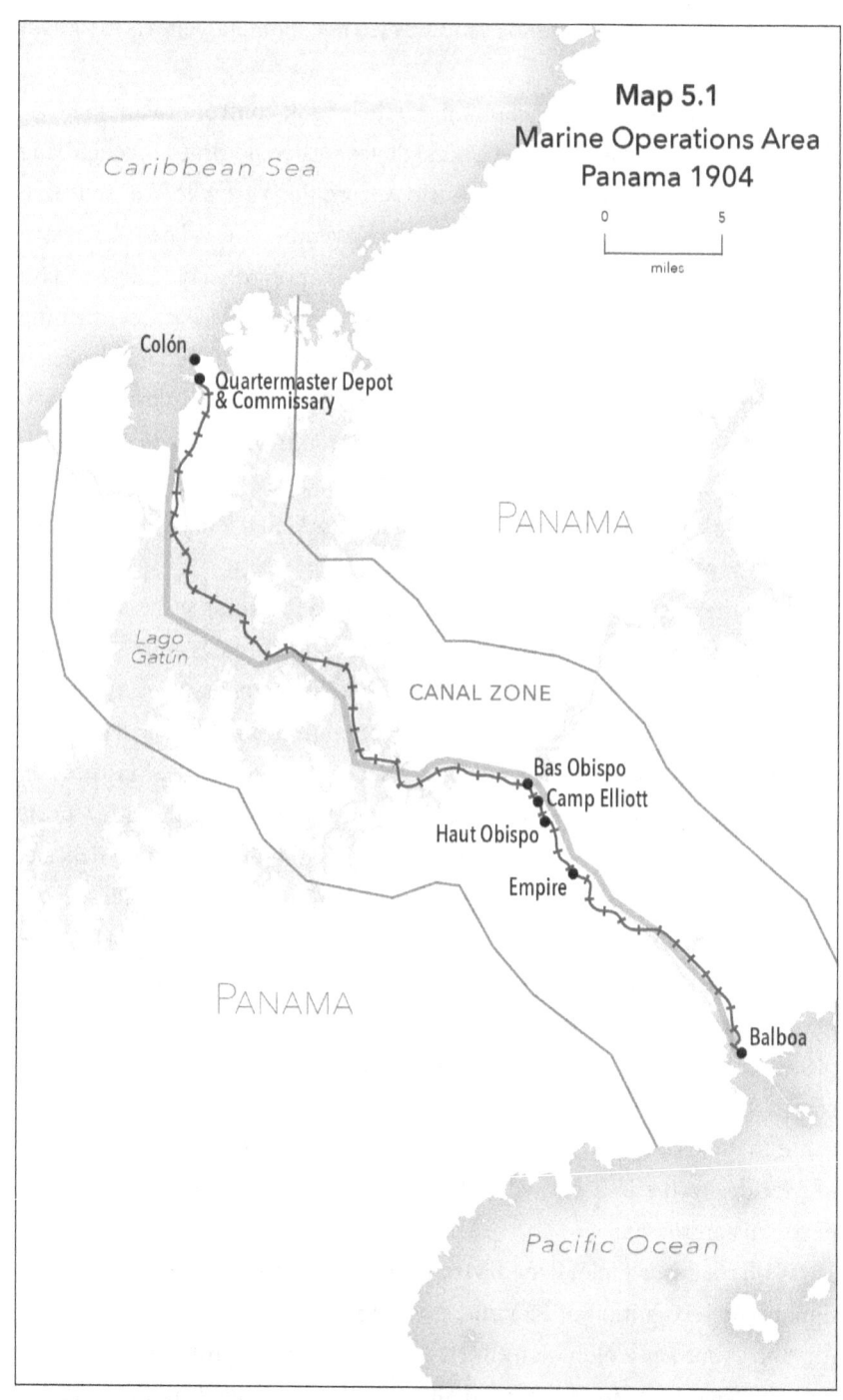

also growing tension in Panama arising from treaty provisions seen as unfair and an infringement on Panama's newly acquired sovereignty. The growing Panamanian unrest and the possibility of threats to the Canal Zone project prompted action in the Navy Department. Secretary of the Navy William H. Moody ordered Brigadier General Commandant G. F. Elliott to assemble a brigade-sized expeditionary force, "with medical officers and hospital Corps men," and move on Panama without delay. Elliott ordered a battalion under Major John A. Lejeune, already in the West Indies, to embark on the USS *Dixie* for Colón, arriving there on November 5, 1903. Lejeune moved into camp at Empire, thirty-five miles along the railroad from Colón (see Map 5.1). The *Dixie* departed immediately after landing Lejeune and his Marines, bound for Philadelphia with orders to transport the rest of the brigade back to Colón. On December 28, a second battalion under Major Lewis C. Lucas arrived at Colón on the transport ship USS *Prairie* from Guantanamo Bay, Cuba and occupied Bas Obispo, not far from Empire. There, the two battalions waited for the additional two battalions, brigade headquarters, and auxiliary units then assembling at League Island in Philadelphia.[14]

Meanwhile, word reached Waller at his recruiting offices in Philadelphia that he would command the Second Regiment of the brigade. He packed his

USS *Dixie* (1898–1922), a screw steamer, was used extensively for movement of Marines especially as events required deployment during the early days of the Panama Canal. *Courtesy of U.S. Naval History and Heritage Command.*

gear and reported to the force command at League Island. There he found intense preparations underway for the expedition that must have reminded Waller of loading his Marines aboard the USS *New York* at Cavite, for the voyage to Samar, just a few years earlier. In Panama, Waller would find that the Navy would be better prepared for operations in the tropical environs surrounding the railway along the canal and across the Isthmus.

Armed with the knowledge of the difficulties with tropical diseases during the earlier French canal attempt in Panama, and the continuing medical casualties among its own personnel serving in the Caribbean, the Navy Department took no chances. "On December 18, 1903, the Bureau was informed that a medical outfit . . . for a field force of 1200 men would be required." At League Island, quartermasters organized "medicines, hospital stores, appliances, and filters" for the coming expedition. "Tentage, cots,

Officers of the 2nd Regiment of Marines, at Bas Obispo, Panama, January 1904, on the steps of De Lessipa house. 1. Lieutanant Commander Dudley N. Carpenter (MC), USN. 2. Major Jame E. Mahoney. 3. Colonel L. W. T. Waller. 4. Major Lewis C. Lucas. 5. Captain George C. Reid. 6. Captain William Hopkins. 7. Captain Robert F. Wynne. 10. Captain James T. Bootes. 11. 1st Lt. Herbert J. Hirshinger. 12. 2nd Lt. Harry O. Smith. 13. 2nd Lt. Davis B. Wills. 14. 2nd Lt. Fred D. Kilgore. 15. Lt. Francis W. Furlong (MC) USN. 16. 2nd Lt. Samuel A.W. Patterson. 17. 2nd Lt. Ellis B. Miller. 20. 2nd Lt. Cleyburn McCauley. *Courtesy of the National Archives.*

Camp Elliott, Panama. *Courtesy of the National Archives.*

mosquito nettings, etc." were added to the cargo holds aboard the USS *Dixie*. Soon General Elliot arrived, and with Waller and the rest of the headquarters staff, the loading of two additional battalions began. By December 27, 1903, the expedition was aboard the *Dixie* and ready for the voyage. The next morning, the deck crew cast off all lines, and the *Dixie* maneuvered away from the pier, easing into the river, bound for Colón in Panama, "arriving at that place after a quick and pleasant trip of six days."[15]

Waiting for the return of the *Dixie* at Colón in early January 1904, the two battalions of Marines at Empire and Bas Obisbo occupied Panama Canal Company properties along the rail line inland from Colón. Commandant G. F. Elliott planned to use Empire as headquarters for the First Regiment, under the command of Lieutenant Colonel William P. Biddle and ordered Lieutenant Colonel Littleton W.T. Waller to Bas Obispo to command the Second Regiment. Elliott established brigade headquarters and his staff organization nearby at Haute Obispo with the brigade quartermaster and commissary depots at Colón, with access to the port and the rail lines connecting all of his outposts along the inland communications line (see Map 5.1).[16]

On January 7, 1904, Lieutenant Colonel William P. Biddle, his regimental staff, and one battalion under Major Eli K. Cole disembarked the *Dixie* and entrained for Empire. At Empire, Biddle organized the First Regiment headquarters, with two battalions under Lejeune and Cole. Biddle found that sufficient Canal Company huts were not available to house all of Cole's newly arrived battalion, "consequently the overflow was put under canvas."

The next day, Waller went ashore with a battalion commanded by Major James Mahoney and joined the battalion under Lucas, already operating at Bas Obispo. Waller assumed command and organized the Second Regimental headquarters, arranging for quarters for men in company houses belonging to the Panama Canal Company at the outpost (see Map 5.1).[17]

Determined to minimize health issues emerging from poor sanitary conditions, both Waller and Biddle hired "large numbers of natives ... to cut undergrowth and clear away rubbish around the various camp sites." The company huts were "thoroughly disinfected with a strong carbolic solution and were subsequently scrubbed out." Regulations required the use of mosquito nets, and inspection routines were developed to ensure that these regulations were followed. Throughout the brigade, medical personnel were proactive in making sure that preventative measures were monitored in all camps and treatment of infected patients were swiftly delivered. These procedures guaranteed success in the field, and the effectives available remained high throughout operations in Panama.[18]

During their expeditionary service in Panama, the Marines focused on "the requirements of security and information" and "numerous scouting parties were sent out" to produce surveys and a series of comprehensive topographical maps that included the trails, settlements, and geographical features of "the surrounding country." The perceived threats from Colombians and tensions from Panamanians never were realized so the Marines' activities remained routine in nature. In just a few weeks, "in the judgement of the Department [of the Navy]," the situation in Panama no longer required a brigade of Marines, so Commandant Elliott received orders for the relief of most of the brigade. Beginning on February 14, 1904, Major Lucas and his battalion were detached to Guantanamo, Cuba. Two days later, Elliott and the remainder of the brigade began a staged departure from Panama, leaving Major Lejeune's battalion of ten officers and 407 men behind. It would not be long until that force would be further reduced.[19]

Waller remained in Panama until March 7, 1904, when he reported on board the *Dixie* for the voyage to the United States. Waller returned to his recruiting duties at Philadelphia on March 26, but a few days later, he received the welcome orders to command the Marine Barracks at the Norfolk Navy Yard. Departing Philadelphia immediately and, after a few days at his Norfolk home, he reported in at Marine Barracks on April 12. His assignment to Norfolk brought him home to family and friends, once again beginning a lengthy assignment in the city where he grew up. Waller had prospered during his brief assignment in Panama. He returned home without the debilitating consequences that he had suffered in the camps and jungle operations on Samar.[20]

At Norfolk, Waller spent the next two years overseeing routine training, equipping his men for expeditionary duty, and supervising the construction of a new Marine barracks and officers' quarters on just over thirty-one acres allotted for the purpose. The new construction "proposed to make Norfolk a post for two, if not three battalions, with storage capacity" in support of what a large expeditionary multibattalion force at Norfolk needed for emergency service. The new construction ensured that "a command of from 300 to 600 men can promptly be equipped and embarked for any destination." Such planning proved timely. Within the next year, Waller would be ordered to command a provisional expeditionary brigade in Cuba, where disabling events were swiftly moving toward a crisis for Roosevelt's foreign policy and the fledgling Cuban republic.[21]

## THE CUBAN PACIFICATION CAMPAIGN

During the years since the war with Spain, American big business expanded its operations across Cuba, taking advantage of vast amounts of inexpensive land and the power of the American dollar on the agricultural landscape. As the political turmoil developed into insurrection and instability in Cuba in 1905 and 1906, the problem for the Roosevelt administration centered not only on preventing foreign intervention on the island but on protecting American lives and economic interests in Cuba.

Historian James H. Hitchman wrote that "by 1906, Americans reportedly owned between seven and fifteen percent of all Cuba." These American holdings in Cuba represented a significant share of wealth-producing operations that drained profits and revenue away from Cuba. These American-controlled assets "consisted [of] 632,000 acres of sugar lands, 25,000 [acres] of tobacco, 700,000 [acres] of fruits," and included, "2,750,000 [acres] of mining, [containing both] improved and unimproved land." But the American hold on the Cuban economy went well beyond the land: "Americans owned one-fourth of the banking industry (Spain, Germany, and Great Britain held the rest)." U.S. companies "shared railroading with the British, and monopolized the mines, electric railways, fruit, and cattle industries." Just eight years after the end of the war with Spain, these economic interests brought large populations of Americans into Cuba, building homes, businesses, and establishing social, economic, and cultural institutions that set them apart from the Cuban population. For Roosevelt and American business leaders, the growing political unrest in Cuba posed a real threat to the American lives and property scattered across Cuba, in the cities and throughout the rural countryside.[22]

For Waller and the Marines, the upcoming mission would be similar to many of their duties carried out in Panama in 1904, but the Cuban expedition promised to be more daunting in scope. The presence of an insurrection against the Cuban government, an immense American civilian population scattered across an urban and rural landscape, and the growing American business holdings in Cuba demanded a well-conceived and significant logistical network to solve the political crisis, and at the same time, protect American lives and property. At Norfolk, Waller waited for orders that would soon come.

The trigger point for the growing political unrest in Cuba began with the presidential election in 1905. Tomás Estrada Palma and the Moderate Party won reelection with the results fiercely contested by Palma's opponent, José Miguel Gómez and the Liberal Party. Gómez claimed that Palma had used "bribery, intimidation, and violence in order to keep in power." Both Palma and Gómez wanted President Roosevelt to intervene in Cuba to assist each side in putting down the other. Roosevelt first tried diplomacy and sent Secretary of War William Howard Taft and Assistant Secretary of State Robert Bacon[23] to Cuba to attempt a diplomatic solution, but Palma refused to join

Tomás Estrada Palma (at right foreground at head of table) and his cabinet in the Palace, Havana, Cuba, 1902. *Courtesy of the Library of Congress.*

talks with Gómez, and it soon became clear that Palma could not control events. The situation in Cuba soon pressured the reluctant Roosevelt toward intervention.[24]

In September 1906, two ships dispatched by Roosevelt arrived in Cuba as a small, first step in protecting American lives and property. The USS *Marietta* reached Cienfuegos on September 11 and the USS *Denver* arrived in Havana the next day (see Map 5.2). Neither captain had specific instructions from Roosevelt, but the appearance of the two ships convinced both the Moderates and the Liberals that "the landings [were] the first step of an

Jose Miguel Gómez, leader of the Liberal Party in the 1905 election. *Courtesy of the Library of Congress.*

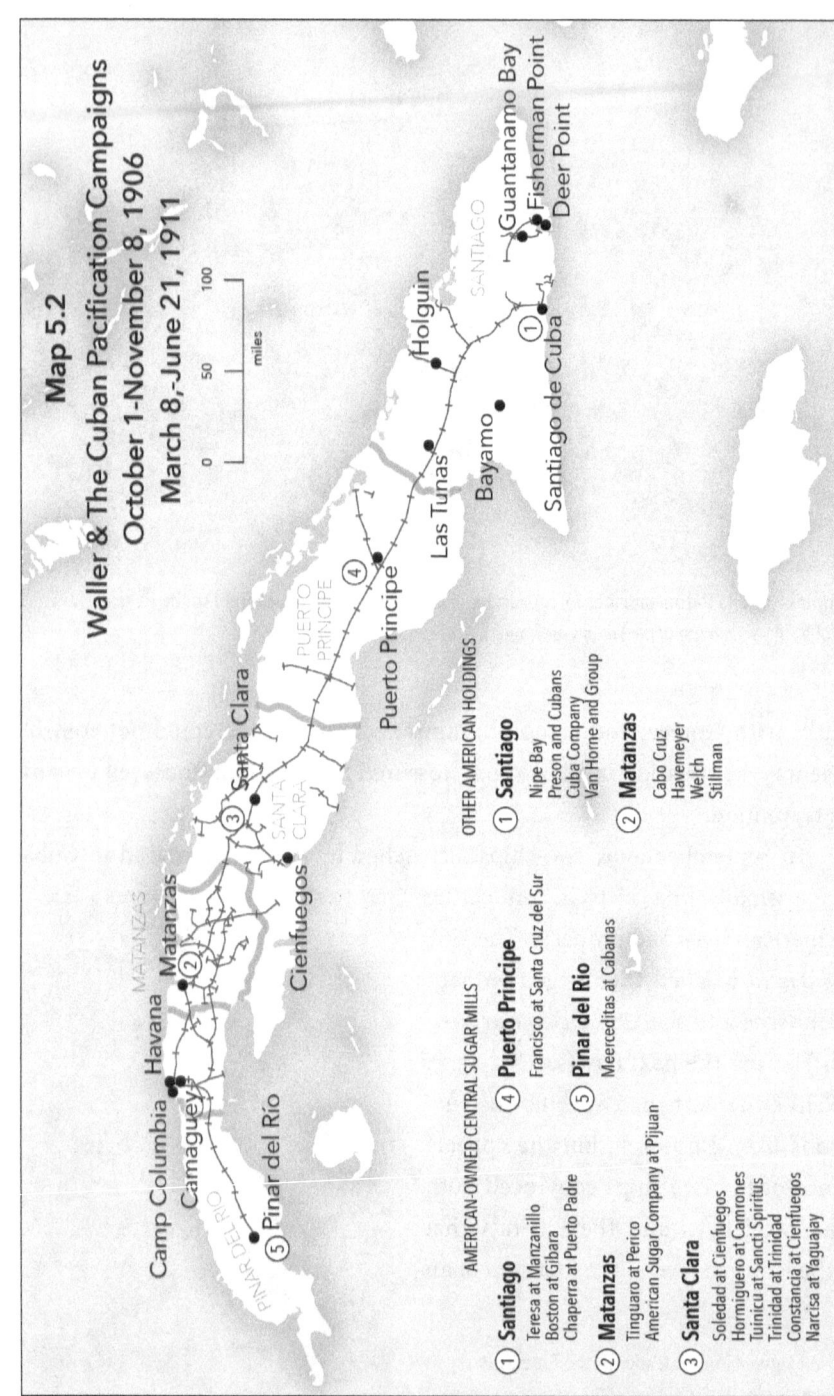

Map 5.2 Waller & The Cuban Pacification Campaigns October 1–November 8, 1906 March 8–June 21, 1911

American military intervention" and prompted Palma and Gómez to step up "their efforts to insure that intervention would serve their purposes."[25]

Meanwhile, word reached Roosevelt that conditions in Cuba were deteriorating with Palma's threats to dissolve the government and resign—placing the island nation on the brink of anarchy. On September 12, Roosevelt sent a warning to Bacon in Cuba that "we should have a large force of Marines in Havana at the earliest possible moment on any ships able to carry them." Roosevelt indicated that the Marines' mission would be for "the protection of American life and property."[26]

During the first two weeks of September, tenuous mediation efforts between Palma and Gómez continued with few results and growing tension. Roosevelt grew convinced that "Estrada Palma's unpopularity and military weakness made it unwise to intervene on his behalf." The deteriorating situation in Cuba persuaded Roosevelt that he needed to have immediate resources off the coast of Cuba should threats to American lives and property escalate. Earlier, the War Department informed Roosevelt that a large Army force would take weeks to organize and transport to Cuba, so Roosevelt decided that a provisional Marine brigade organized for immediate service in Cuba could begin pacification operations until the Army arrived.[27]

During the last two weeks of September 1906, Roosevelt began the immediate movement of Marines to Cuba, while the Army organized a larger pacifying force that would arrive in Cuba in November. The Marines fielded "a total strength of ninety-seven officers and 2,795 men," most of whom originated from League Island and Norfolk, along with Marine Guards from the Atlantic Fleet. Waller received orders to command the brigade and proceeded to Miami, Florida, for transport on the USS *Miami*, arriving in Havana on October 1.[28]

Meanwhile on September 28, Palma and his government resigned, "leaving the threat of general anarchy heavy in the air." With the *Marietta* and the *Denver* already in Cuba, the incoming Marine brigade's two regiments occupied Camp Columbia in Havana, and in the west at Cienfuegos. Waller arrived at Camp Columbia on October 1, took command of the brigade, and ordered the two regiments "out across the countryside to guard sugar properties and railway facilities." Waller organized his Marines into "company detachments" to occupy towns and communities throughout Cuba, with small units to ride the trains as guards and serve as sentries at American mills and farms. Waller's deployments created a network designed to ensure his command and control over the island and dampen the tension between the militia remnants and the insurgents. Map 5.2 provides an overview of the rail network and many of the American holdings in Cuba. There were many other smaller mills and company operations where Waller dispatched Marines during the early days of pacification.[29]

During October, Waller and the Marines continued pacification duties across Cuba while waiting for the Army's expedition to arrive. The first Army units began to reach the island early in October, but it took most of the month to transport the five-thousand-man army to Cuba, unload the men and equipment, and dispatch the soldiers to assignments across Cuba. By November 1, the pacification Army had successfully taken up their duties and one thousand Marines joined the pacification force. For Waller and the rest of the Marine brigade, their assignment came to an end. The brigade was dissolved, and the remaining Marines returned to the United States. Waller

Officers of the 2nd Regiment, U.S. Marine Corps, Camp Columbia, Marianao, Havana Province, Cuba, Army of Cuban Pacification, September 1906. Colonel Waller arrived to take command on October 1. *Courtesy of the Library of Congress.*

departed Cuba on November 8 for Norfolk, where he resumed his command at Marine Barracks.[30] Waller's brief expeditionary service in Cuba was at an end, but a lingering problem soon resurfaced as a new battle appeared on the horizon for Waller and the Marine Corps. This time, not in the tropics or ashore in Asia, but in the halls of Congress.

## MARINES ON SHIPS

During the decade following the Samar expedition, the courts-martial, and the expeditions to Panama and Cuba, Waller and his fellow Marines faced another threat, one that grew out of earlier efforts in the 1890s by Navy reformers to remove the Marines from ships, and which now intensified with President Theodore Roosevelt determined to remove Marines from ships and President Taft pursing a more drastic course amalgamating the Marine Corps into the Army.

The troubles began years before, in 1894, when a small number of naval officers led by W. F. Fullam pushed for removing Marines from ships. Fullam's group was "opposed by not only by a majority[,] but by the leading officers of the Navy."[31] The Navy Department ruled against the Fullam's "movers" and soon after, petitions addressed to the Congress began appearing aboard all commissioned ships, urging the enlisted personnel to sign their names and support for removal of Marines. Added to the petition campaign was a digest of inflammatory quotations published in various newspaper articles aimed at belittling the bluejacket and revealing the hostile relationship between sailors and Marines on ships.[32] The document concluded with an impassioned argument for removal of the Marines.

W. F. Fullam, early in his career. He was promoted to rear admiral in 1914. *Courtesy of U.S. Naval History and Heritage Command.*

Stationed at Marine Barracks at Norfolk during this time, Waller discovered that two "papers" had been brought ashore "from the *Detroit*," by a petty officer and posted in the barracks. Waller made copies and mounted an investigation.[33]

Waller wrote the commandant that "each ship at this yard has or had one [petition and quotation set of documents] circulated for signatures." He reported that the "petty officer stated that the object of the petition at this time was to defeat or 'block' the recommendation . . . for the increase of the Marine Corps." The petty officer indicated that he expected to be the "delegate" from Norfolk "<u>to present the petition to the Congressional Commission</u> [Waller added underlining for emphasis]."[34] Two weeks later, the Secretary of the Navy issued Special Order 16 designed to put a stop to the maneuvering of the few officers behind the agitation for removal. "[A]fter maturely considering the subject," and taking into account the long and faithful service of the Marine Corps since 1775, the Department "is convinced of the usefulness of the corps, both ashore and afloat, and of the propriety of using it in service on shipboard." Fullam and his cohorts were stopped for the moment, but the issue would later surface again, this time with assistance of the president.[35]

Later that same summer, the petitions found their way to the Senate and soon two senators introduced Senate Bill 2324 that called for "five regiments of Army artillery . . . [to] be consolidated with the Marine Corps," forming a "Corps of Marine Artillery and be transferred into the Army."[36] Fullam's efforts fared no better in the Senate. The bill soon languished in the Senate Naval Affairs Committee, and Senate Bill 2324 never came to the floor for a vote. Although stalled for the time being, Fullam and his coterie worked behind the scenes to achieve their goals. As the momentum grew within the ranks of the Navy Department, proponents of removal in the Navy found a friend in President Theodore Roosevelt. Roosevelt had long become convinced that the Marines' "downfall is due largely to themselves." In a private note to his military aide, Archibald Butt, Roosevelt explained that the Marines "have augmented to themselves such importance, and their influence . . . has given them such an abnormal position for the size of their corps that they have simply invited their own destruction."[37]

On November 8, 1908, Roosevelt's Executive Order 969 shocked the Marines and their supporters into action. The executive order outlined the new relationship for the Marine Corps within the Navy Department. Marines were:

- To garrison the different Navy yards and naval stations, both within and beyond the continental limits and naval stations of the United States.
- To furnish the first line of the mobile defense of naval bases and naval stations beyond the continental limits of the United States.
- To man such naval defenses, and to aid in manning, if necessary, such other defenses, as may be erected for the defense of naval bases and naval stations beyond the continental limits of the United States.
- To garrison the Isthmian Canal Zone, Panama.
- To furnish such garrison and expeditionary forces for duties beyond the seas as may be necessary in time of peace.[38]

With the executive order in force, the Navy began removing Marines from ships. As 1908 closed, the Marines had just three months before the new naval appropriations bill came to a vote. The key to blocking Roosevelt's move lay in the House Committee for Naval Affairs, headed by Thomas Butler, Waller's old friend and father of Smedley Butler. As 1909 unfolded, Congressman Butler organized a hearing of a subcommittee on the status of the Marine Corps, and Waller was there as both sides prepared to fight it out on the hearing floor.[39]

The hearing opened with Thomas Butler chairing the session,[40] with arguments for removal from ships from the Secretary of the Navy Truman H. Newberry and Rear Admiral John E. Pillsbury, who headed the Bureau of Navigation. There followed nine other admirals, active and retired, who testified in favor of removing the Marines from ships and argued that Executive Order 969 set out the proper role for Marines in the Navy. While each witness explained his reasons for removing the Marines from ships, all were opposed to removing the Marines from the Navy Department.[41] However, not all the Navy witnesses supported Roosevelt's decision to remove the Marines.

General Elliott, Waller, and a series of Marine and naval officers presented testimony in favor of Marines on ships. Historian Robert Heinl pointed out that all the naval officers supporting removal had graduated from the Naval Academy before 1881, the first class year that Marine officers were appointed from the Academy. After 1881 Marines had academy classmates who supported them over the years in various fights. Ironically, Waller, who saw the Academy Marines as a threat to himself and others of the old Corps, became a part of the coalition of naval and Marine officers to block removal efforts in the Navy Department.[42]

The power of the purse blocked Roosevelt and his executive order when the naval appropriations bill became law on March 3, 1909, and stipulated "that no part of the appropriations herein made for the Marine Corps shall be expended . . . unless officers and enlisted men shall serve . . . on board all battleships and armored cruisers" and onboard "other vessels of the navy as the President may direct," where such assignment of Marines are "in detachments of not less of eight per centum of the strength of the enlisted men of the navy on said vessels."[43]

Despite the victory won in Congress in the fight over Roosevelt's Executive Order 969, officers in the Marine Corps remained wary of future efforts that could threaten the Corps. Roosevelt's successor, William Howard Taft, harbored an animosity against the Corps that many feared would bring about the dissolution of Marine Corps entirely. Officers saw an urgent need to organize, and in 1911 at Deer Point at Guantanamo Bay, Waller's officers in the First Provisional Brigade organized what would eventually become the Marine Corps Association. "We met to discuss defenses against being abolished by the Navy and to raise funds for travel to Washington by selected officers to see members of Congress" to secure political support in favor of the Marine Corps. "The first steps taken toward" a permanent Marine Corps Association at Deer Point in 1911 began a process that two years later resulted in the creation of a permanent association. The 1913 founding document included "publishing a periodical journal for the dissemination of information concerning the aims, purposes and deeds of the Corps, and the interchange of ideas for the betterment and improvement of its officers and men." That proposed journal became the *Marine Corps*

*Gazette*.⁴⁴ For Waller, the year 1911 brought new prospects as he began his last decade of service.

## COMMANDANT OF THE MARINE CORPS

Outspoken and often derisive, Waller alienated many who shared his attitudes on the American empire, his view of opponents, and his record as a field commander. Waller was quick to criticize, and he often failed to grasp the subtleties required of him as he rose to higher levels of leadership. His was a style acceptable and much sought after in an earlier era, but as the Naval Academy graduates began to dominate leadership roles, many regarded Waller as part of the "Old Corps" at a time when professionalization in the Marine Corps matured. Since many of the officers with whom Waller competed had Naval Academy educations, successful shared networks, and were more socially adept, Waller's portfolio failed to convince government officials to appoint him commandant in 1911 or in 1914. As 1911 opened, opportunity beckoned to Waller, but the vagaries of political power checked his reach for his ultimate goal.

In 1910, Waller's rise to supreme Marine command seemed imminent. Commandant George F. Elliott decided to retire during an intraservice controversy,⁴⁵ leaving the position open for President Taft's appointment. Most observers, including Waller, thought he would get the post. He had the reputation and support within the Marine Corps, making him the obvious choice. His protégé, Smedley Butler, had lined up his influential father, Congressman Thomas Butler, to forward Waller's name for the post, and Secretary of the Navy George von Lengerke Meyer recommended Waller as well. Taft agreed to make the appointment, but as events unfolded, Waller's selection began to unravel. He did not have sufficient political leverage to unseat a plan mounted to stem Waller's bid for commandant. For Waller, it would be the first real test of his political acumen where the stakes were at the highest levels, the players included the best politicos in and out of the Marine Corps, and the game was political hardball.⁴⁶

Archibald Butt, military adviser to both Theodore Roosevelt and Taft, recalled the outrage Taft felt as he was blackmailed into withdrawing Waller's name and selecting William P. Biddle in his place. Butt complained that the

Captain Archibald W. Butt, military aide to President Taft, May 4, 1909. *Courtesy of the Library of Congress.*

president was "grouchy," all because of this business of the appointment of a commandant. "He [Taft] says he feels as if he were held up on the public road and relieved of his purse and his watch." Butt explained that Taft had planned to name Waller who was "the idol of the Corps and certainly the only man . . . who has any fitness for the position at the present time," but although Meyer and Taft agreed and the appointment was "practically written," Senator Boies Penrose of Pennsylvania then interceded and "in five minutes Waller was sidetracked and Colonel Biddle elevated to the place in command." It was no coincidence that Biddle was Penrose's cousin and a member of a prominent Philadelphia family, long active and strong in Pennsylvania Republican politics.[47]

Congressman Butler, Waller's champion, fell under Penrose's withering political fire. Butt pointed out that "Penrose is a gentleman by birth, but a guttersnipe by instinct." The senator "owns Pennsylvania, and every member from that state in the House and every office holder back in the state is an abject tool to him in politics." Butler's own political fortunes were at stake when Penrose told him, 'See here, I want you to withdraw from this Marine Corps fight at once,' and Butler fell from it as if he had fallen

Senator Boies Penrose, circa 1911. *Courtesy of the Library of Congress.*

William Howard Taft, governor-general of the Philippines, circa 1901. *Courtesy of the Library of Congress.*

from a ladder." With one stroke of the political brush, Penrose eliminated Waller's formidable support in the House. With Butler removed, Penrose confronted the president to secure Biddle's nomination.

In a meeting in the White House with President Taft, Penrose moved quickly to the point: "I want this appointment for Biddle." Taft replied that Biddle was not considered for the post due to his "unfitness." To this Penrose countered that Biddle was the "ranking officer of the corps" and from his state. Biddle's family ties to Penrose went unmentioned. Taft told Butt later that "he never saw a man more vulgar in his demand," but at the end of the conversation, Taft told Penrose that he could not select Biddle, regardless of his arguments. Penrose responded that he would not support the president's legislative program if he did not give Penrose the "appointment which is mine by rights as far as I can see." Taft could not afford to alienate Penrose so Waller was dropped, and Biddle named in his place. Butt summed up his thoughts on the matter: "Presidents have always used the army and navy for trading stamps, but I had hoped that the President would throw down the glove to Penrose or rather pick up the one Penrose threw at his feet; but it was not to be."[48] Looming just ahead, another retirement brought Waller one last chance to be commandant of the Marine Corps.

On February 14, 1914, Commandant Biddle retired one year short of the end of his four-year term. Waller was once again considered for the position of commandant. After the perceived injustice of 1911, many of Waller's friends in the Corps thought his elevation could not be denied, and on the surface, it appeared they were right. Waller, a Southern Democrat who traced many of his 1911 problems to Penrose and the Republicans, felt secure now that the

Senator Claude Swanson of Virginia, 1910–1915. *Courtesy of the Library of Congress.*

Democrats were in power. Waller and his friends left nothing to chance and pursued the nomination with determination. Claude Swanson, the senior senator from Virginia, assumed the responsibility for managing the Waller campaign for commandant. Senator Swanson wrote President Woodrow Wilson that "I have filed with his papers a petition signed by thirty-four Democratic senators[49] requesting [Waller's] promotion to" major general commandant. Swanson promised Wilson that he could also "obtain a large majority of the Republican members of the Senate." This was no idle boast, for Swanson had mounted a campaign to gain the appointment.

On December 17, 1913, Republican Senator Boies Penrose, who had thwarted Waller's almost certain appointment in 1910, wrote that "many prominent people in Pennsylvania are interested in the promotion of Colonel Waller to be Major General and Commandant of the United States Marine Corps." He informed Daniels that Pennsylvania knew Colonel Waller and [we] esteem him highly.[50]

Earlier, during the first week of December 1913, Republican Senator Henry Cabot Lodge had written Daniels a brief letter of support for Waller.

Secretary of the Navy Josephus Daniels, circa 1914. *Courtesy of the Library of Congress.*

Senator Henry Cabot Lodge, circa 1912. *Courtesy of the Library of Congress.*

"During my long service as Chairman of the Philippine Committee I had occasion to know a great deal about Col. Waller and defended him from criticisms which were made upon him after the Samar expedition." Lodge told of the investigation he made into the allegations and the circumstances surrounding the trial and came to the conclusion that Waller was not only "unjustly criticized but that he was a very gallant officer of unusual capacity." After the first of the year, Lodge wrote a lengthy letter to Swanson about Waller, who attached it to his own letter promoting Waller to the president.[51]

Swanson had Waller making the rounds as well. Lodge wrote Swanson that he "had never met [Waller] until yesterday, when he came to thank me for having written in his behalf to the Secretary." Waller's visit to Lodge prompted the expanded letter of support to Swanson the next day. Lodge explained that newspaper accounts suggested that perhaps Waller would be passed over again, a situation that Waller obviously pointed out to the senator. "I was afraid a great injustice might be done to a distinguished officer," he explained. As chairman of the committee investigating "Colonel Waller's expedition in Samar," Lodge

President Woodrow Wilson, circa 1916. *Courtesy of the Library of Congress.*

had concluded that "not only were the charges against him unfair" but that he had, in a campaign of "great difficulty and danger, conducted himself with great gallantry and had shown the utmost efficiency." Lodge concluded that Waller was a "first rate officer deserving of high recommendation instead of censure or abuse." Certain that Swanson would lay his missive on the president's desk, Lodge went to the crux of the matter, saying that "to use that expedition in Samar as a reason for not appointing [Waller] commandant of the Marine Corps would be an act of great injustice." The next day as the decision on the nomination neared, Swanson attached the Lodge letter to the president with his own request "to present Colonel Waller's case before you personally before any decision is reached."[52]

The momentum seemed to be going for Waller. After all, Josephus Daniels, the Secretary of the Navy, was a southerner from nearby North Carolina. With the two Virginia senators "urgently" pressing Daniels to send Waller's name up for the nomination, with a large block of Democratic and influential Republican senators supporting him, and with Congressman Butler again pushing the colonel's case in the House, Waller's appointment seemed imminent. But Daniels had reservations.

"During the war in the Philippines, General[53] Waller had been charged with cruelty, not personal cruelties but military harshness." Daniels saw Waller as "the old-type officer" who viewed the Filipinos as "an inferior people." When confronted with Waller's record in the Philippines, "it seemed to me to be unwise to appoint as" commandant of the Marine Corps "an officer who was alleged to have needlessly caused the death of Philippine soldiers, though in the trial he had been acquitted."[54]

Daniels took a decidedly anti-imperialistic view of American involvement in the Philippines, and he applied his personal perspective to the selection process. In addition to his distaste for Waller's attitude toward colonial policy and operations, Daniels was also aware that President Wilson wanted to establish "a new policy looking to independence of the Philippines." Concerned with establishing policies that would lead to "a larger voice [for Filipinos] in the government of their own country," Daniels was reluctant to recommend as commandant someone whom the Filipinos associated with the harsh treatment of the earlier era. The secretary wanted to exorcize that image and forge a new relationship with the Philippines, based on cooperation and the spirit of goodwill.

Daniels admitted that "in light of experience, . . . Waller deserved the place," but the secretary explained that "except for my intense hostility to the war upon the Filipinos and my zeal that they be given the right of self-government, I would have favored him." Despite Daniels's respect for Waller's "high qualities as a man and officer," he felt that the nation could not afford a man such as him at the helm of the Corps. Daniels saw Waller and officers like him as useful for the nation at critical times but believed that they should be placed in reserve during other periods. Daniels wrote that he "trusted [Waller] with important duties. He more than measured up to every assignment and duty." In the end, Waller's past and his reputation as a bush fighter in the "Old Corps" did not serve him well as questions of a political nature decided his fate, questions over which he had no control.[55]

Instead, Daniels turned to George Barnett, who had "heavy Republican backing." Daniels had little choice in the matter after deciding against Waller. With Waller out of the race, Colonel Lincoln Karmandy had the most political support for the position, with Academy classmate Senator John Weeks of Massachusetts his champion. Furthermore, retiring Commandant William P. Biddle favored Karmandy and despite being junior to Waller, Karmandy would have been the nominee had it not been for an embarrassing divorce that brought distaste to the ascetic Marine community. Other nominees were too junior to be seriously considered, so Barnett, another classmate of Karmandy's, became the dark horse who ousted Waller from the race.[56]

Meanwhile, while Waller involved himself with the politics of command, he continued his work at Norfolk. During the first two months in 1911, Waller was detached temporarily to serve with courts-martial panels at Philadelphia in January and at Washington, D.C., in February, before resuming his duties at Norfolk. Soon events required a Marine brigade once again to land in Cuba with Waller in command.

## EXPEDITIONARY WORK IN THE CARIBBEAN
In the years since the first pacification campaign in Cuba, political unrest and corruption continued to be a source of threat to Americans living in

Cuba and for the growing number of American companies scattered across the island. "Under José Miguel Gómez, who became president when the provisional government was withdrawn in 1909, there was graft and political favoritism in all branches of the [Cuban] administration." Year after year, issues of corruption and inept economic policy, brought protests and complaints from the Department of State, along with veiled threats of renewed intervention. Between 1909 and 1911, Marines landed small forces in Cuba on several occasions to quell uprisings or suppress unrest. In March 1911, in response to instability and continued threats to American interests, a Marine brigade once again embarked for Cuba with Waller in command.[57]

Waller departed Norfolk for Philadelphia and organized a provisional brigade "for temporary foreign shore service in Cuba." Waller and the brigade boarded the USS *Prairie* at the Navy Yard at Philadelphia on March 8, 1911, and sailed the next day for Guantanamo Bay. Five days later, the Marines disembarked in Cuba and "established Brigade Headquarters, First Provisional Brigade, US Marines, on Fisherman's Point, Guantanamo Bay, Cuba" (see Map 5.2, p. 154).[58] The brigade remained in Cuba just over three months, with Waller back at Marine Barracks in Norfolk by June 22.

Two months later, Waller transferred to command the Marine Barracks at Mare Island, California, where he remained until April 1914. Events in Mexico soon created a crisis for Wilson and brought a new expeditionary assignment for Waller. The Mexican troubles began at Tampico on April 9, 1914, with the arrest of a small party of sailors from the USS *Dolphin*, loading gasoline supplies at a warehouse about ten miles from their ship. Unknown to the sailors, the warehouse was located in a restricted area, and Mexican Federales suddenly appeared and arrested the seven Americans at the warehouse and two sailors who were still on their boat loading the gasoline. The Mexicans took their nine prisoners to their headquarters. The Mexican commander, Colonel Ramón Hinojosa, "was aghast at what his men had done" and ordered the sailors returned to their boat at the warehouse. His superior arrested Hinojosa for "negligence" and sent an apology to Admiral Henry T. Mayo aboard the *Dolphin*. Not satisfied, Mayo demanded a formal apology and that the American flag "be publicly hoisted in a prominent position on shore and salute it with twenty-one guns." These actions set in motion a

Rear Admiral Henry T. Mayo, circa 1910–1914. *Courtesy of the U.S. Naval History and Heritage Command.*

series of events raising tension levels in Mexico City and in Washington, D.C.[59]

Meanwhile, President Wilson received news that a German freighter, the *Ypiranga*, carried a large cargo of arms consigned for Veracruz, in violation of an American arms embargo.[60] With the failure of President Victoriano Huerta[61] to meet the American demands for redress for Tampico, and the fear that the *Ypiranga* cargo would be unloaded at Veracruz and shipped inland to Huerta in Mexico City. Wilson directed that the fleet move from Tampico to Veracruz. In Washington, officials decided against intercepting the German freighter at sea and risking conflict with Germany. Instead, Wilson opted for landing a naval and Marine force in Veracruz and taking control of the customs house, warehouses, and the city. The plan called for allowing the *Ypiranga* to deliver the arms to Veracruz and seizing the cargo once it was unloaded at the docks.[62]

At 11:50, on the morning of April 21, a landing force transferred on board the *Prairie* from ships laying off Veracruz. Under the command of Lieutenant Colonel Wendell C. Neville, the force included two naval battalions, Marine guards, and a Marine battalion. As soon as the transfer was complete, the *Prairie* maneuvered past the breakwater in the harbor, opposite Pier Four (see Map 5.3). Neville landed his force in whaleboats at Pier Four and quickly moved into the wharf area. Neville assigned the Marines the northern section of the waterfront and ordered the bluejackets to move on objectives on the southern side. The American forces occupied the Customs House, Post Office and Telegraph Station, the Terminal Hotel, the American Consulate, and the Cable Office. Within the hour, snipers, Mexican civilians, and enemy military elements began to resist the Americans as they moved into Veracruz from Pier Four.[63]

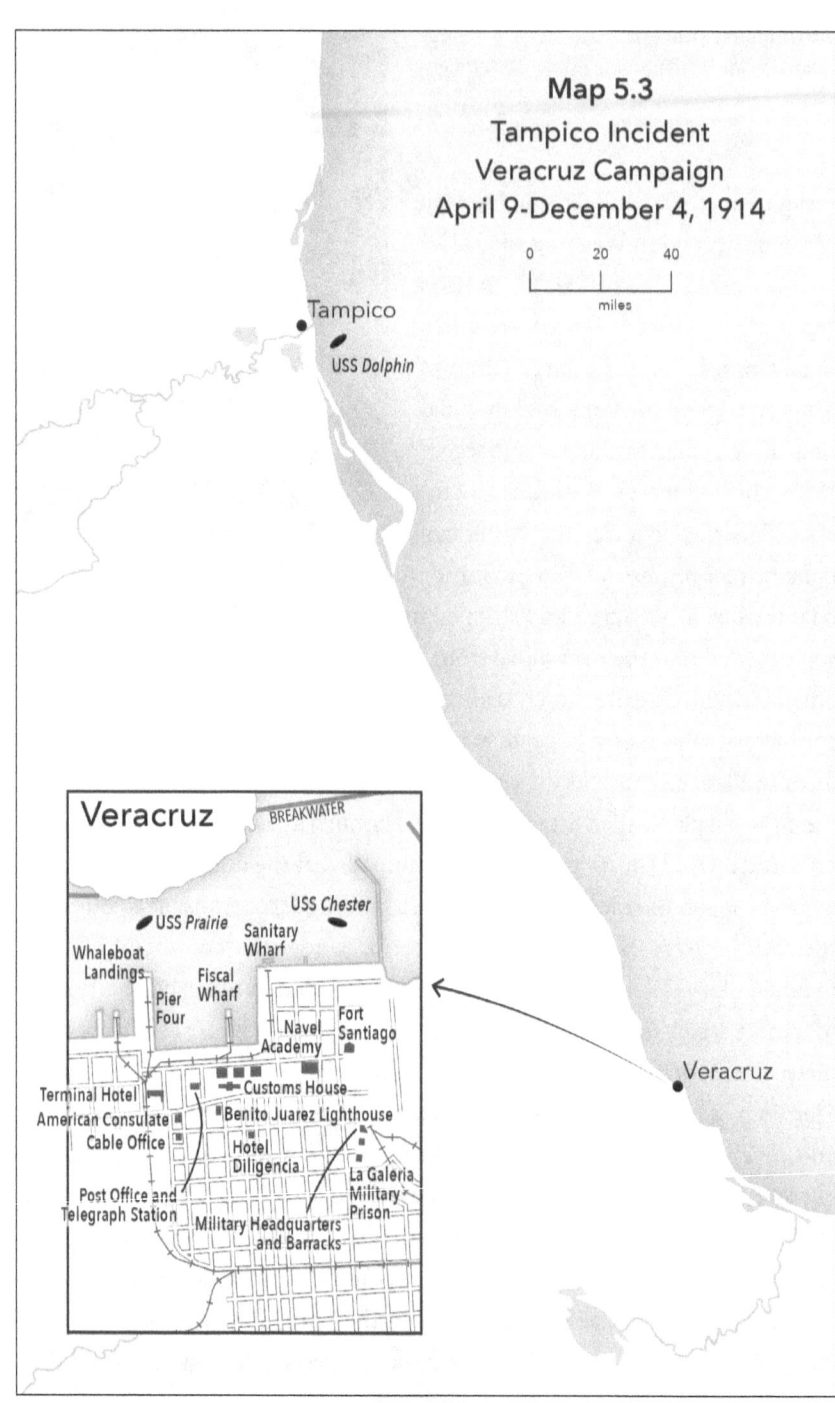

**Map 5.3**
Tampico Incident
Veracruz Campaign
April 9–December 4, 1914

Lt. Colonel Wendell C. Neville, circa 1914. Neville later served as major general commandant. *Courtesy of the Library of Congress.*

The next day, the Marine and naval force continued the street fighting, building by building, street by street, as the Mexican defenders failed to hold the line. The naval brigade suffered an ambush at the Mexican Naval Academy in the southern sector, calling on the Marines for support. Naval casualties were high, with "thirteen killed" and several wounded. The Marines in the northern sector fared much better as the fighting there was "slow but routine against the amateurish Mexicans." By the end of April 22, the overwhelming force in Veracruz, together with supporting gunfire from ships anchored off the city, had eliminated most of the resistance. Snipers continued to be a problem, but soon the Marines overpowered them, and as the final days of April played out, the Marines

USS *Prairie*, in service from 1898 to 1923, later designated AD-5. *Courtesy of the U.S. Naval History and Heritage Command.*

Colonel L. W. T. Waller with field glasses and Marine officers near Veracruz, Mexico, 1914. *Courtesy of the National Archives.*

"cleared buildings, patrolled the streets, and outposted the city limits." Meanwhile, events accelerated at home as Waller and other Marines posted at various Marine barracks across the United States received orders to move on Veracruz.[64]

At the Marine Barracks at Philadelphia's League Island Navy Yard, the Navy Department organized an additional regiment of Marines for Veracruz. Colonel R. M. Moses commanded the new regiment and supervised the preparations and boarding on the chartered transport, *Morro Castle*. On April 23, 1914, the transport cleared the port, loaded with the Marine regiment and "with a full supply of stores and ammunition." The *Morro Castle* picked up additional Marines as it steamed down the eastern seaboard and reached Veracruz on April 29.[65] Waller was not far behind.

At Mare Island, Waller followed the fast-moving events at Tampico and Veracruz as the situation rapidly spiraled into intervention and landing at Veracruz. Waller received orders detaching him to his next command at League Island in Philadelphia. The street fighting and the battle for Veracruz continued as Waller made his way across the heartland by train,

Colonel L. W. T. Waller shortly after arrival at Veracruz, Mexico, 1914. *Courtesy of the National Archives.*

arriving at Philadelphia on April 26. That same day, Waller joined the USS *New York* at New York for passage to Veracruz. Just two days after commissioning, the new battleship steamed out of New York with Waller and additional Marines on board. As Waller and reinforcements made their way toward Veracruz, activities in Mexico and on the Texas coast moved swiftly in response to the volatile events in Veracruz.[66]

Meanwhile at Galveston, the harbor was teeming with countless ships arriving and departing for Veracruz. At the Galveston and the nearby Texas City harbors, transports were loading equipment, supplies, and Army expeditionary forces for the 734-mile voyage to Veracruz. Other vessels arriving at Texas ports carried refugees eager to leave Mexico for safer environs. After unloading the refugees, some of these civilian liners were chartered by the Army for the return trip to Veracruz. As the Army organized its expeditionary brigade along the Texas coast, events were moving quickly as the Marine expeditionary force began arriving at Veracruz from points across the Caribbean and elsewhere.[67]

The Marine brigade under Colonel John A. Lejeune arrived off Veracruz more quickly than Funston and the Army Expeditionary force steaming to Veracruz from Texas. From Pensacola and New Orleans, the Marine brigade relocated quickly to the Mexican eastern coastline. Lejeune's reinforcements landed swiftly at Veracruz, augmenting Neville's Marines and consolidating the lines of control across the city. As April closed, Waller and the *New York* continued the voyage down the eastern coastline near Florida and arrived at Veracruz on May 4, where he assumed command of the Marine brigade from Lejeune.

Commanders at Veracruz expected orders from Wilson to move from Veracruz inland toward Mexico City, but the president "had lost his taste for military intervention." Once it was apparent that the intervention would move no further than Veracruz, Waller spent the next six months in Veracruz in routine command and control activities. The brigade "trained and manned the city's outpost line, leaving the problems of military government" to General Funston and the Army. For Waller, the Cuban pacification campaigns and the occupation of Veracruz proved to be but a prelude for his next major expedition, one that would serve as a final conclusion to his long and extensive expeditionary service across the globe. In November 1914, he left Veracruz and assumed command of Marine Barracks at League Island in Philadelphia, a brief respite before his final posting as an expeditionary brigade commander. As conditions in Haiti deteriorated, orders would soon arrive in Philadelphia for Waller to land a brigade one last time.[68]

Marine camp near Veracruz, Mexico, 1914. *Courtesy of the National Archives.*

US Marines on outpost duty at Vergara, near Vera Cruz, 1914. *Courtesy of the National Archives.*

CHAPTER 6   # A VIRGINIA ARISTOCRAT IN HAITI

As the sweltering summer days of 1915 slowly passed, American naval forces stood off Haiti's Port-au-Prince capital city, poised to respond to the volatile affairs fired by the overthrow and murder of the President and the massacre of political prisoners in the government prison and its aftermath. The chaotic events of July 27–28, 1915, stemmed from generations of political strife and recurrent civil wars grown endemic in Haitian life. Admiral William B. Caperton, commanding the United States flotilla offshore, assumed his mission would be a brief one, to establish law and order and protect American interests until a new government could stabilize the situation. It proved not to be. The American intervention lasted nineteen years, until Depression problems at home forced a reconsideration of imperial prerogatives and responsibilities.[1]

While Waller commanded the First Marine Brigade at the Philadelphia Navy Yard, concerning himself with routine training activities and his ever-present political maneuvering, events were moving swiftly that would again propel Waller into the national limelight. Now that he had been passed over twice for commandant, Haiti would be his last expeditionary assignment. Facing economic collapse and

Rear Admiral William B. Caperton, Commander Cruiser Squadron, U.S. Atlantic Fleet In his cabin on board his flagship, USS *Washington*, circa 1915. *Courtesy of the U.S. Naval History and Heritage Command.*

political anarchy, the tropical nation again had plunged into its traditional throes of revolution and chaos. Since gaining independence from France in 1804, Haiti had suffered a century of civil war and instability. Washington, long convinced that Germany schemed to secure concessions in Haiti and determined to protect its new Panama Canal, regarded the island of Hispaniola as strategically positioned for a coaling station or other imperial posts that required close American control. In Haiti, Wilson would throw down the gauntlet—the Monroe Doctrine and the Roosevelt corollary could justify intervention should Germany threaten encroachment.

While Wilson drew up plans for an American-dependent democracy for Haiti, the islanders seemed no closer to unity and stability than they had been in 1804. Of its population of over two million, "ninety percent . . . were Creole-speaking blacks, the large majority of them illiterate."[2] The other 10 percent constituted the nation's governing mulatto elite who endorsed French culture, adopting the arrogance of class-based corruption and power. Both secretaries of state under Wilson expressed decidedly biased views of the Haitian and his capacity to operate on the world's stage. William Jennings Bryan once sneered, "dear me, think of it, [n----s] speaking French," while his successor, Robert Lansing, dismissed the potential of Haitian elites, suggesting that "the experience of Liberia and Haiti show[s] that the African race are devoid of any capacity for political organization and [have no] genius for government."[3] Such perspectives comfortably accommodated the southern prejudices of President Wilson, other high government officials, and Marines of like mind such as Colonel Waller. As the Haitian crisis worsened in July and August 1915, patterns of corruption and decades of instability led to President Jean Vilbrun Guillaume Sam's inevitable downfall and accelerated American intervention at Port-au-Prince and across the island nation.

The story of the impending disaster in Haiti began with yet another insurgency from the north. By the end of 1914, Haiti neared bankruptcy as devalued currency and a rising Caco[4] rebel militancy forecasted the evitable. Wilson dispatched the gunboat *Machias* to Port-au-Prince in December 1914 to load the Haiti's gold reserve aboard the vessel and prevent the Cacos from storming the bank and spiriting away the bullion. Meanwhile, a new revolutionary leader, General Guillaume Sam, had surfaced in the north, acquiring endorsements from northern Caco chiefs before pushing south. Wilson responded and ordered Admiral Caperton to proceed with his flagship, the battleship *Washington*, to Cap-Haïtien at once. Using vessels under his command, Caperton dogged Sam from port to port until Sam's rebels surrounded Port-au-Prince and forced President Davilmar Théodore into exile. Sam's accession to power brought to a temporary end the need for Caperton's presence in Haitian waters, and the *Washington* sailed for Mexico soon after.[5]

During Caperton's absence, General Sam enjoyed a few weeks without much difficulty. He used treasury gold to pay off Caco obligations, while beginning to fund government debts with tax monies collected from import duties. On the surface, Sam appeared to be the chief executive that Wilson needed for Haiti, one who could establish stability and accept American influence in that vital sector of the Caribbean. However hopeful American diplomats may have been, Sam's grip on presidential power proved short-lived.

Sam soon ran out of money, undermining his influence with his Caco constituents in the north, and by April, Dr. Rasalvo Bobo had captured Cap-Haïtien, a first salvo in a bid to depose Sam. While Sam had engineered a spectacular rebellion without the usual bloodshed, Bobo's brand of insurgency ran the gamut of Caco depredations. Torture, beheadings, and casual executions by Bobo himself quickly spurred the United States to action. Wilson initially tried diplomacy to secure an agreement with Sam, in exchange for American assistance against Bobo and the Cacos. Rebuffed at every turn, Wilson determined to act independently. "Action is evidently necessary, and no doubt, it would be a mistake to postpone it long." The first day of July found Caperton once again at Cap-Haïtien with orders to secure the city. But events soon took a more ominous turn.[6]

Meanwhile, Sam prepared to defend himself and mount an operation against Bobo and his supporters. He ordered the arrest of about two hundred elites whom he considered likely to support Bobo, imprisoning them at Port-au-Prince. His henchman then dragooned old men and boys into a patchwork force to send northward to block Bobo's expected attack on Port-au-Prince. Sam imposed martial law in the city to eliminate saboteurs and suspected enemies. The first strike at the Palace, however, came not from Bobo in the north, but from enemies within Port-au-Prince.

The recurring problem confronting sitting Haitian presidents lay historically in the presence of numerous remnants of former regimes in Port-au-Prince still seeking a return to power. One such operative was Carles de Delva, who had served former president Oreste Zamor, and who had spent the last few years enjoying sanctuary in the Portuguese legation. Ousted officials frequently took advantage of the sovereignty of the foreign legations, biding their time until a turn in their fortunes prompted a return to political action. Judging the chaos as his opportunity, de Delva left the legation in the early morning hours of July 27 and organized an attack on the Palace. His men set fires on the grounds and besieged the Palace where President Sam lay wounded from an earlier assault. In spite of his injuries, Sam evaded de Delva's force and made his way to the French legation before the attackers knew that he had slipped through their lines. The raid on the Palace and Sam's flight signaled the collapse of the government, and with all authority absent, Haiti descended into its darkest hour.[7]

Meanwhile, Sam's Chief of Police Charles-Oscar Etienne ordered all political prisoners executed. Jailers left no killing tool unused in their frenzy to butcher their captives, hacking, bayoneting, disemboweling, shooting, and tearing their luckless charges to pieces. "There were enough . . . bleeding and dead [prisoners], so that the blood was running down and out under the penitentiary wall, into the outside gutters." The blood attracted a mob who gathered up several "great big sugar kettles . . . , and stuck them under the outflow to catch the blood." Pouring large quantities of rum into the gory pots, the crowd mixed a ghastly cocktail, and promptly "got drunk on the combination."[8]

Chief Etienne, fearing that he had gone too far, fled for safety to the Dominican embassy. But a grieving father, posing as an official caller, entered the embassy and fired three shots into Etienne from close range. A mob then broke into the legation and dragged the body into the street where "it was shot at, hacked at, and defiled by every passer-by. . . . By evening Etienne had become an unrecognizable pulp of flesh." Now only Sam was left, himself the quarry of a mob, growing angrier as preparations were made for the burial of the massacre's victims.[9]

This increasing violence stirred American action, prompting Admiral Caperton's return to Haiti's troubled waters. The day following Etienne's

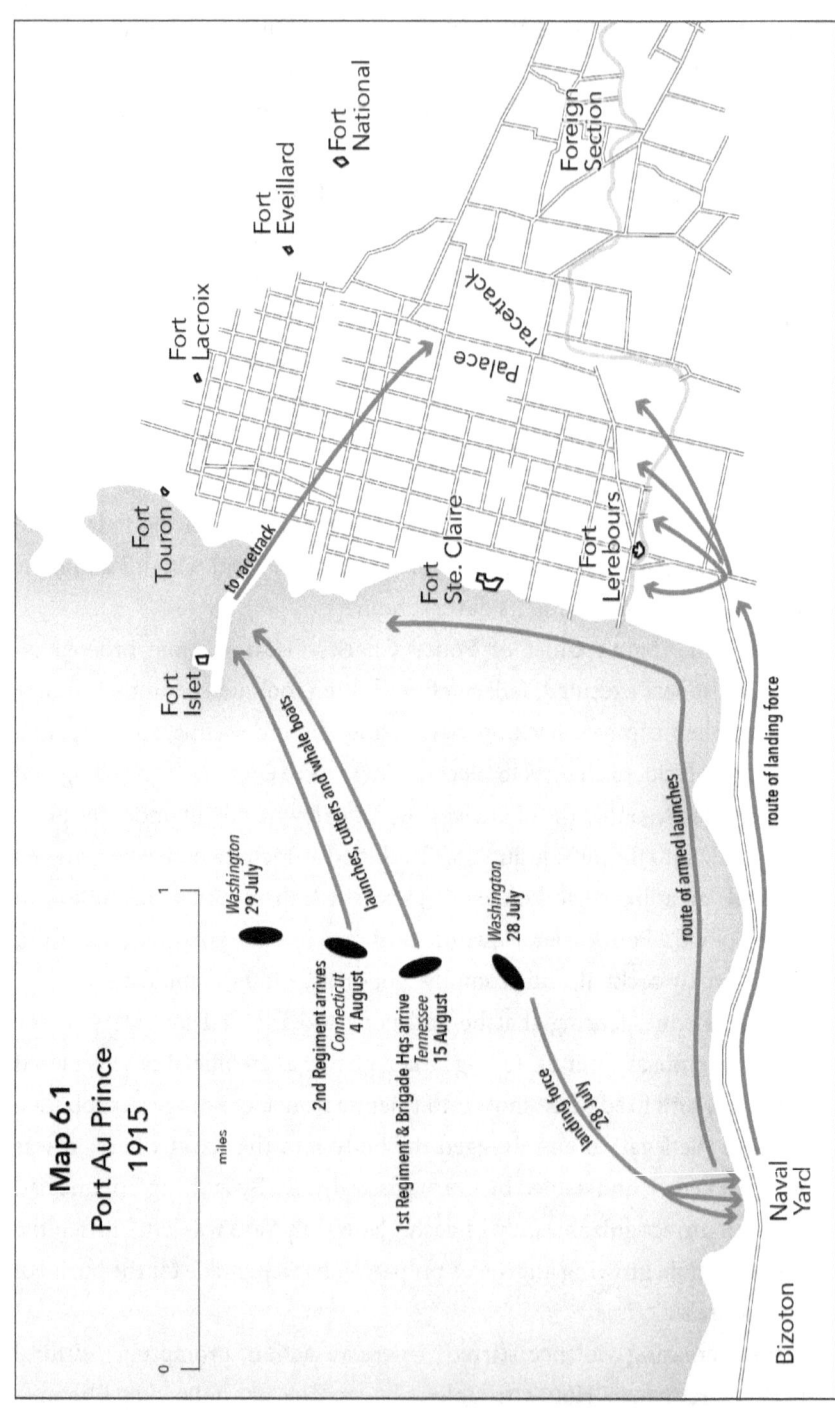

Map 6.1 Port Au Prince 1915

slaughter, Caperton and the *Washington* neared Port-au-Prince, raising fears by many Bobo supporters that Sam might find sanctuary on board the American vessel. A mob quickly rushed into the French legation, found the president cowering in the Ambassador's bathroom, and dragged him to the street outside.

> I could see that something or somebody was on the ground in the center of the crowd, just before the gates, . . . when a man disentangled himself from the crowd and rushed howling by me, with a severed hand from which the blood was dripping . . . . behind him came men with the feet, the other hand, the head, and other parts of the body displayed on poles, each one followed by a mob of screaming men and women. The portion of the body that remained was dragged through the streets by the crowd.[10]

The savagery convinced Caperton that he must act quickly. Finding "no government authority . . . to exist in the city," and fearful of the growing unrest throughout Haiti, the next day he ordered a landing force ashore at Port-au-Prince. Caperton hastily organized two battalions of Marines and bluejackets and landed them along the western approach at Port-au-Prince to quell the rioting and protect foreign nationals and their property (see Map 6.1). Friendly fire killed two Americans while Haitians suffered twelve casualties. Over the next few days, the American force swiftly brought the capital under control, and by week's end, some two thousand Americans stood guard in Port-au-Prince and Cap-Haïtien.

Caperton ordered the Twenty-Fourth Company of Marines at Guantanamo Bay, Cuba, to move to the Haitian capital as reinforcements for the landing party. The admiral then reported to Washington that the "masses of the Haitian people" welcomed the Americans and the landing force encountered only "slight resistance." At the French consul's urging, "Caperton ordered twenty men from the USS *Eagle* to land at Cap-Haïtien to protect the French Consulate."[11]

That same day, Caperton radioed Washington for "a regiment of Marines from the United States at once for policing and patrolling."[12] Caperton's request and the growing urgency of the situation resulted in the first of two major deployments of Marines from the United States and soon led to Waller's direct involvement in Haitian affairs.

## EXPEDITION TO HAITI

At 9:30 a.m. on July 30, Colonel John A. Lejeune, acting commandant during General George Barnett's absence, wired Philadelphia Navy Yard First Brigade commander, Colonel Littleton Waller, that the Second Marine Regiment would be detached for expeditionary service to Haiti. Lejeune ordered Major Eli Cole, commanding Marine Barracks at Annapolis, to leave immediately for Philadelphia and take command of the Second Regiment. In the meantime, the battleship USS *Connecticut* had arrived at League Island ready to embark the Marines for Haiti.

A few hours later, Officer-of-the-Day Marine Lieutenant Adolph B. Miller had just mounted the guard at Seaman's Barracks at the Navy Yard when Colonel Wendell Neville "passed the word to stop all liberty [and] to stand-by to sail for Port-au-Prince, Haiti at 9 a.m. Saturday morning [July 31st]." Miller spent the rest of the day getting his "gear together" before going home to spend a few hours with his wife Holly and their newborn baby. At midnight,

The Marine Band at League Island playing the Marines aboard the USS *Connecticut* while friends and families watch the boarding. *Courtesy of the Waller Family Archives.*

The 2nd Regiment, USMC, going aboard the USS *Connecticut*, League Island, July 1915. *Courtesy of the Waller Family Archives.*

Miller reported back to the Seaman's Barracks for a few hours' rest. As he slept through the early morning hours, the regiment worked feverishly to ready itself for boarding later that morning. By 5:00 a.m., Miller reported that everyone was up, with officers on leave having reported, and at 8:00 a.m., Miller's fifteenth Company of the First Battalion formed up under Captain William P. Upshur and "marched to the *Connecticut*." Wives and families crowded along the wharf, watching the men filing in columns onto the pier as Colonel Waller and his wife, Clara, waited to send the regiment on its way. Mrs. Waller "invited Holly [Miller] to her auto," so Miller said his goodbyes and boarded the ship.[13]

Colonel Cole arrived an hour before departure and found the ship loaded with men and gear ready to sail. By 9:40 a.m., just one day after the regiment had received its orders, the *Connecticut* got underway for Haiti. At New York, other officers on leave joined the ship before it moved out into the Atlantic and made a starboard turn to the south. With a brief stop the next day at Hampton Roads to take on an additional 125 enlisted men and two officers, the expedition steamed on toward Haiti. During the day, weapons classes and drill for "new recruits" kept the men busy while at night there were movies on deck and always good Navy food all around. Miller and the other officers spent the evening hours reminiscing. "We have quite a number of officers on this expedition who were out at China when I was there. It seems like a big family reunion."[14]

The Second Regiment arrived off Port-au-Prince at 3:30 p.m. on August 4 as the *Connecticut* anchored near Caperton's flagship. Cole immediately unloaded, using "sailing launches, cutters, and whale boats." The men landed at the Customs Wharf, shifting their gear and equipment onto railroad flatcars under the watchful eyes of the bluejackets standing guard. "A heavy [steam] engine took us through the town out to the race track," and through the city, "the natives all cheered and seemed very glad to see us, al[though] quite a number of brick bats were heaved at us from dark places along the line."[15] The next day, the Marines plunged into expeditionary duties (see Map 6.1).

Caperton duly reported the Second Regiment's arrival but requested another one thousand Marines for service on the island. Two days after the Second Regiment's disembarkation at Port-au-Prince, Colonel Waller received orders from the Navy Department. "Proceed via USS *Tennessee* to Port-au-Prince, report Commander Cruiser Squadron temporary duty in command First Brigade U.S. Marines and other United States Naval forces on shore in Haiti."[16]

As early as 1877, long before the 1915 Haitian intervention, the United States had applied a policy of assigning Black diplomats as representatives to the Caribbean nation. But beginning with Waller's administration in 1915, Wilson appointed "white marines and civilian officials ... from the southern states on the theory that from long acquaintance with Negroes, they could handle them better."[17]

In the midst of this turmoil and the emerging new staffing prerogatives for Haiti, President Woodrow Wilson ordered Colonel Littleton W. T. Waller and the First Marine Brigade to Haiti with an eye on Waller's long imperial experience. Despite Wilson's earlier political reticence to name him as commandant, Waller's unparalleled field experience in Egypt, China, the Philippines, Panama, Cuba, and Mexico made him the logical choice for the command. Short, tenacious, often cocksure and aggressive, the Marines' foremost bush fighter was disliked by many but loved by the men who served under him. Waller, not Caperton, would decide the operational realities of America's first two years of occupation in Haiti.

Since the 1890s, the emerging American empire had shouldered broad responsibilities, offering new opportunities for military leaders who brought their own cultural perspective to a changing imperial landscape. Chief among them, Waller performed these duties in a manner consistent with his aristocratic southern mores. The scion of a Virginia first family with members long in public service, he approached his assignment in Haiti with the hauteur and determination characteristic of his class. Such attitudes may have helped him attain immediate goals in Haiti, but they undercut his long-term reform efforts and set him at odds with the changing Marine Corps leadership.

Charged with stabilizing Haitian society following the financial, social, and political crisis of 1915, Waller rooted out corrupt government officials, while ruthlessly suppressing banditry and rebellion. At the same time, he was appalled by the insensitivity of Haiti's ruling mulatto elite toward the suffering of their country's masses, who were almost all of pure African heritage. Horrified by the squalor around him, Waller wielded his command authority to implement public health programs, develop educational facilities, and establish an effective national transportation system. Committed to these reforms out of a patrician sense of noblesse oblige, Waller still held a patronizing contempt for the very people he benefitted.

Waller's assignment in Haiti also stirred old rivalries and tensions as the Corps struggled to incorporate its own internal reforms. Waller grappled with a continuing and increasing competition from a class of new officers equipped with a Naval Academy education, a better grasp of planning and staff work, and the diplomatic skills necessary for the Navy's ever-widening imperial responsibilities.[18]

Waller's attitudes regarding race and class strongly influenced his administration in Haiti. Bred a southern aristocrat, he could not countenance the perceived corruption of a Black oligarchy; Africans he deemed incapable of developing a proper ruling ethic. "Thes[e] people are [n----s]," he wrote to his superior in October 1915, "in spite of the varnish of education and refinement. Down in their heart, they are just the same happy, idle irresponsible people we know" back home.[19] Waller subsequently implemented reforms under the assumption that only the supposedly progressive Anglo-Saxon race could save the blighted isle from its squalid morass.

Waller's appointment and subsequent administration demonstrate that by the early twentieth century, the American government had accepted as valid the southern white views on race and class. With the Virginian Woodrow Wilson in the White House, and North Carolina's Josephus Daniels heading the Navy Department, American imperialists established policies whose ramifications would be felt through the remainder of the early twentieth century.

By the time the Navy ordered Waller to Haiti, decades of disorder had scarred the Caribbean nation. Patterns of upheaval and chaos dominated Haiti since the revolution against France in 1804. Since that time, the Haitian people had lived under twenty-six presidents, only two of whom had completed their full terms. The latest chief executive, suffering the fate of many of his predecessors, had been dragged from his refuge and hacked to death by a furious crowd exerting the traditional method of a Haitian mandate.[20]

For the eager Waller, this episode meant a continuation of his service in the American empire as he answered the call to bring the American brand of order to lands torn by chaos and terror. His previous imperial service had well prepared him for the demands of Americanization his Haitian assignment would bring. So once again Waller left Clara behind as he sailed for the next campaign.

On August 10, as the *Tennessee* pushed away from the wharf at League Island, easing into the Delaware River and making way for open sea, Waller scribbled a quick note to his second son, John B. Waller, and handed it to the pilot to mail. He wrote that his oldest son "Littleton dropped in Saturday evening but had to go back yesterday so Mama was alone this morning." Waller worried that "I have no idea how long the duty will last, but I fear it will be quite a while," so "in the meantime do everything you can to cheer Mama." With Philadelphia disappearing in the distance, Waller looked ahead to Haiti and his final expedition. In the beleaguered Haitian cities along the coastline, and in the hostile mountain country to the north, Waller would draw on his vast experience and continue his career, filled with both success and conflict.[21]

Philippe-Sudré Dartiguenave, president of Haiti, Port-au-Prince, circa July 1915. *Courtesy of the U.S. Naval History and Heritage Command.*

On August 15, 1915, Waller's First Marine Brigade landed in Haiti, a force which included eighty-eight officers and 1,941 enlisted men. Waller ordered Colonel Eli Cole and the First Battalion, First Regiment, to Cap-Haïtien and established his own headquarters with the remainder of the brigade at Port-au-Prince.[22] Waller's most pressing task was the establishment of order in a country where insurgent activity plagued the northern areas, even as anarchy wracked the cities to the south.

Three days earlier, on August 12, the Haitian Congress elected Philippe-Sudré Dartiguenave to succeed Sam as president. The American chargé d'affaires, Robert B. Davis, met with Dartiguenave and gave him a draft of a proposed treaty "that in effect made Haiti an American protectorate." Dartiguenave responded to the draft in a positive way, assuring Davis that he intended "to give the United States everything that it desired in the treaty, and stated his belief that the Haitian Congress would interpose no serious objections."

The proposed treaty reflected American aims to address corruption, instability, and the continuing deteriorating conditions for ordinary Haitians and their prospects for a better life. The treaty "provided for American control of Haiti's finances, the creation of an American-officered national constabulary," and called for an ambitious plan to deploy "American engineers and public health officials to reform the public works and sanitation systems" in Haiti. The treaty draft also prohibited the Haitian government from selling land to any foreign governments. Dartiguenave's optimism for the treaty's reception in the Congress in Port-au-Prince was not well founded. American actions the next day guaranteed to frustrate the negotiations and treaty ratification in Haiti.[23]

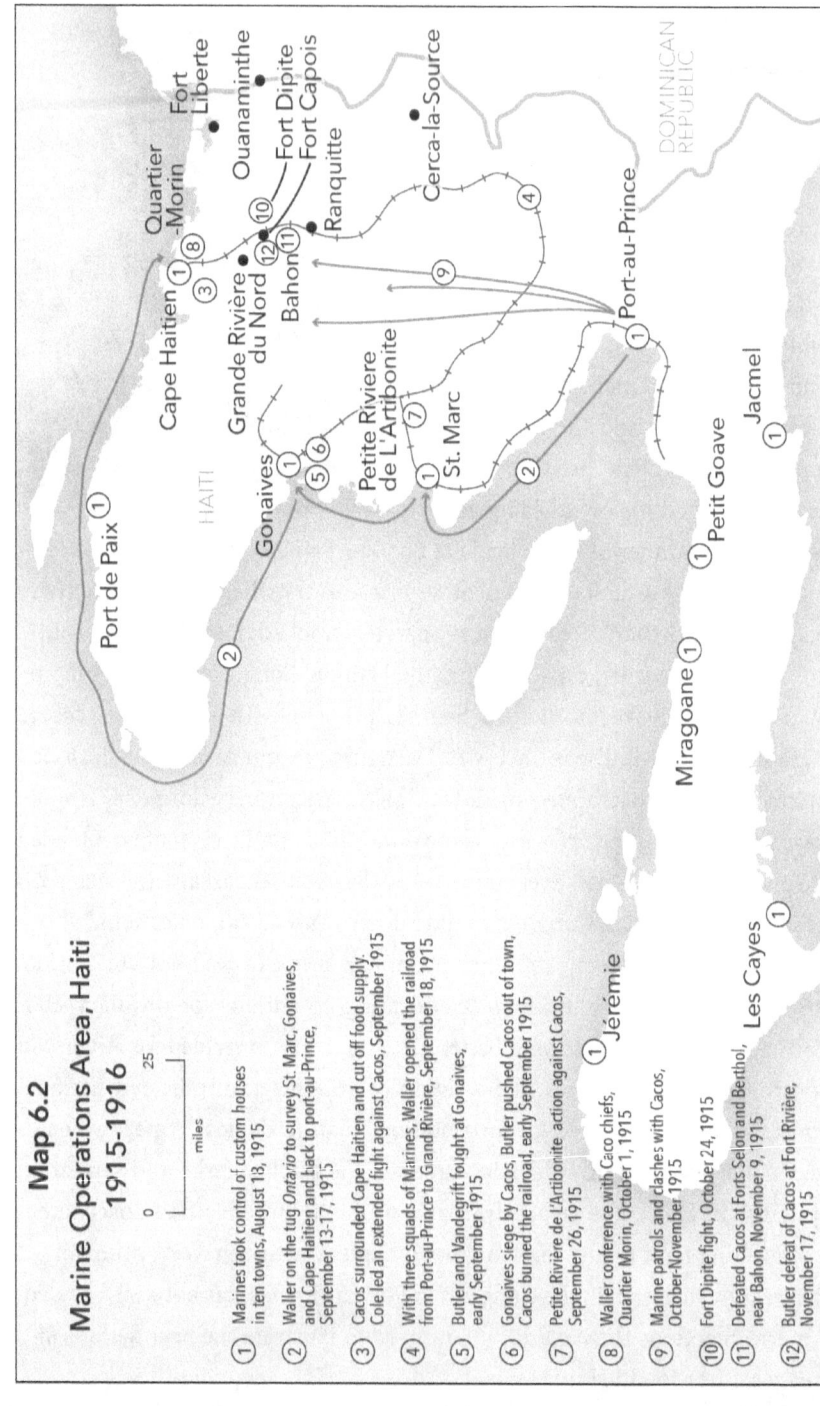

Map 6.2
Marine Operations Area, Haiti
1915–1916

1. Marines took control of custom houses in ten towns, August 18, 1915
2. Waller on the tug *Ontario* to survey St. Marc, Gonaives, and Cape Haitien and back to Port-au-Prince, September 13–17, 1915
3. Cacos surrounded Cape Haitien and cut off food supply. Cole led an extended fight against Cacos, September 1915
4. With three squads of Marines, Waller opened the railroad from Port-au-Prince to Grand Rivière, September 18, 1915
5. Butler and Vandegrift fought at Gonaives, early September 1915
6. Gonaives siege by Cacos, Butler pushed Cacos out of town, Cacos burned the railroad, early September 1915
7. Petite Riviere de L'Artibonite action against Cacos, September 26, 1915
8. Waller conference with Caco chiefs, Quartier Morin, October 1, 1915
9. Marine patrols and clashes with Cacos, October–November 1915
10. Fort Dipite fight, October 24, 1915
11. Defeated Cacos at Forts Selon and Berthol, near Bahon, November 9, 1915
12. Butler defeat of Cacos at Fort Rivière, November 17, 1915

Marines in lineup in front of Marine Barracks, Port-au-Prince, Haiti, circa 1915. *Courtesy of the National Archives.*

On August 18, the State Department sent a directive to the Navy Department to assume control of all custom houses in Haiti (see Map 6.2). The next day Caperton "received a radiogram from the Navy Department" ordering him take "charge of the custom houses at Jacmel, Les Cayes, Jereme, Miragoane, Petite Goave, Port-au-Prince, St. Marc, Gonaives, Part de Paix, and Cap-Haïtien." His orders instructed him that custom duties collected were "to be used for the organization and maintenance of an efficient constabulary for conducting such temporary public works." The funds "will afford immediate relief through employment for the starving populace and discharged soldiers, and finally for supporting the Dartiguenave government."[24]

On September 1, Admiral William B. Caperton ordered Colonel Waller to establish martial law in areas under American control. Soon after Waller arrived, Caperton cabled his superiors asking "that military government be

Brigade Headquarters Detachment, USMC, Port-au-Prince, Haiti, circa 1915. *Courtesy of the Waller Family Archives.*

A section of the 6th Company camp, USMC, Port-au-Prince, Haiti, 1915. *Courtesy of the Waller Family Archives.*

established" with Waller "as military governor" until a more stable "government can be established." Caperton instructed Waller to "issue the necessary regulations and appoint the necessary officers to make this martial law effective."[25] These orders derived from communications with Washington concerning threats by Haitian officials to resign should the United States continue to push for a treaty designed to make sweeping changes in Haiti while establishing new relationships with the United States.

A detachment of Third Signal Company, USMC, establishing communications in the capital city, Port-au-Prince, Haiti, 1915. *Courtesy of the Waller Family Archives.*

Caperton soon would regret, however, that Waller would command all American forces ashore. He grew convinced that Waller sought "to swipe all Haiti" for the Marines and use every "effort of the Marines ... to get control of the public utilities and increase their influence in Haiti."[26] In the months ahead, this all too common and often bitter sort of interservice imperial rivalry grew into a clash of "domineering personalities," as both Waller and Caperton used back channels to Washington to poison the well against each other. Waller denounced Caperton as "insane" and moved by paranoia, complaining that "instead [of] backing up men who are working for him[,] he knifes them when they do well." Waller peppered his correspondence with complaints about Caperton and derogatory references about "the old fool." Caperton, for his part, complained repeatedly that Waller acted unilaterally and kept him (Caperton) in the dark. Jealous of Waller as a competitor, Caperton maneuvered and contested Waller at every turn. In this environment of growing distrust and disdain, the work of the Marine brigade began in earnest.[27]

On September 4, Caperton cabled the Navy Department that "in northern Haiti, the Cacos situation is becoming critical because ... [they] will not come within our lines and surrender arms and will not disband." At Cap-Haïtien, the Cacos were blockading the town, preventing the entry of trade and transport and threatening the people. Waller had to act decisively and quickly.²⁸

While Admiral Caperton's vessels landed small groups of Marines to occupy isolated seaports along the coastline, Waller left Port-au-Prince on September 13 to survey conditions at St. Marc, Gonaives, and Cap-Haïtien (see Map 6.2). "I went aboard the seagoing tug, *Ontario*, to make inspections of the northern ports," planning on interviewing "the Caco chiefs and reconnoitering around Cap-Haitien." Arriving at St. Marc, Waller "found the town clear and the people happy and contented and having a thorough confidence in Captain Fay who commands there." Throughout his correspondence, Waller repeatedly depicts the Haitians as a "happy and contented" people who were "very docile," and who welcomed him as both protector and commander. He saw little difference between the "Negroes" of his Virginia childhood and the Blacks and mulattos he encountered in Haiti: "I say this without any spirit of egotism, I know the [n-----] and how to handle him."

After a week's reconnoiter through northern Haiti, Waller returned to Port-au-Prince, having extracted promises from the Caco chiefs not to interfere with the Marines and "to be good." Satisfied that the situation in the north would stabilize, he expected that the Cacos could be easily managed.

USS *Ontario*, an ocean-going tug used for transportation along the Haitian coastline, 1915–1916. *Courtesy of the U.S. Naval History and Heritage Command.*

Waller and Marines at Quartier Morin to meet with Caco chiefs, October 1, 1915. *Courtesy of the Waller Family Archives.*

Impressed with Waller's fieldwork, Caperton cabled Washington that "on September 18, with three squads of Marines, two machine guns and wrecking material, Colonel Waller opened the railroad to Grand Riviere without difficulty." While danger loomed over the expedition, Caperton reported

Caco General Morencey and Jeter Horton in Haiti, about October 1915. *Courtesy of the National Archives.*

that in the end, the "Cacos [were] much excited but offered no resistance"[29] (see Map 6.2).

Waller positioned Marines in ten towns across Haiti and later added other towns to the occupation plan. From these settlements, frequent Marine patrols contested Caco operations against the government's control of towns and deep into the rural countryside. In early September, Cacos laid siege to the Marine garrison at Gonaives. "Major Smedley D. Butler and Lieutenant Alexander A. Vandegrift sped there in a small boat; and Butler led the local Marine detachment . . . in pushing the Cacos out of town." Later that night, word reached Butler that the Cacos "were burning the railroad." With fifty Marines, Butler attacked the rebels at the rail yard and pursued the Cacos into the countryside where the Marines took the Caco commander into custody. The Gonaives fight was just the beginning of action in the mountain region in northern Haiti (see Map 6.2).[30]

At Cap-Haïtien, Cacos surrounded the city and cut off food supplies from the countryside. In response Colonel Cole sent out three "strong patrols," but when the Cacos surrounded the three patrols, Cole brought bluejackets ashore from the *Connecticut* to replace Marine sentries in the city, and then "he led out the rest of the Marines to join the fight." The Cacos put a good showing, but they "were finally driven off, leaving 40 dead on the field." Marine casualties numbered just ten wounded (see Map 6.2).[31]

Further south at St. Marc, on September 26, Captain R. O. Underwood and "a half company of mounted Marines" responded to a "disturbance" at Petite Rivière de L'Artibonite to the east (see Map 6.2). The Marines defeated the Cacos but suffered the first Marine killed in action in Haiti. The next day, the patrol worked their way back to St. Marc. "All along the route in returning, the inhabitants turned out everywhere, expressing regret at the loss of the Marine." Underwood reported that "women followed the corpse for some distance chanting a native hymn." In the fight at Petite Rivière and in operations all along the coastal areas, Marines pursued attackers deep into the north central mountains as the leathernecks responded to the Cacos' hit and run tactics. The rebels used the rugged mountain terrain as a refuge against the better trained and equipped Marines who dogged their tracks as the Cacos tried to disappear into the wilderness (see Map 6.2).[32]

September's end found Waller again traveling north to negotiate with the Caco chiefs. On October 1, he conferred with their leader at Quartier Morin and secured a written agreement that the Cacos would "disarm immediately, turn in all arms and ammunition to United States Forces, go to their homes, and not interfere with railroads, telegraphs, telephones, commerce, agriculture or other industries of the country." But Waller soon realized that the Cacos had no intention of keeping their promises, and he immediately launched operations against the northern strongholds. Although the Cacos' guerilla tactics proved challenging for the American Marines, Waller quickly subdued the uprising. On November 9, the colonel radioed Caperton that "Forts Selon and Berthol captured yesterday. Cacos fled at sight of our men." He reported that "all houses in Caco country now displaying white flags and people say they have had enough, no ammunition, and leaders have fled." Waller planned a sweep "westward of the railroad towards Ranquitte," mopping up the remnants as his men advanced. He boasted that the "mobile columns have averaged fifteen miles a day for nine days, are hard as nails and fit for anything."[33]

Eight days later, Waller dispatched a force under Major Smedley Butler that stormed Fort Rivière, capturing the stronghold with heavy Caco causalities. Josephus Daniels ordered a suspension of operations "in view of the heavy losses received by the Haitians in recent engagements in order to prevent further loss of life." The fighting at Fort Rivière marked an end to Caco resistance in the north. Caperton radioed Daniels in Washington on November 19 that "operations against Cacos bandits in North Haiti during [the] last three weeks" had destroyed their ability to fight and isolated the Caco insurgents, "capturing many of

Major Smedley D. Butler, a few years before he arrived in Haiti. *Courtesy of the Library of Congress.*

their strongholds, destruction [of] quantities [of] arms and ammunition and bringing peaceful conditions throughout Cacos country."[34]

Meanwhile, Waller and the State Department sought to expand American control of Haiti through the expansion of the Haitian gendarmerie (a constabulary with Marine officers under Smedley Butler at its helm) to control "Haiti's public works." Waller reasoned that with the gendarmerie's continuing successes over public roads, communications, sanitation, education, and the post office, the Haitian economy would have a sound foundation, and the United States would continue in a position to ensure stability and protect against foreign encroachment.

Anticipating that the treaty with Haiti would approve a gendarmerie with American officers, Waller assigned Smedley Butler with the task of "organizing the Gendarmerie on December 3, 1915." Early in 1916, when the treaty was ratified by the U.S. Senate, Butler already had the gendarmerie in place with "1,500 Haitian enlisted men garrisoning 117 posts" across Haiti. By the time formal agreements were signed and ratified, Butler had the gendarmerie engaged in a variety of nation-building projects designed to reduce corruption and inefficiency and develop important resources in Haitian communities and across the rural landscape. Waller saw the Haitian gendarmerie as the key to success for American policy in Haiti. The State Department agreed with him.[35]

As November and December 1915 closed, Waller found Port-au-Prince a hotbed of intrigue, involving both the Haitian politicos and officers of the naval service under Caperton. For the next year, Waller focused on establishing public services and stabilizing the political situation while pursuing his own career goals. Waller's administration improved conditions in the short term, yet the American occupation failed ultimately to obtain its goal of lasting reforms. Walter H. Posner suggests that too many changes in the American leadership cadre during the first seven years doomed the project to failure. "From 1915 to 1922 the Marines in Haiti had nine commanding officers, and the gendarmerie four chiefs," with "five senior naval officers directing affairs from the Dominican Republic." In Washington, the executive branch suffered similar instability and over the same period, leadership included "six chiefs of the Division of Latin-American Affairs in Washington,

... four secretaries of state, and two American presidents." Often distracted, Waller's administration in Port-au-Prince faced difficult challenges in Haiti while he negotiated a maze of intrigue within the Corps as he maneuvered for promotion and recognition. His most difficult adversary often proved to be himself.[36]

"Short, pugnacious, hard-drinking, and very energetic," Waller had fixed ideas on almost everything, with himself very often the center of his point of view. His subordinates loved him for his aggressive, hands-on leadership that placed him among the troops, suffering the hardships of the campaign and assuming the same risks. The loyal and impressionable young officers who served under him often shared his optimism and vanity. Years after his service with Waller, Smedley Butler wrote that Waller was "the greatest soldier I have ever known.... Waller may have liked to talk about himself, but he had plenty to talk about."[37]

Waller's officers were quick to defend him, never forgot the injustices against him, and fought to protect his reputation. In September 1930, four years after Waller's death, Lieutenant Colonel Gerard M. Kincade, who served under Waller in 1904 as a second lieutenant, wrote to Waller's oldest son, still complaining about Taft's failure to name Waller commandant in 1911: "Those who knew your father, all the old crowd who had dealings with him, knew that he should have had it [major general commandant], and knew that he was deprived of his just deserts through politics." Waller never had trouble getting along with his men or winning over officers who looked to him for leadership. To these men, Waller represented the "Old Corps," and all the traditions and myths surrounding that vision. In Haiti, it was the new, educated elite—the technocrats—with whom Waller found fault, and they reciprocated.[38]

Waller criticized the men of the new Navy unrelentingly and often allowed his disparaging remarks to be heard by casual listeners who then relayed the conversation to interested parties. In the Marine Corps, a small and exclusive club, Waller's targets quickly heard of his coarse and often harsh denunciations. His relationship with Eli K. Cole illustrates the kind of political damage Waller reaped with his intemperate remarks when careful political maneuver and discreet words could instead have created valuable allies.

Major Cole enjoyed a reputation as a staff officer, particularly by producing influential studies on the Advanced Base Force. Waller had known Cole for years, periodically having him under his command. In Haiti, in 1915–1916, Cole had the demanding task of serving under Waller in the pacification work. Waller publicly embarrassed Cole several times by remarks to others and by often placing Smedley Butler, Cole's junior, in command of operations, plainly bypassing Cole in the chain of command. Before Waller departed the United States for Haiti, the Marine commandant had authorized an unofficial line of communication for Waller's use to gain a clear view of operations in Haiti. Waller so laced his "unofficial" letters to Assistant Commandant John Lejeune[39] with derogatory observations concerning Cole that Lejeune cautioned Waller to temper his comments concerning the reputations of officers. As Waller's friend, Lejeune sought to shield the old bush fighter from himself.[40]

Waller's treatment of Cole reflected his impatience in dealing with any of the staff types he so enjoyed criticizing. Waller spent his career competing with Marines who were Naval Academy graduates who, in Waller's view, caused all that was wrong in the Corps, and he held them directly responsible for many of the problems that demanded his attention in Haiti and other assignments. In a letter to Lejeune, in September 1915, Waller reached the point of exasperation with Cole and others in northern Haiti: "Frankly, if my instructions are not carried out by Cole and the others . . . I shall be obliged to ask that the timid individuals be removed to the United States." Waller alerted Lejeune not to be too surprised if he took some drastic measures. "Hesitation at this time with . . . [the Haitians] means bloodshed. Positive firmness means that they will give up." Waller warned Lejeune that "if Cole can't hold his position without the support of a gunboat and battleship[,] I will bring him down here and send a younger and more active man up there."[41]

Much of Waller's correspondence to Clara and his sons during the Haiti operation comprised copies of his letters to Lejeune, with brief postscripts at the end in long hand. Yet, even notes to his wife included complaints of others' perceived shortcomings. "The night passed without trouble all along the line, although Cole is again asking for help . . . . It doesn't look as though he had much red blood in his veins." When Cole later requested two additional companies, Waller acidly observed that "things must have quieted down considerably for Cole to want to go out and attack. Of course, he knew that [Washington] had forbidden any offensive move." In a handwritten note added to one of the copies that he sent to his son, Waller condemned the fainthearted conduct of Cole and others during operations to curtail banditry in the north, noting that "[Edward H.] Durell of the *Connecticut* blames Cole for all the timid conduct at first, and Cole blames Durell. The fact is they frightened each other." Cole "does pretty well when there is someone there to make him keep up to his work."[42]

Waller showed no more circumspection in disparaging his immediate commander, Rear Admiral William B. Caperton. Caperton "is always making errors that I have to correct.... He does not understand the things that are reported to him." Waller complained that he often had to spend time correcting mistaken impressions generated by the admiral. This assignment was "very much the most unsatisfactory work I have ever done in any line."[43]

In February 1916, Caperton appointed Captain Edward Beach his chief of staff and a few days later, Beach called on Waller with the news that Caperton "felt that I was growing away from him" and wished to redefine "my duties." Fearing that Waller would not accept a revision of those duties authored by Caperton, the admiral sent word that Waller should "draw up an order," which Caperton would then sign. Waller informed Beach that "the Navy Department had defined my duties, and I did not see how I could change them." He then threw down the gauntlet, saying "that if the Admiral was dissatisfied with my manner of performing duty," Waller would ask to be "relieved by a senior officer" or be "sent home." He pointed out to Beach that Caperton had recently refused Waller leave because he "could not do without my services for the three weeks necessary for me to go home." The colonel wondered "who was trying to influence the Admiral against me" since he "was rather in the dark as to the cause of the sudden change" in Caperton's attitude.

Beach assured Waller that "personal relations between" the admiral and Waller "were fine but the Admiral thought he ought to be told more of what was going on" ashore. Caperton was annoyed that Waller had signed a proclamation to the Haitian people and failed to give him (Caperton) credit or standing with the Haitians. This continuing problem dated back several months. Waller could not convince Caperton that "it was entirely according to custom and military propriety" to put Waller's name on proclamations and agreements since he held the authority and "made all the arrangements" and so should "do the signing." Since October, Waller had carried on the negotiations with the Haitians on the treaty and other legal notices and proclamations. These efforts irritated Caperton, as he sought to control events as the ultimate American occupation authority on the scene. The two never ceased jousting for credit and standing, and the issue continued as an aggravation until Caperton left Haiti.[44]

## MARINE CORPS EXPANSION ON THE EVE OF WAR

In late February, Waller was ordered home for congressional hearings concerning the 1917 appropriations budget. As the senior Marine colonel, Waller testified about conditions in Haiti and his views on the proposed personnel increases for Marine Corps. The Corps functioned under an authorization for 342 officers with only one general officer, a major general who served as the commandant. Waller testified in support of a plan calling for expanding the general officer category to a total of four, one major general and three brigadier generals. The proposals centered on a new ratio of four officers for every one hundred enlisted men and included three options involving the number of enlisted men in the Corps: (1) maintaining the current strength of 9921 with no increase, (2) an increase of 1500 enlisted men, and (3) an increase of 2379 enlisted men. All three plans meant increases in every officer rank category, using the new four to one hundred ratio (see Figure 11). For Waller and his fellow colonels, every proposal included an increase in the brigadier general category, representing future promotion opportunities for many of these senior colonels. As it stood in 1916, the only avenue to general's stars was to be named commandant, the only general officer in the Marine Corps. That would soon change.[45]

As the senior colonel, Waller anticipated receiving his first star should Congress adopt any one of the three proposals. Lacking further opportunities to be named commandant and without the legislative increase for the

FIGURE 11

## Marine Corps Personnel Increase Proposals Based on the Ratio of Four Officers per 100 Enlisted Men for Federal Year 1917

| | CURRENTLY AUTHORIZED | PROPOSAL 1 (NO INCREASE IN ENLISTED MEN) | PROPOSAL 2 (ENLISTED INCREASED BY 1500 MEN) | PROPOSAL 3 (ENLISTED INCREASED BY 2379 MEN) |
|---|---|---|---|---|
| MAJOR GENERAL | 1 | 1 | 1 | 1 |
| BRIGADIER GENERAL | 0 | 2 | 3 | 3 |
| COLONEL | 10 | 13 | 15 | 16 |
| LIEUTENANT COLONEL | 12 | 16 | 19 | 29 |
| MAJOR | 26 | 45 | 53 | 80 |
| CAPTAIN | 107 | 119 | 137 | 148 |
| LIEUTENANT | 156 | 201 | 230 | 248 |
| TOTAL | 342 | 397 | 457 | 492 |

Corps, Waller would have left the Marine Corps as a long-serving colonel. But the proposals came at a time when the European war threatened to involve the United States, and within four years, Waller would retire a major general.

Congressman Thomas Butler, Major Smedley Butler's father and an influential member of the Naval Affairs Committee, chaired the hearings. After several days of testimony by Commandant George Barnett, Assistant Commandant John A. Lejeune, and others, Waller appeared before the committee on March 2, 1916. "I have been before the Naval Committee and made my little spiel," Waller wrote his oldest son, Littleton.

With the Haiti campaign still prominent in the minds of the nation and prospects freshening for war in Europe, Waller enjoyed a sympathetic audience, greatly interested in what the combat veteran had to say. "I was questioned about the needs of the Marine Corps at first, and then about the Haitian situation." Waller left with the "impression that the committee was very favorable to us on both the questions." He confided to his middle son, John Beresford, "I may be mistaken, but I hope that we will get the immediate increase needed that amounts to [adding] 2379 [enlisted] men and 156 officers including the brigadiers." Waller was not mistaken.[46]

The clouds of war prompted Congress to expand the Marine Corps request, and on August 29, 1916, Congress "increased the authorized strength of the Marine Corps from 344 officers and 9,921 enlisted men to 597 officers and 14,981 enlisted men, and the President was authorized in an emergency to further increase the corps to 693 officers and 17,400 enlisted men, which he did by Executive order on March 26, 1917." By the end of World War I, only two years later, the permanent authorized Marine strength loomed even higher.[47]

While on this temporary duty in Washington, Waller seized the opportunity to make certain that nothing would go wrong with his bid for a brigadier's star. With two failed campaigns for commandant behind him, he lined up strong support for his case. Although confident that his seniority and his military record gave him the edge over all competitors, he meant to leave nothing to chance. "Mr. Butler told me that the committee was determined that I should be made a brigadier, and I learn that the Department is of the same opinion." Smedley Butler had also returned to Washington on temporary orders to shore up support for increases in the new personnel budget hearing in Congress. As always, the longtime Waller protégé served as conduit to his father for Waller.

With Smedley Butler working behind the scenes, and the congressional front moving in his favor, Waller canvassed the other colonels who would be his competitors for brigadier. "All the officers of the rank of colonel in the Corps" indicated their support that Waller should be "the first brigadier." Only Colonel Lincoln Karmany, who remained silent on the question, proved an unknown factor. "I have no doubt that he will fight for the place, not to hold it but to retire soon with that grade." Waller found one senator who "opposes his [Karmany] advancement to any grade. This on account of the moral character of the man."[48]

The Washington interlude also allowed Waller some time at home with Clara in Philadelphia. "I do not know whether I shall have to go back to Haiti or not. The President and the Admiral [William S. Benson, Chief of Naval Operations,] both want me there but Benson told me not to hurry." Grateful for the respite, Waller wrote that Benson "thought I had done enough there and should have a rest. I am not kicking about that in the least." In one of his last letters to his wife before departing Haiti, Waller had grown pensive as he took stock of his three and half decades on the campaign trail. "Passing into the silver leaf of life I would like to be at peace with all men. All my life has been a battle. . . ." and, longing for the joy that peace brings, Waller declared that "I am tired of war and its consequent suffering."[49]

Although he was now over sixty years of age, his long separations from Clara continued. As he wrote the letter, he remarked that it was the thirty-first anniversary of their wedding in New York City. "I long to be with you today darling to pass this anniversary." He mused that "I would like to go over to New York to our church and at twelve o'clock offer a prayer of thanksgiving for the blessings that have been ours." Regret for loss filled his letter to Clara, underscored by the tender poetry of his devotion to her. When he found himself at home with leisure moments, the couple made up for lost time. "We have been very gay here and next week every night is taken."[50]

## RETURN TO HAITI

Despite Benson's orders for Waller "to rest," Barnett wanted Waller back in Haiti where he could hold the line against Caperton and the Navy. On March 27, at 2:32 p.m. at Marine Headquarters at 8th and I Streets, Waller received orders to "proceed by rail, via Key West, Florida," to the Naval Station, Guantanamo," and take passage to Port-au-Prince. Waller left later that same evening and arrived in Key West on March 29. Two days later, he came ashore at Guantanamo to find the auxiliary cruiser USS *Prairie* waiting for him. The next day, Waller returned to Port-au-Prince and immediately went into conference with Caperton, renewing the old clash yet again.[51]

Twelve days after his return to Haiti, Waller wrote Lejeune that "everything is moving smoothly, and if we could only get rid of the Admiral, it would be fine." Waller's earlier thoughts of "peace with all men" clearly excluded Caperton. Waller shared his pointed comments on the admiral, warning that Caperton was losing "the little mind he has. I hope so anyhow."

He confided that "I am very hard pressed at times to keep my temper and show him the respect due his position."[52]

At the close of 1915, despite Caperton's annoyance with Waller, the admiral submitted excellent ratings for Waller for the period ending September 30, 1915. He reported that Waller served as "special representative of" Caperton and "the Haitian government" where he "arranged disarmament of [the] Cacos in Haiti. Excellent 4.0." Caperton scored Waller with "excellent 4.0" marks in every category of duty. He described Waller as "calm, forceful, active, bold, and painstaking."[53]

A month later Caperton submitted a commendation for Waller with the Navy Department, describing Waller's work as "excellent and effective service." For service against the Cacos in northern Haiti in October and November, Caperton wrote that Waller commanded the "expeditionary force of Marines and . . . seamen" and "effectively crushed all armed resistance to the American Occupation and the Haitian Government, and has maintained peace and order in all parts of the country." Caperton concluded with a hearty endorsement of Waller's loyalty and fidelity. "Colonel Waller has most efficiently and willingly supported me in all operations and negotiations in Haiti," he wrote, adding that "his bearing and conduct throughout this duty has added distinction to his already long and efficient service to the United States."[54]

No further fitness reports written by Caperton appear in Waller service jacket, but telegrams from Major General Barnett requesting the post-September 1915 fitness reports yielded communications from Caperton with scores that were used in Waller's examination for brigadier general later that fall. Barnett's telegram in November 1916 stated that no fitness reports had been received for Waller since the September 30, 1915, period. Caperton telegraphed Barnett that Waller's scores since that date would average 3.96, slightly lower than his previous assessments for Waller. At no time during his command of the South Atlantic Fleet did Caperton's official reports and commendations ever reflect the animosity and personality conflicts that existed between the two. Among the officers serving with Waller and Caperton, however, the widening breech between the two was evident and often public. Only Caperton's promotion and departure from Haiti brought the episode to an end. A crisis was brewing in the neighboring Dominican Republic, and Caperton moved his headquarters to Santo Domingo City to oversee the impending American invention there. With Caperton's departure, Waller assumed more control of Haitian affairs while the admiral's "role shrank drastically." Soon Waller would leave as well.⁵⁵

Never interested in an aggressive investment program and partnership in Haiti, the State Department was content to use the Marines to maintain the new order on the island and let matters remain where they were. Promises of loan packages and investments in Haiti remained unfulfilled as the State Department sought to "consolidate the intervention under a more effective structure rather than relax its grasp." With expanded Marine controls in place, the State Department reasoned that the continuing situation provided guarantees against upheaval and unrest in Haiti. Despite Caperton's arguments for a more active rebuilding of the Haitian economy and other institutions, Waller's plan for a Marine-led infrastructure reflected the State Department's policy for Haiti. With Caperton in San Domingo, Waller moved swiftly and with a firm hand, and set out to extend the military occupation through an accelerated public works program while maintaining a vigorous occupation of the island.⁵⁶

Upon Caperton's relief by Rear Admiral Charles Pond, however, Waller found the new man even more insufferable than Caperton. Waller grumbled to his son that he had "been very busy and very much annoyed for about two weeks. . . . We had the [n-----] about where we wanted them when along came the collection of admirals and balled up the whole business." Infuriated by two admirals giving secret and confidential information to the Haitians, he complained that "we will have to use a club on the [n-----]s before they get back into line."⁵⁷

Waller never came to grips with the fact that although he commanded all forces ashore, the Navy held overall command of the theater. He resented any intrusions and felt that the admirals only stole his thunder: "There is an article in the *New York Herald* of the 9th that I think must have been inspired by him [Caperton]. It does mention me once but that is all." Waller worried that "the people of the United States will believe him [Caperton] the greatest fighter we have" and that "if there is any trouble," the public would demand

Officers at Headquarters, Port-au-Prince, Haiti, in August 1916. Left to right, front row: Surgeon Richard B. Williams, USN; Lieutenant Colonel William C. Dawson, USMC (Paymaster); Colonel Littleton W. T. Waller, USMC (Commanding Officer); Lieutenant Colonel William B. Lemly, USMC; Major Louis J. Magill, USMC. Back row: Captain Joseph A. Rossell, USMC; Major Percy F. Archer, USMC; Lieutenant Randolph Coyle, USMC; and Passed Assistant Surgeon George L. Wickes, USN. *Courtesy of the Waller Family Archives.*

Caperton for the job. "Now they have sent us Pond. I want to go home—It is not fair to us or to the people of the two countries to send freaks."[58]

Despite his frustration with the Navy and his continuing campaign against the "staff types" in the Marine Corps, toward the end of his service in Haiti, Waller saw great promise in the work done by the Marines. "We are certainly doing a lot for this country and the people are beginning to appreciate it." He reflected that "it will be a fine thing to look back in the years to come and see" how the work helped Haiti evolve into a "prosperous country with a stable government." He reasoned that with the great natural resources present in Haiti, an efficient government dedicated to its people could use those resources to "pay its public debt and have a big surplus for the internal improvements, roads, water supply, irrigation and other purposes."

Convinced that the Haitian people were destined to enjoy such a future, Waller exclaimed that "we are certainly having some work over it, but it is fun as long as the old fool [Caperton] is absent." Much of his optimism came from the early work of the gendarmerie and from the leadership Waller and his officers invested in the brigade's efforts fighting against the generations of corruption. Waller's early successes in the various areas of public rehabilitation held great promise for the future that, in the long term, were not realized or sustained.[59]

November 22, 1916, found Waller back in Washington before a Marine Examining Board convened to consider him for brigadier general. With the new appropriation increases approved for the Marine Corps, Waller, as expected, stood for his first star.

Despite the rigors of his thirty-six years of service and his advancing age, Navy doctors found Waller in good physical health. The physicians discovered a hearing loss in both ears, "about one half of normal," but found the impairment not incapacitating for active service. The medical report indicated that the damage occurred from gunfire aboard the USS *Indiana* during the battle for Santiago during the Spanish-American War in 1898. With general efficiency scores of 3.90 from each of the reviewing officers, the panel recommended Waller for promotion to brigadier general. Despite his failure to reach the commandancy, Waller's long campaign for a general's star had come to fruition. His return to his Port-au-Prince command was met with celebration from old friends and the officers and men in his command. While Waller would never be the major general commandant, he would soon become a major general, yet another milestone for the aging general. During the short time left in Haiti, Waller's position as a newly minted brigadier brought him a sense of vindication and redemption.[60]

Outspoken and impudent, Waller often alienated many who shared his view of the Navy, his deep distrust of opponents, and his great admiration of himself. Waller refused to temper his words and saw great value in a frank exposition of his position. He rarely grasped the subtleties required of him as he rose to higher levels of leadership. His was a style acceptable and much sought after in an earlier era, but as Naval Academy graduates began to dominate the Marine Corps, an emerging professional officer corps demanded a different style of leadership and social skills. Faced with these changing dynamics in the Marine Corps, with a growing schism between Waller and his younger peers, the aging general confronted an officer corps who would not countenance the vagaries of the past that failed to assume the social graces inherent in the new modern Corps. These conflicts followed Waller to Haiti and, despite his operational successes during his tenure there, had continued to undermine his influence and position.

Bing by far the most distinguished Marine in the Corps, in the fullness of time Waller should have retired as commandant. But by 1916, at the close of his Haitian assignment, his blunt style, his pragmatic and often forceful approach to problem solving, and the controversy that blighted his Philippine service denied him that ultimate honor. His successes in Haiti failed to bring him a command in the coming war. A man who had long and faithfully served his country and the Marine Corps concluded his career, not at the front leading Marines in France, but in the war's backwaters pushing papers in Philadelphia.

CHAPTER 7  **THE CURTAIN CLOSES**

Ensconced next to General John J. Pershing, commanding the American Expeditionary Force in France, Marine Brigadier General John Lejeune was assigned the command of the Thirty-Second Brigade and later led the Fourth Marine Brigade in France and soon rose to command the Second Division under Pershing. Even as he grew in rank and honor, his mentor Brigadier General Littleton W. T. Waller languished in exile, far from action and far from the honors that his long and distinguished career demanded. While history gave Waller extraordinary opportunities and placed him on battlefields that stretched across the globe, by 1917 his time had passed. Like a comet that streaked across the heavens burning brightly on its journey, Waller's career had reached its zenith and faded into the night.

Leading the parade, possibly a Preparedness Parade, in the 400 block of East Main Street in Norfolk, Virginia, circa 1913–1916. *Courtesy of the Waller Family Archives.*

209

Waller recognized that the end was near. Writing from Philadelphia in July 1918 to the Marines in France, Waller reminded them that they were part of something larger than the moment:

> Fate has denied me the honor of leading you, my own people, in this great struggle, but I want you to know and feel that I am with you in spirit. Your splendid achievements in the recent fighting during the early part of June forces the admiration of the world and the deep gratitude of your comrades at home, in that you have lived up to the best traditions of our beloved Corps and have made a brilliant page in its history. You will go on with this work in the same spirit.[1]

Over the course of his career, Waller enjoyed a strong and loyal following from his men and those officers who admired his successes in the field. For Waller this was proof of his achievements across his career and the value of his service as he looked back from his concluding years. For Waller, his words to the Fifth Regiment voiced the essence of what it meant to be a soldier and Marine. His words spoke to a cause that brought righteousness in the midst of pain and chaos and brought clarity to their achievements of the battlefields of Europe:

> All honor to you living men and the peace of God which passeth all understanding to the souls of our beloved comrades who have given their lives in this great cause. May the pain of the wounded be alleviated by the full realization that they have stood for righteousness, truth and the honor of country and Corps. Always faithful, always ready. In all the world there is no better precept, no better aim.
>
> May the God of battles have you in his keeping and bring victory to your banners.
>
> As "you have stood as a stone wall between the Hun and Paris," you will always stand for the liberty of the world.
>
> Your old leader and always friend,
>
> Littleton W. T. Waller
> Brigadier General, USMC[2]

On March 17, 1920, at Waller's request, Major General Commandant George Barnett ordered Waller to Washington, D.C., on the next Monday to appear before the Marine Retiring Board. His old friend, John Lejeune, was serving as the president of the board. A mere formality, within a week, Waller received orders retiring him from active service, effective June 16, 1920. On that day, Waller turned over the records of the First Advanced Base to the commanding officer of the First Regiment and departed for home to "assume the status of a retired officer." It was finished.[3]

His retirement years were brief but filled with activity and work. In the time surrounding his retirement, the occupation of Haiti continued and in 1919 a firestorm erupted in the American press led by the *Nation* and newspapers such as the *New York Times*. Republicans were quick to latch onto the news of the alleged atrocities and illegal executions against Haitians at the hands of American Marines. Candidate Warren G. Harding "told election crowds that thousands of native Haitians have been killed by American Marines." Although the truth included a few cases of such action, the press continued to press the issue with exaggerated facts and falsehoods. In an interview in the *New York Times* with Harry Franck, a travel writer, the article repeated Franck's claims that the Marines in Haiti, "largely made up and officered by Southerners," had used airplanes to open "fire with machine-guns . . . upon defenseless Haitian villages" and murdered "men, women, and children in the open marketplaces." Franck described how Marines killed Haitians routinely "for sport by a hoodlum element among these same Southerners." Such stories inflamed the public and were published as fact without evidence or verification. Harding and other Republicans "looked upon the Haitian matter as a gift right off the Christmas tree."[4]

Earlier, Commandant George Barnett had fueled the fire when he routinely reviewed two courts-martials in Haiti and discovered that Marine misconduct had occurred. In a letter to Colonel John H. Russell, Barnett complained that there had "been indiscriminate killings" by Marines and ordered Russell to put a stop to it. Barnett's correspondence with Russell was leaked to the press, and his words gave weight to a growing outcry by those who opposed Wilson's occupation of Haiti. In 1921, Senate hearings were scheduled, and Barnett and Waller were among those called to testify.[5]

Although the charges of atrocities and indiscriminate killings took place in 1918 and 1919, long after Waller had left Haiti, he appeared before the committee and provided testimony on a variety of issues. Waller laid out the pattern of American control in the cities and in the rural areas as the Marines came ashore to deal with the chaos facing the Haitian people. He described the conditions in Port-au-Prince during his tenure there, the Caco unrest in the north, operations against guerrilla forces, losses on both sides, and Waller's efforts for nation-building and development of infrastructure in Haiti. Waller came prepared and addressed questions put to him and demonstrated his grasp of the details of his operations in the years before 1917, in much the same way he would have presented a legal brief before a court of law. His testimony was precise and to the point. It proved to be his last formal activity relating to his Marine Corps service. From now on, he would be content to watch the careers of his three sons and focus on his farming and his business interests.[6]

The Senate committee concluded that there had been a small number of illegal executions and atrocities by Marines in a "restricted" area in Haiti and "limited in point of time to a few months." The hearing found no sweeping patterns of mass killings or Marines engaged in the sport of killing Haitians. The committee argued that most Marines during occupation had "restored order and tranquility under arduous conditions of service," and "generally won the confidence of the inhabitants" as they carried out their duties.[7]

The investigation revealed that lessons needed to be drawn from the history of the occupation, and that "lack of communications and the type of operations conducted by small patrols" prevented timely revelations of serious cases. The committee found that when executions were reported, the record indicated that "investigations were held with no apparent desire to shield any guilty party" and that "such executions were unauthorized and directly contrary to the policy of the brigade commanders."[8]

Waller and other Marines were elated to see the Senate "condemn the process by which biased or interested individuals and committees and propagandists have seized on isolated" courts-martials, and in the process, promoted "as true any rumor, however vile or baseless, in an effort to bring into general disrepute the whole American naval force in Haiti." The senators

Retirement lasted six years, filled with lingering memories and busy times on the farm and with family. *Courtesy of the Waller Family Archives.*

exposed the critics for what they were, irresponsible purveyors of unfounded charges based on rumor and innuendo. Worse yet, the target of the attacks were the Marines who, the committee reasoned, had earned the "admiration" of the American people "for the manner in which our men accomplished their dangerous and delicate task."[9]

Meanwhile Waller moved rapidly into his retirement routine, splitting his time between his Philadelphia home and the York Pine Lodge near Williamsburg, Virginia. His letters to his sons revealed a Waller engaged in a new busy life that included farming and other business interests. No longer did he have the benefit of an aide or enlisted men to do daily tasks for him, although Clara had a cook who usually worked in the house. By 1923, his life was filled with routine as he and Clara established housekeeping in a new way at the Lodge. "The work here has been rather hectic for one reason or another," Waller explained in a Fourth of July letter to his three sons, "and I have been pretty busy all the time and have had no time for pleasure, except the pleasure of work."[10]

Waller slept late in celebration of the holiday: "I got up late, seven fifteen, got breakfast" since the cook did not work on the Fourth of July. Waller's description of his activities during the day provides some clues to his interests and his life as a retired Marine. After breakfast "I then cleaned up things and filled all the burners, straightened out my tool chest and swept up the porch," then drew water for a bath from the artesian well, "came back and had a nice warm bath," and then carried in a bucket of water for Clara's bath. Waller described their intention to rest and enjoy the day, but that "about a thousand things turned up requiring attention and when we finished these," Clara and he went berry picking together. His description of the stroll into the berry patch brought into focus Waller's well-being and enjoyment in his life. He was no longer the man who struggled for survival across Samar, or the officer who fought his way to Peking or took the fight to the Cacos into the north of Haiti. That life was gone, and a new one had replaced the responsibility and the risk.[11]

"By the way, a mockingbird has a nest in the wonderful bush [where we pick berries,] and we disturb each other a good deal. There are no eggs yet," but the protective bird "makes quite a little fuss when I go for the berries." Waller reported that "they are beginning to see that I am not going to disturb them as they make much less row than at first. In fact, today they simply watched us." All around the Lodge, Waller marveled at the wildlife, and it came to be a source of joy for him. "We have quite a number of songbirds around the house, and two of the most pugnacious Bee Martins." His letter was filled with reports on the lively world of the delicate creatures who shared his home. "A dear little Song Sparrow has a nest nearby, and he sings a great deal." Waller was astonished that "I saw a Robin a few days ago, and it is a rare thing to see them so far south in summer." His return to the Virginia country where he grew up as a boy brought him peace and pleasure in the simple things of life. His responsibilities now revolved around family and the simple daily routines where his decisions no longer had life and death consequences. With Clara at his side, he spent these brief years surrounded by family and old friends in comfortable surroundings.[12]

There was a stability to Waller's retirement brought on by his long service in the Marines, his high rank, and the pension he enjoyed. Waller no doubt remembered the early days of boyhood and enjoyed the satisfaction of the knowledge that he had made something of his life and ensured the future for Clara and himself. In Williamsburg, he was not far from those growing up years where his mother, Mary, had to rely on her wealthy sisters for support and assistance. Somehow Waller had compensated for the financial failures of his father, the struggles of his mother to raise her boys, and repaid the benevolence of his wealthy aunts many times over by his service to the nation. Still, Waller was not so affluent that he could not be watchful of living within his means and making smart decisions when it came to money.

"We had a visitation from some people yesterday who were anxious to put in an *acetylene* plant for cooking and lighting" at Waller's York Pine Lodge. "It would be very nice and comfy, but I have just bought a Ford truck and the plant for lighting this house, the farm house and the barn would cost about $350.00." Despite the offer of an interest-free installment schedule, Waller "told them that we could not consider it at this time." He had other improvement plans that needed to come first.[13]

"The biggest thing I would like to do is to [deepen] the artesian well and connect it up with the tank at the barn." The steady flow of water from the well was a constant problem since "the well is pumped dry in about fifteen minutes. I do not believe the pump pipes go deep enough in the well." Waller was determined to get the project done "as soon as I finish the work around the house," which he promised to complete within the week. He complained that even fishing had been work recently. "I have been fishing only once and that was for food, and not for fun." He reported that "spot, hog fish and perch are running now, and I think a few blackwills." Waller's idyllic retirement days would be short-lived. The strenuous nature of the combat trail, the tropical climates, and his suffering on many difficult and successful campaigns would make an early claim upon him. Over the next three years, a series of strokes presented new battles for the old Marine. The curtain was beginning to close.[14]

On Friday morning, July 9, 1926, Littleton Waller, Jr. was working in his office when he received an urgent telephone call from his mother, Clara. His parents were vacationing in Atlantic City on the Jersey shore. Clara told him that "Dad had had another attack [Thursday night]. She did not know whether or not it was necessary for me to come right away, but the doctor thought Dad very sick." Littleton and wife Sadie were planning to join his parents the next day, and Clara thought that would be soon enough. But Littleton "went home [and] packed a bag," told his wife, Sadie, the news, "and left for the shore, getting there about 6 p.m." When Littleton arrived, he found his father "fairly rational—the first time since his attack," according to Clara. The doctor gave Waller a "large dose of morphine, and he had been in a coma ever since." On Friday, while Littleton ministered to his father, youngest brother Tazewell was traveling and unaware of his father's illness. Beresford, a naval officer, was at sea serving in the Mediterranean, also unaware of his father's attack. Beresford's wife, Agnes, was at home near Boston, pregnant with their second child. Over the next two days, all the family, except Beresford who was at sea, gathered at the Crescent Hotel in Atlantic City and waited.[15]

Littleton wrote brother Beresford that throughout Saturday "Dad's condition apparently did not vary much." His vital signs improved marginally and "his kidneys began to work a little," prompting some small optimism from the family. Waller "was unable to keep anything on his stomach and was very miserable." Sadie arrived from Meadowbrook, and the doctor advised Littleton that his brother Tazewell "should be sent for. Just then we received a telegram from Taz that he was on his way to New York." Littleton quickly responded and "caught him by telegram" and Tazewell, instead, "stopped in Philadelphia, coming to Atlantic City on an early train Monday. By that time Dad was in a coma and did not recognize anyone."[16]

Worried about Agnes coming to Atlantic City with her late pregnancy, Littleton kept her informed of Waller's illness with a series of telegrams, "telling her there was nothing she could do. We doubted the advisability of her coming on in her condition." Earlier, Agnes had received a birthday card from Clara with the news of Waller's attack. "But she didn't seem very concerned about it as she said it wasn't nearly as bad as his others had been, in fact she wrote in quite a cheerful strain." That same evening, Agnes received the first of Littleton's telegrams "saying condition far from satisfactory but not hopeless." Then on Monday another telegram from Littleton, "saying doctor held out no hope." The next morning, Agnes opened the final telegram telling her it was just a matter of time. "It is so hard for poor dear Mus [Clara], but luckily Littleton, Taz, and Sadie are there. Think of it—three years to the day from the first stroke." In the end, Agnes traveled to Philadelphia for the funeral and on to Washington, D.C., for the internment ceremony at Arlington. Littleton later wrote Beresford that she "came anyway as you know and apparently no damage was done."[17]

By Sunday, Waller was "weaker, he could take nourishment," but the doctor expressed concern at the high fever that developed that day and "he feared pneumonia." By evening the doctor's fears were confirmed. "The left lung had consolidated at the bottom and all hope was over." Littleton remembered that "we still hoped against hope as Dad had so often staged almost impossible rallies, but reason showed the utter hopelessness of the situation." The family understood that Waller's condition was worse than previous attacks and that pneumonia was the factor that made it hopeless. The fever rose higher in the evening, Waller was in and out of a coma, and "could only mutter a few words. By the time Taz arrived, his coma was complete, the left lung fully consolidated and the right [lung] affected." The night passed into Monday with no change.[18]

"Monday night we sent out a hurr[ied] call for the doctor as Dad was sinking fast. He rallied, however, but we knew it could not be for long." Most of the family "was exhausted" and went to their rooms for a few hours' sleep. Littleton remained with his father for a time but slipped into Sadie's room to sleep. The nurse remained with Waller, monitoring his condition. At 2 a.m. she called the family to Waller's bedside, telling them that he "was manifestly much weaker" and that the old general did not have long. Fifteen minutes later, Waller breathed his last. "It was very peaceful—no struggle, he simply stopped breathing. We were all there." His long journey was done.[19]

Littleton called Oliver Bair Funeral Home in Philadelphia and "they had their men at the Creston just before six" Tuesday morning and transported Waller directly to the funeral home in Philadelphia. Meanwhile, the family "packed up Tuesday morning," had lunch, and left the hotel for home. Littleton telegraphed Arlington Cemetery, the family in Norfolk, and Beresford that the end had come. Littleton and mother Clara left for Philadelphia and stopped by Bair's on the way home and "selected the casket—a lovely black cloth one—plain but of good lines, and made the preliminary arrangements."

Before they left the funeral home, Clara wanted to see Waller and "was disappointed in the way he had been fixed up. They had made him very heavy jowled. This was fixed, and he looked very well." Littleton remembered that "one hour after he died, the lines of pain had disappeared and a sweet, peaceful expression had come over his face." The next two days would be busy ones, with the funeral services set on Thursday afternoon at Bair's and the departure for Washington, D.C., the next day. Waller's final military ceremony would be an impressive one.[20]

The family arrived at the funeral home early on Thursday morning to prepare for the service that afternoon. "We put Dad's medals, sword, etc. on . . . and many people came in to see him—quite a few of his old men." At 4:30, with a "terrific thunderstorm" blowing outside, the service began in the Bair Funeral Chapel, packed with family, old friends, and those who had served with Waller across the years. "A detail of six N.C.O.s were sent up from the Marine Barracks, and they stood at attention all during the service and for an hour or so before." Clara, with her two sons Littleton and Tazewell on either side of her, "stood it very well." As the service closed, plans moved forward for the procession the next morning, when Philadelphia crowds turned out for Waller's final journey to Arlington.[21]

"I have never seen anything more impressive or inspiring than the procession from Bair's to the Broad Street Station." Outside the chapel, a regiment of Marines waited with a battalion of seamen and the Marine Band, while inside the pallbearers placed a flag on the casket from the regiment of Marines at Waller's old command in Philadelphia. "[Eight] Marines in blues" carried the casket to the hearse on Chestnut Street. "The hearse was all glass sides, [and] back so you could see the flag draped coffin" inside. The procession began moving down Chestnut to Broad Street north to the train station. "The band played *Semper Fidelis* and *Nearer My God to Thee* and *Lead Kindly Light*" as Waller made his way to the station. Crowds lined the sides of the street, and "they all stood with hats off, heads bowed as the hearse went by—all sorts and kinds of people—oh so impressive." Police were "out in force and the line [kept] clear, including the station entrance, stairway and route along the platform to the train." As the procession neared the station, "the hearse stopped and the [eight] Marines carried the

Pallbearers exited the Oliver Bair Funeral Home, carrying General Waller's coffin to the waiting hearse on Chestnut Street, July 16, 1926. *Courtesy of the Waller Family Archives.*

coffin to the train" and the family "all marched behind it." The final journey had begun.[22]

The trip to Washington "passed by very quietly," arriving in Union Station at 12:55 p.m. Family and friends met the Wallers and stood by as the casket was unloaded by Marines to a waiting hearse. "We went straight out to Arlington following Dad's body" and on the approach to the cemetery, "again there were miles of Marines, it seemed to me . . . the horses attached to the waiting caisson were stunning too." At Arlington, the hearse slowed to a stop near the caisson, and "while they were fixing the hearse to the caisson, we waited at the Lee Mansion, then trailed behind the caisson to the" assigned lot, next to where "Admiral Dewey was buried." It was a "truly lovely spot and as always, Arlington impresses me as being so calm, peaceful with the lovely big trees, and rolling ground."[23]

The Tenth Regiment from Quantico formed the escort at Arlington and the procession slowly moved to the beat of the dirge as the caisson wound its

Procession down Chestnut Street to Broad Street, en route to the train station for the trip to Washington, D.C., and Arlington National Cemetery, July 17, 1926. *Courtesy of the Waller Family Archives.*

way among the headstones to the burial plot. The somber formation was led by "the full Marine Band, the Tenth Regiment, an artillery caisson, a man carrying a major generals flag who turned out to be First Sergeant Glenn," together with the "pall bearers, body bearers and a very large procession of motors." Soon the crowd gathered around as the Marines carried the casket forward. "The interment ceremonies were short, but very hard on Clara. It was also quite hot." As soon as the closing taps sounded across the rolling green meadows, old friends and family surrounded Clara, offering condolences and well wishes. "As soon as possible, we got her away and to the Lafayette Hotel where we had rooms." It was finished.[24]

The next day, late on Saturday morning, the family began making plans to return home. Littleton escorted Clara and everyone back to his home at Meadowbrook, taking the train after lunch. "Agnes went home [to Boston] on Sunday and Taz left for New York." Clara remained at Meadowbrook for a

Major General Littleton W. T. Waller and his wife, Clara, are buried in Arlington National Cemetery, Section 4, Grave 3311. Clara Waller lived thirty-two years beyond Waller's death. *Courtesy of Anne Cady.*

time, assisting in probating the will and "getting things cleared up." Waller's long journey was over.[25]

As the curtain closed in his seventieth year, it was just forty-six years since he resigned his position in the Norfolk Blues and accepted his commission as a second lieutenant in the Marine Corps. His service led him to the Mediterranean where he met Clara in Lisbon, to Alexandria in Egypt, points along the North African coast, to Cuban waters in the Spanish-American War, the Philippines, the Boxer Rebellion in China, "numerous revolutions in South and Central American republics," the pacification campaign in Cuba, and active operations at Veracruz and in Haiti. Along the way, he served under officers who molded Waller into the officer that he came to be. Later Waller became a mentor for new generations of officers who made their mark upon the Corps and on history. Waller argued before the U.S. Supreme Court, was a contender for commandant in 1910 and 1914, fought political battles in a changing and evolving Marine Corps and together with other Old Corps Marines, helped build the foundation upon which the modern twentieth-century Marine Corps stood. Waller was part of the old guard left behind, but the warrior qualities he brought to his service remain part of his legacy that Marines evoke today, in missions that stretch across the globe. He was a product of his time, a failure in the minds of many who judge him on his temperament, his failure in reaching commandant, his decisions on Samar, and his battles with the rising cadre of new leadership in the Corps. His story is filled with flaws, but great achievement as well. In the end, one must judge both to properly assess Waller the man, the officer, the Marine.

# APPENDIX: WALLER CHRONOLOGY, 1856–1926

September 26, 1856, born in York County, near Williamsburg, Virginia.

December 1857, Matthew Page Waller family moves to Norfolk, Virginia.

October 11, 1861, death of Matthew Page Waller, Norfolk, Virginia.

April 20, 1877, Norfolk Light Artillery Blues voted membership for twenty-one-year-old Littleton W. T. Waller.

June 24, 1880, accepted appointment as second lieutenant in the Marine Corps. Assigned to duty at Marine Barracks, Washington, D.C. Joined June 26, 1880.

August 30, 1880, detached to Marine Barracks, Norfolk, Virginia. Joined August 31, 1880.

August 10, 1881, detached to USS *Lancaster*. Joined August 20, 1881.

July 1881 met Clara Wynne in Lisbon, Portugal, while en route to Egypt for expeditionary duty.

May 2, 1882, detached to USS *Nipsic*. Joined May 2, 1882.

November 20, 1882, detached to USS *Lancaster*. Joined November 20, 1882.

July 16, 1884, detached to USS *Powhatan*. Joined July 16, 1884.

August 26, 1884, detached to Marine Barracks, Norfolk, Virginia. Joined August 30, 1884.

February 17, 1885, married Clara Wynne at the Church of the Ascension in New York City. On leave of absence from February 6–March 1, 1885.

April 11, 1885, on temporary duty at Brooklyn, NY, from April 11 to May 16, 1885.

January 25, 1886, promoted to first lieutenant, to rank from September 26, 1885.

December 20, 1886, death of Mary T. Waller at Norfolk, Virginia.

May 16, 1887, detached to USS *Iroquois*. Jointed May 30, 1887.

March 6, 1888, detached to Marine Barracks, Mare Island, California. Joined March 6, 1888.

April 9, 1888, detached to USS *Pensacola*. Joined May 14, 1888.

August 31, 1888, detached to Marine Barracks, Norfolk, Virginia. Joined September 1, 1888.

October 19, 1888, detached to USS *Kearsarge* bound for Montevideo, Uruguay, with relief officers and men for the side-wheeler *Tallapoosa*. Joined November 1, 1888.

January 31, 1889, detached to USS *Tallapoosa*. Joined January 31, 1889. Commanded guards at American Legation at Buenos Aires, Argentina, during unrest related to revolution of 1890.

November 26, 1890, detached and granted one month leave of absence (at Lisbon, Portugal), and at its expiration to report at Norfolk, Virginia, for duty. Reported March 2, 1891.

August 1, 1895, temporary duty with Judge Advocate-General's Office, Navy Department, Washington, D.C. Commended by Department of Justice for arguing case of M. L. Johnson, U.S. Navy vs. David B. Sayre before the U.S. Supreme Court. Duration of service: August 1–September 6, 1895. Waller prepared and filed the printed brief and presented the oral argument before the Supreme Court.

September 7, 1895, detached to USS *Lancaster*. Joined September 12, 1895.

March 20, 1896, detached to USS *Newark*. Joined March 20, 1896.

July 1, 1896, promoted to captain, to rank from June 14, 1896.

September 13, 1896, detached to USS *Indiana*. Joined September 20, 1896.

May 12, 1898, participated in an engagement with the enemy at San Juan de Puerto Rico.

June 22, 1898, participated in an engagement with the enemy at Santiago de Cuba.

July 2, 4, 1898, participated in an engagement with the enemy at Santiago de Cuba.

July 3, 1898, participated in the destruction of Admiral Cervera's fleet during the naval battle at Santiago, Cuba.

August 20, 1898, ordered to report to Marine Barracks, Norfolk, Virginia.

September 16, 1898, detached to Marine Barracks, Norfolk, Virginia. Joined September 17, 1898.

October 20, 1898, ordered to temporary duty at League Island, Pennsylvania.

November 22, 1898, detailed as judge advocate of Court of Inquiry, Norfolk, Virginia.

August 28, 1899, promoted to major, to rank from July 25, 1899.

October 23, 1899, alerted to hold himself in readiness for orders to command a battalion for the island of Guam.

October 25, 1899, reported to Commodore Silas Casey, USN, and Col. R. W. Huntington, USMC, for duty with Marine battalion.

October 25, 1899, detached to Third Battalion, for Cavite, Philippine Islands. Joined November 1, 1899.

December 15, 1899, arrived Manila, Philippine Islands. Commanded, Second Battalion, First Marine Regiment at Marine Barracks, Cavite.

June 18, 1900, arrived off Taku, China.

June 20, 1900, began advance toward Tientsin to relieve the besieged legations.

June 25, 1900, began a successful joint rescue operation to the Hsi Ku Arsenal, outside Tientsin.

June 27, 1900, supported a multinational attack on the East Arsenal at Tientsin.

July 13, 1900, participated in the multinational attack on the Walled City at Tientsin.

August 4, 1900, began advance from Tientsin to Peking.

August 6, 1900, battle of Yang Tsun.

August 14–15, 1900, battle for Peking. The Forbidden City falls to relief expedition.

September 14, 1900, Waller appointed provost-marshal of Tartar City, Peking.

September 28, 1900, Marines ordered back to Cavite in the Philippines.

March 28, 1901, appointed lieutenant colonel by brevet, in the Marine Corps of the United States, for distinguished conduct and public service in the presence of the enemy near Tientsin, China, from July 13, 1900.

March 28, 1901, advanced two numbers in rank on the list of majors, for eminent and conspicuous conduct in battle on June 21 and 23, and July 3 and 9, 1900, at Tientsin, China, from March 8, 1901.

September 18, 1901, under suspension for ten days from September 18, 1901, for being under the influence of liquor and thereby unfit for the proper performance of duty.

October 22, 1901, embarks on USS *New York* at Cavite for Samar. On duty in Samar, Philippine Islands, from October 22, 1901, to March 2, 1902.

November 16, 1901, begins Sojoton Cliffs Operation from Basey into the interior of Samar.

December 27, 1901, begins fateful expedition across the interior of Samar.

January 20, 1902, Waller orders eleven Filipinos shot.

March 17, 1902, reported to Major General A. R. Chaffee, U.S. Army, Commanding Division of Philippines. On duty with the Army from March 17 to April 28, 1902, undergoing trial by general court-martial on charge of "Murder, in violation of the 58th Article of War." Found "not guilty" and acquitted of said charge.

May 2, 1902, detached to United States. Arrived at San Francisco, California, on June 12, 1902, and at New York City on June 30, 1902. Detached from the Marine Barracks, New York, and ordered to his home. Granted three months leave of absence from July 10, 1902.

July 15, 1902, Norfolk Blues Dinner at Armory Hall where Waller was presented with a ceremonial sword and welcomed home.

July 18, 1902, traveled to Warm Springs in Bath County, Virginia, for rest and recuperation from the fevers and travails suffered on Samar.

October 9, 1902, ordered to assume command of recruiting district of Pennsylvania, Delaware, and Western New Jersey with headquarters at 1628 Market Street, Philadelphia, Pennsylvania. Joined and assumed command October 13, 1902.

March 23, 1903, promoted lieutenant colonel, to rank from March 3, 1903.

December 23, 1903, ordered to report on December 26, 1903, to the Commandant, Navy Yard, League Island, Pennsylvania, for duty in command of a provisional regiment of Marines for service on the Isthmus of Panama. Departed December 28, 1903, on board the USS *Dixie*, bound for Panama.

January 3, 1904, arrived at Colón, Panama. On duty ashore as commander, Second Marine Regiment from January 6–March 7, 1904, at Bas Obispo, Panama.

March 26, 1904, rejoined recruiting office at Philadelphia, Pennsylvania.

March 31, 1904, detached to Marine Barracks, Norfolk, Virginia. Joined April 12, 1904.

March 31, 1905, promoted o colonel, to rank from March 11, 1905.

March 10–17, 1905, observer in connection with the combined Army and Navy exercises at Fort Monroe, Virginia.

September 26, 1906, ordered to command the brigade of Marines that was first to land in Cuba and which formed the first part of the Army of Cuban Pacification.

September 29, 1906, departed Miami, Florida, for Cuba.

October 1, 1906, landed at Havana, Cuba.

November 8, 1906, returned to Norfolk, Virginia.

January 4, 1911, member, general court-martial at Philadelphia Navy Yard, Pennsylvania. Duration of service: January 4–13, 23–25, 1911.

February 9, 1911, president, general court-martial at Washington, D.C. Duration of service: February 9–13, 1911.

February 1911, Waller passed over for commandant. William P. Biddle receives the appointment.

March 8, 1911, commanded the First Provisional Brigade of Marines at Guantanamo Bay, Cuba. Duration of service: March 8–June 21, 1911. Embarked on USS *Prairie* at Navy Yard, Philadelphia, Pennsylvania, on March 8, 1911, sailed March 9, 1911. Arrived at Guantanamo Bay, Cuba, on March 13, 1911, and disembarked same day and established Brigade Headquarters, First Provisional Brigade, U.S. Marines, on Fisherman's Point, Guantanamo Bay, Cuba.

April 26, 1911, while at Guantanamo Bay, Waller and other officers formed the Marine Corps Association. Commanded the brigade until June 17, 1911. Embarked on USS *Washington* at Guantanamo Bay, Cuba, June 17, sailed June 18, arrived at Hampton Roads June 21, 1911, and detached from temporary expeditionary service to resume former duties at Marine Barracks, Norfolk, Virginia. Rejoined that post June 22, 1911.

August 10, 1911, detached to Marine Barracks, Mare Island, California. Joined August 25, 1911, as commanding officer.

February 25, 1914, Waller passed over for commandant. George Barnett receives the appointment.

April 22, 1914, detached to Marine Barracks, Philadelphia, Pennsylvania. Joined April 26, 1914.

April 26, 1914, absent on temporary foreign shore service to command First Marine Brigade at Veracruz, Mexico. Duration of service: April 26–December 4, 1914. Embarked on *New York* at New York City on April 26, 1914, for Mexican waters. Arrived at Veracruz, Mexico on May 4 and assumed command of First Brigade that date for duty with Army forces ashore. Embarked on transport *Denver* at Veracruz and sailed on November 23 en route to Philadelphia, arriving on December 4. Resumed duty at Marine Barracks, Philadelphia, Pennsylvania.

June 9, 1915, in camp with First Marine Brigade at West Chester, Pennsylvania. Duration of service: June 9–12, 1915.

August 10, 1915, absent on temporary foreign shore service to command all U.S. expeditionary forces ashore in Haiti. Duration of service: August 10, 1915–January 8, 1917. Sailed on August 10, 1915, from Philadelphia on USS *Tennessee* with First Marine Brigade and arrived at Port-au-Prince, Haiti, on August 16. Waller returned to the United States on February 24, 1916, to confer with headquarters and for a leave of absence. He returned to Haiti and resumed duty on April 1, 1916. He remained there until his final departure in November 1916.

January 6, 1917, commissioned a brigadier general, to rank from August 29, 1916.

January 8, 1917, detached from Marine Barracks, Philadelphia, Pennsylvania, and from command of the U.S. naval forces on shore duty in Haiti and from all other duties connected therewith, to command the Marine Corps Advance Base Force, with headquarters in the city of Philadelphia, Pennsylvania. Assumed command January 8, 1917.

August 20, 1917, inspecting officer, Mobile Artillery Force at Marine Barracks, Quantico, Virginia. Duration of service: August 20–22, 1917.

August 28, 1918, temporarily promoted to major general, to rank from July 1, 1918. Accepted appointment and executed oath of office August 30, 1918, at Philadelphia, Pennsylvania.

March 22, 1920, appeared before a Marine Retiring Board at Headquarters Marine Corps, Washington, D.C. Retired on March 27, 1920, but continued on active duty at Headquarters, Advance Base Force until June 16, 1920, on which date relieved of all active duty.

November 8, 1921, testified before a Senate select committee on Haiti and Santo Domingo, 67th Congress, 1st and 2nd sessions.

July 13, 1926, died at Atlantic City, New Jersey.

# NOTES

### CHAPTER 1

1. Major General Littleton W. T. Waller had three sons, each beginning a career in the military during the latter stages of General Waller's career. His oldest son, Littleton W. T. Waller, Jr., rose to the rank of major general in the Marine Corps; his middle son, John Beresford Wynne Waller, who is the author of the telegram to the captain and crew of the *Waller*, ended his career in the Navy as a rear admiral; and his youngest son, Henry Tazewell Waller, served as a brigadier general in the Marine Corps.
2. John Beresford Wynne Waller to E. H. Frost, September 30, 1942, Waller Family Papers (hereafter cited as WFP), San Diego, California.
3. Service Record, Littleton W. T. Waller, National Personnel Records Center (hereafter cited as NPRC); William H. Stewart, ed. and comp., *History of Norfolk County, Virginia and Representative Citizens* (Chicago: Biographical Publishing Company, 1902), 584–586; Harold P. Clark et al., "Line of Succession of Title to the House," in *History of the Tazewell House: Talisman from the Wishing Oak.* (Virginia Beach, VA: W. S. Dawson Company, 1991), 42–43; Virginia Waller, compiler, Waller family genealogy records, WFP.
4. Clark, "Line of Succession of Title to the House," 42–43; Harold P. Clark et al.,"Notes from the Norfolk City Directories," in *History of the Tazewell House*, 85–87; Mary Waller to Clara E. Wynne, November 12, 1884, WFP.
5. Mary Waller to Clara E. Wynne, November 12, 1884, WFP. Waller married Clara E. Wynne the next year in New York City.
6. Waller to Wynne, November 12, 1884, WFP.
7. Clark, "Line of Succession," 42–43; Clark, "Notes from the Norfolk City Directories," 85–87.
8. Mary Waller to Mary H. Byrd Claiborne, circa November 1866, Jones Family Papers, Mssl-J735b23-40, Virginia Historical Society, Richmond, Virginia (hereafter cited as VHS).
9. Littleton W. T. Waller, Jr., to James T. White, copy of biographical sketch sent to the editor of National Cyclopedia of American Biography, circa October 1926, WFP; W. H. T. Squires, "Norfolk in By-Gone Days," typescript, WFP; Service Record, NPRC; Littleton W. T. Waller Biographical File, Reference Section, Marine Corps Historical Center (hereafter cited as MCHC); *Virginian Pilot*, July 14, 1926; City Directory for Norfolk, Virginia, 1859–1880, Sergeant Memorial Room, Norfolk Public Library (hereafter cited as SMR); Waller to Wynne, November 12, 1884, WFP.
10. First organized in 1829, the Norfolk Light Artillery Blues enjoyed a long and distinguished history as a Virginia militia company and venerable social club. During the Civil War the Blues fought at Gettysburg, Chancellorsville, the Wilderness, and in other significant actions under Robert E. Lee in the eastern theater. They were present at the war's end at the siege of Petersburg and with Lee at Appomattox Courthouse.

During the postwar years, the unit made much of its combat reputation but served primarily as a ceremonial and social organization for Norfolk's elite sons.

11. Minutes Ledger, Norfolk Light Artillery Blues, 1875–1875, SMR.
12. Littleton W. T. Waller to Hugh Blair Grigsby, April 13, 1880, Grigsby Papers, Mssl-G878263091-3094, VHS.
13. Waller to Grigsby, April 13, 1880, Grigsby Papers, Ms-sl-G878263091-3094, VHS. Grigsby noted on the reverse of Waller's letter the date of Waller letter to him and the date of his reply (April 16, 1880). Grigsby's April 16 letter to Waller was not found in the Waller personal papers in the Marine Corps Historical Center or in the extensive private collection still held by the family in La Jolla, California. It must be assumed that it did not survive.
14. Waller to Grigsby, May 15, 1880, Grigsby Papers, Mssl-G878263091-3094, VHS.
15. Waller to Grigsby, May 22, 1880, Grigsby Papers, Mssl-G878263091-3094, VHS. Waller's use of family connections was especially apparent in his attempt to gain the commandancy in 1911 and 1914 (see Chapter 5).
16. "Under the provisions of section 1599 of the Revised Statutes, 'no person under twenty or over twenty-five years of age shall be appointed from civil life as a commissioned officer of the Marine Corps." Richard W. Thompson to Littleton W. T. Waller, June 5, 1880, WFP.
17. Thompson to Waller, June 7, 1880, WFP.
18. Jack Shulimson described the initial training of new officers three years after Waller's entry into the service. Jack Shulimson, *The Marine Corps' Search for a Mission, 1880–1898* (Lawrence, Kansas: University Press of Kansas, 1993), 51. Waller's first training took place at Eighth and I Avenue, in Washington, D.C. While the 1883 group were all graduates of the Naval Academy and had finished two years at sea, Waller's group in 1880 all came from civilian life and their training probably included a more ambitious curriculum. Waller left no reflections on his training in Washington or on his earliest assignment in Norfolk. His protégé Captain Henry C. Cochrane managed to mention him in several letters home and, it seems, paid social calls on the Wallers during that first year.
19. Cochrane's activism in Marine Corps politics prior to 1880 is well documented in Shulimson, *Search for a Mission*, 17–18.
20. "Military History of Colonel Littleton W. T. Waller, United States Marine Corps," February 9, 1914, NPRC.
21. Frederic M. Wise, *A Marine Tells It to You* (New York: J. H. Sears & Company, Inc., 1929; repr. 1981 by the Marine Corps Association), 3.
22. City Directory, 1880–1881, SMR; C. F. Goodrich to Henry C. Cochrane, August 12, 1881, Box 7, Folder 26, PC1, Henry C. Cochrane Papers, P.C. 1 (hereafter cited as HCCP), MCHC.
23. Entries for October 22–November 23, 1881, Logbook, USS *Lancaster*, volume for August 26, 1881–February 25, 1882, RG 24, Logbooks of U.S. Navy Ships, ca. 1801–1940, National Archives, College Park, Maryland, copy in Waller Papers, Lancaster Logbook Collection, Old Primero Historical Foundation, Abilene, Texas (hereafter cited as WOPHF).
24. Cochrane Diary, January 1, 1882, HCCP.

25. Cochrane Diary, January 2, 1882, HCCP.
26. Cochrane Diary, January 15, 1882, HCCP.
27. Cochrane Diary, January 16, 1882, HCCP.
28. Cochrane Diary, January 24 & 26, 1882, HCCP.
29. Cochrane Diary, February 4-8, 1882, HCCP.
30. Cochrane Diary, February 9-March 26, 1882, HCCP.
31. Cochrane Diary, April 9, 1882, HCCP.
32. Cochrane Diary, May 2, 1882, HCCP. Waller commanded the Marines aboard the *Nipsic* for just over six months, returning to the *Lancaster* on November 20, 1882. Personnel transfer log in Logbook, USS *Lancaster*, volume for August 27, 1882-February 28,1883, WOPHF.
33. Entries for April 27-June 5, 1882, Logbook, USS *Lancaster*, volume for February 26-August 26, 1882, WOPHF.
34. Handwritten notes, 1882, WFP; career biographies, various typescripts, WFP; "Military History of Colonel Littleton W. T. Waller," February 9, 1914, NPRC.
35. Cochrane to Naiman, August 4, 1882, HCCP; Littleton W. T. Waller to Henry C. Cochrane, September 9, 1882, HCCP. Waller's handwritten account of the hunt did not include the location or port of the episode, other than to mention that local Moors were involved and that it took place on the cruise into the Moroccan ports and towns.
36. Henry C. Cochrane Diary, June 1, 1882, HCCP, Marine Corps Research Center, Quantico, Virginia; Oral Interview, Littleton W. T. Waller II by Vernon L. Williams, March 22, 1990, La Jolla, California; guestbook, Lisbon, Clara Wynne Waller Historical Collection, Waller Family Papers.
37. Entries for June 6-23, 1882, Logbook, USS. *Lancaster*, volume for February 26-August 26, 1882, WOPHF.
38. Robert L. Robinson, "Gunboat Diplomacy 1882: The United States Navy and the Bombardment of Alexandria," *Warship International*, 19, no. 1 (1982): 48, 55;
39. Harry A. Ellsworth, *One Hundred Eighty Landings of United States Marines, 1800-1934* (Washington, D.C.: History and Museums Division, Headquarters, U.S. Marine Corps, 1974), 75; Henry C. Cochrane to W. T. Naiman, August 4, 1882, Box 7, Folder 27, HCCP.
40. Contemporary maps during the last half of the nineteenth century vary on the spelling and labeling of the central plaza area in the commercial center at Alexandria, Egypt. I have elected to use as a convention for the space, the Place of Mohamed Ali. Other naming variations found on maps of the period include: Mohemet Ali Place, Place Mohamed Ali, Place Mehemet Ali, and other variations.
41. Collum, *History of the United States Marine Corps*, 218-219. Eyewitness accounts of the Marines ashore in the city center are drawn from a British journalist's accounts published in the *New York Times*, August 18, 1882, 2; August 20, 1882, p. 1; *New York World*, July 19, 1882, 1; Karl Baedeker, *Egypt and the Sudan: A Handbook for Travelers*, 7th edition (Leipzig, Germany: Karl Baedeker, 1914), 15-16.
42. *London Telegraph* dispatches carried in the *New York World*, July 19, 1882, 1, 8.
43. Cochrane Diary, July 16-20, 1882; *New York World*, July 19, 1882, 1, 8.
44. Wise, *A Marine Tells It to You*, 7.
45. Personnel transfer log in Logbook, USS *Lancaster*, volume for August 27, 1882-February 28,1883, WOPHF.

46. Cochrane Diary, July 6, 16, 1884, HCCP; Service Record, LWTW, NPRC.
47. Cochrane Diary, July 16-18, 30, 1882, HCCP.
48. Cochrane Diary, July 20-23, 1884, HCCP.
49. Cochrane Diary, July 24-30, 1884, HCCP.
50. Clara Wynne Waller to Henry C. Cochrane, July 21, 1887, Box 7, Folder 32, HCCP; Henry C. Cochrane to Martha Wynne, December 31, 1887, Box 7, Folder 32, HCCP.
51. Cochrane to Martha Wynne, December 31, 1887, HCCP; Henry C. Cochrane Diary, July 27, 1884. Cochrane referred to the birth of the Waller's first child, Littleton W. T. Waller, Jr., who later became a major general in the Marine Corps.
52. Cochrane to Martha Wynne, December 31, 1887, HCCP; Clara Wynne Waller to Henry C. Cochrane, July 21, 1887.
53. Clara Wynne Waller to Henry C. Cochrane, July 21, 1887.
54. Merrill Barlett, in his biography of John Lejeune, reported that "unlike most of his contemporaries . . . [Lejeune] chose marriage at a young age and began a family." Barlett observed that many of Lejeune's [and Waller's] contemporaries "adopted lifestyles of hard-drinking womanizers or dandies, claiming that the lengthy periods at sea or abroad forced them to remain perpetual bachelors." Merrill L. Bartlett, *Lejeune: A Marine's Life, 1867-1942* (Columbia, South Carolina: University of South Carolina Press, 1991), 3.
55. Oral Interview, Littleton W. T. Waller II, March 22, 1990; Cochrane Diaries, 1882-1888, HCCP; S. Dudley to Henry C. Cochrane, February 13, 1885, HCCP.
56. Cochrane Diary, July 30, 1884, HCCP.
57. Waller to Cochrane, March 15, 1883, HCCP; Waller to Cochrane, March 20, 1883, HCCP; Waller to Cochrane, March 28, 1883; Littleton W. T. Waller to W. E. Chandler, February 9, 1883, Letters Received, Marine Corps Commandant, RG 127, National Archives, Washington, D.C.; Littleton W. T. Waller to Edward E. Potter, December 6, 1883, HCCP; "career biographies," WFP; "Military History of Colonel Littleton W. T. Waller, February 9, 1914, NPRC.

**CHAPTER 2**

1. For example, the commissioned officer distribution in the Marine Corps in 1885 was: 2 colonels (including the colonel commandant), 2 lieutenant colonels, 7 majors, 22 captains, 30 first lieutenants, and 21 second lieutenants. Ten years later in 1895 the distribution had changed little: 2 colonels (including the colonel commandant), 2 lieutenant colonels, 7 majors, 22 captains, 30 first lieutenants, and 30 second lieutenants. Department of the Navy, *Register of the Commissioned and Warrant Officers of the Navy of the United States and of the Marine Corps* (hereafter referred to as *Navy Register*) (Washington, D.C.: Government Printing Office, 1885) 138-142; *Ibid.*, 1895, 124-129.
2. *Navy Register*, 1885, 142; marriage license, WFP; Mary Waller to Clara E. Wynne, November 12, 1884, WFP; Waller family biographical files and genealogy records, WFP.
3. Mary Waller to Clara E. Wynne, November 12, 1884, WFP.
4. *Gallia* history, http://www.theshipslist.com/ships/descriptions/ShipsG.html; Charles Fisk, "Graphical Portrayal of New York Central Park Daily Temperatures, Precipitation, and Snowfall, by Year (1876-Present)," http://home.att.net/~ny_climo

/NY1885.gif; Brian T. Hill, February 1885 entries, "Ice Charts and Ship/Iceberg Database," http://researchers.iot.nrc.ca/~hillb/icedb/ice/ice_charts/1885jf.htm; *Passenger Lists of Vessels Arriving at New York, New York, 1820–1897*, Microfilm Publication M237, roll 483, Washington, D.C.: National Archives; marriage license, WFP; Waller family biographical files and genealogy records, WFP; *Gallia* tow attempt, February 23, 1885 entry, http://www.norwayheritage.com/p_ship.asp?sh=geise; "Fighting Their Way Across: Incoming Steamers Reporting Violent Storms at Sea," *New York Times*, February 13, 1885, 8.

5. Waller family biographical files and genealogy records, WFP; Cochrane to Martha Wynne, December 31, 1887, HCCP.

6. *U.S. Statues at Large*, 47th Congress, 1881–1883, volume 22, chapter 391. For a recent and complete discussion of the political efforts to improve the Marine Corps' size and to professionalize the officer corps, see Jack Shulimson, *The Marine Corps' Search for a Mission, 1880–1898* (Lawrence. Kansas: University of Kansas, 1993)—especially Chapter 3. Shulimson's study is the best work by far on the changes in the Marine Corps in the period preceding the Spanish-American War.

7. Vernon L. Williams, Marine Corps Data Base, History Department, Abilene Christian University, Abilene, Texas. The database includes all Marine officers who were commissioned during the period 1861–1900 and were listed in the *Navy Register*, 1865–1900. To be included, an officer had to be listed in the 1865 volume or later. Officers commissioned during the Civil War, who did not remain in service beyond the war or left to serve in the Confederacy, are not within the criteria of the study. Officers are divided into three groups: "NA GRAD," those who completed the course of study at the Naval Academy; "NOT NA GRAD," those who never attended the Naval Academy; and "FAILED NA ST," officers who attended the Naval Academy for any length of time and did not complete the course of study for any reason. In each case, the officer record included data relating to rank, achievement of commandant, commissioning, war or expeditionary service, brevet citations, Naval Academy record, family background, and other personal information. Sources for data compiled in the data base included the *Navy Register, 1865–1900*; *Register of Alumni* (Naval Academy); Callahan (Hamersly), *List of Officers of the Navy of the United States and of the Marine Corps from 1775 to 1900*; and reference files located at the Reference Branch, Marine Corps Historical Center. "Statistical Package for Social Sciences" software was used in this project to produce summary and comparative statistics. Output from such program runs is hereafter cited as SPSS-MCDB.

8. No appointments to the Marine Corps were made in 1881 or 1882. For this reason, these two dates were not included in the charting, primarily for space reasons. Neither year had any impact on either group of commissioned officers.

9. "CTABS1MC," March 1, 1994, 4–23, SPSS-MCDB; "CTABS2MC," March 1, 1994, 4–17, SPSS-MCDB; Allan R. Millett, *Semper Fidelis: The History of the United States Marine Corps* (New York: Macmillan, 1980), 92; Shulimson, *Search for a Mission*, 13.

10. Eleven of the twelve graduated with the class of 1881 and one officer was a recent graduate of the class of 1882.

11. Peter Karsten, *The Naval Aristocracy: The Golden Age of Annapolis and the Emergence of Modern American Navalism* (New York: The Free Press, 1972), 13.

12. "HIGH1898.LIS," March 5, 1994, 4, SPSS-MCDB; Millett, *Semper Fidelis*, 129, 135; Charles Heywood to John Long, July 5, 1898, in Gardner Weld Allen, ed., *Papers of John Davis Long* (Boston: The Massachusetts Historical Society, 1939), 148–149.
13. Until March 3, 1899, the rank of colonel was the highest rank possible in the Marine Corps. The passage of the Naval Personnel Act of 1899 created the rank of brigadier general commandant and in 1908, Commandant Elliott rose to major general.
14. "CTABS3MC," March 3, 1994, 27, SPSS-MCDB.
15. In this instance, the non–Naval Academy group includes both "Not NA Graduates" and "Failed NA Students."
16. Appointment dominance is defined as that period where a particular group of officers dominates acquisition of commissions in the Marine Corps.
17. "NAGVSHIGH.SEL;2," March 18, 1994, 4, SPSS-MCDB.
18. High rank cluster includes colonel, brigadier general, major general, and those officers appointed as commandant.
19. For the purpose of examining promotion success within the modified data group, Non–Academy graduates (forty-six officers) are combined with the Failed NA Student category (six officers) and compared to those officers who graduated from the Naval Academy (fifty officers).
20. Junior rank cluster is defined for this study as second lieutenant, first lieutenant, and captain; middle rank cluster includes major and lieutenant colonel. George Elliott, who was commissioned in 1870, became commandant in 1903. William Biddle, who was commissioned in 1875, was appointed in 1911 over the favored Waller. In 1914 it again was apparent that Waller, who was the senior colonel, would receive the appointment, but Secretary of the Navy Josephus Daniels had reservations, prompting him to recommend George Barnett instead.
21. Decreasing Marine Corps appointments from the South stand in contrast to studies of adjacent groups such as the Naval Academy midshipman population or samples of recent twentieth-century Navy officer corps. Peter Karsten's examination of appointments to the Naval Academy during the late nineteenth century indicated a growing trend toward southern candidates, moving from 5% of the total midshipmen in 1866 to 22% in 1896. Karsten, *The Naval Aristocracy*, 5. In his study of naval leadership, 1910–1950, Morris Janowitz found that southern affiliation for his sample of naval leaders was 38% in 1910, 45% in 1920, 38% in 1935, and 44% in 1950—indicating a long-term stability in southern affiliation for officers in the Navy. Morris Janowitz, *The Professional Soldier: A Social and Political Portrait* (New York: The Free Press, 1971), 88–89. Marine Corps statistics in the last four decades of the nineteenth century exhibited a decreasing tendency toward the South, in contrast to general observations within the Naval Academy admissions record or Navy characteristics in the next half century.
22. "CTABS3MC," March 3, 1994, 4, SPSS-MCDB.
23. "CTABS3MC," 18–19.
24. The Marine Corps lost nearly a third of its officers to the Confederacy; many of these were some of its brightest officers. Millett, *Semper Fidelis*, 92. No Confederates are included in the data base because they are not included in the *Navy Register* for the years 1865–1900, a condition for inclusion in the study (see note 12 for study

specifications). Southern representation in the success categories never achieved equity with the states in the North or to the west. MCDB.
25. "CTABS3MC," 18-19.
26. Military records, Littleton W. T. Waller, National Personnel Records Center, St. Louis, MO, copies in WFP; Fitness Report, Littleton W. T. Waller by James Forney, September 22, 1885, to November 14, 1886, RG 125, Entry 62, Box 785, National Archives, Washington, D.C. (hereafter cited as Fitness, NA).
27. Norfolk Virginian, December 21, 1886, 1.
28. Littleton W. T. Diary, May 1887, WFP. Littleton W. T. Waller Diary, May 1887, WFP. Waller kept a diary on the voyage on the *Iroquois* in 1887.
29. Littleton W. T. Waller to Charles G. McCawley, May 31, 1887, Letters Received, Commandant, 1887–1889, RG 127, Entry 10, Box 389, National Archives, Washington, D.C.
30. Charles G. McCawley to Littleton W. T. Waller, June 14, 1887, and June 15, 1887, WFP.
31. Waller Diary, June–December 1887, WFP; Military records, WFP; Fitness Report, Littleton W. T. Waller by R. P. Leary, May 16, 1887, to March 6, 1888, Fitness, NA.
32. Waller to McCawley, March 27, 1888, April 28, 1888, June 7, 1888, August 24, 1888, August 27, 1888, September 1, 1888, NA.
33. Waller to McCawley, October 11, 1888, NA; "Kearsarge," *Dictionary of American Naval Fighting Ships*, online version, Naval Historical Center, Washington Navy Yard, Washington, D.C., http://www.history.navy. mil/danfs (hereafter cited at DANFS).
34. Waller to McCawley, November 2, 1888, NA; "Tallapoosa," DANFS; Entry for January 31, 1889, Logbook, USS *Kearsarge*, volume for November 2, 1888–May 1, 1889, RG 24, Logbooks of U.S. Navy Ships, ca. 1801–1940, National Archives, College Park, Maryland, copy in Waller Papers, Kearsarge Logbook Collection, Old Primero Historical Foundation, Abilene, Texas (hereafter cited as KOPHF).
35. Waller to McCawley, February 20, 1889, June 11, 1889, June 17, 1889, July 1, 1889, July 22, 1889, September 14, 1889, September 30, 1889, NA; Caspar F. Goodrich, "Desertions in the Navy: A Contribution to the Discussion of the Question," in *Naval Institute Proceeding*, October 1905, 821.
36. Littleton W. T. Waller, "Argentine Revolution," an unpublished manuscript, undated, WFP; Harry Allanson Ellsworth, *One Hundred Eighty Landings of United States Marines, 1800–1934* (Washington, D.C.: History and Museums Division, Headquarters, U.S. Marine Corps, 1974), 13; Edwin N. McClellan to Littleton W. T. Waller, March 24, 1922, WFP.
37. Waller, "Argentine Revolution," undated.
38. Waller to McCawley, October 20, 1890, NA; Military records, WFP; *Passenger Lists of Vessels Arriving at New York, New York, 1820–1897*, Microfilm Publication M237, roll 561, Washington, D.C., National Archives
39. Norwood College in Nelson County, Virginia, was a small preparatory school for the University of Virginia. Vertical file, "Norwood School," Jefferson-Madison Regional Library, Charlottesville, Virginia; Fitness reports, 1900–1920, RG 125, Entry 62 HM1988, Box 784, NA. The face page of the annual fitness report on Waller contained his handwritten biographical and professional accomplishments. He mentioned the study of law at Norwood in most of the reports submitted after the turn of the century.

Circuit Court of the United States of America, Eastern District of Virginia, Certificate of Admittance and Qualification, November 26, 1894, WFP; District Court of the United States of America, Eastern District of Virginia, Certificate of Admittance and Qualification, November 26, 1894, WFP.

40. Military records, WFP; Littleton W. T. Waller to Charles Heywood, May 11, 1894, RG 127, Entry 10, Box 393, NA; Legh R. Page to Littleton W. T. Waller, June 27, 1894, WFP; Waller to Heywood, August 25, 1894, October 22, 1894, October 27, 1894, October 30, 1894, RG 127, Entry 10, Box 393, NA.
41. Case Summary, Johnson v. Sayre, FindLaw Corporation online resource, http://findlaw.com/us/158/109.html; Waller to Heywood, October 22, 1894, October 27, 1894, Letters Received, Commandant, 1894, RG 127, Entry 10, Box 393, NA.
42. Case Summary, Johnson v. Sayre; "Charge and Specification of a Charge Preferred by the Secretary of the Navy against David B. Sayre, a Pay Clerk in the United States Navy," File No. 4622-94, 25 October 1894, copy in WFP; Waller to Heywood, October 30, 1894, Letters Received, Commandant, 1894, RG 127, Entry 10, Box 393, NA.
43. Case Summary, Johnson v. Sayre; Samuel C. Lemly to Littleton W. T. Waller, December 10, 1894, WFP; Hilary A. Herbert to Richard Olney, December 5, 1894, WFP; Lawrence Maxwell, Jr., to Hilary A. Herbert, December 8, 1894, WFP; Assignment of Error, Application of David B. Sayre for a Writ of Habeas Corpus, Circuit Court of the United States for the Eastern District of Virginia, December 14, 1894, WFP.
44. Lawrence Maxwell, Jr., to Francis H. Lassiter, December 20, 1894, WFP; Case Summary, Johnson v. Sayre; Holmes Conrad biographical essay, Department of Justice website, http://www.usdoj.gov/osg/aboutosg/holmescbio.htm.
45. Case Summary, Johnson v. Sayre.
46. Holmes Conrad to Hilary A. Herbert, May 1, 1895, WFP.
47. Case Summary, Johnson v. Sayre; for a list of cases where the Sayre case is cited as precedent, see http://caselaw.lp. findlaw.com; Waller to Heywood, March 7, 1896, Letter Received, Box 395, NA.
48. Waller to Heywood, July 22, 1895, Letters Received, Commandant, 1895, RG 127, Entry 10, Box 394, NA; George C. Reid to Littleton W. T. Waller, August 16, 1895, WFP; Heywood to Waller, September 6, 1895, WFP; Waller to Heywood, August 20, 1895, August 23, 1895, August 27, 1895, August 29, 1895, September 6, 1895, September 7, 1895, September 10, 1895, September 12, 1895, Letters Received, Box 394, NA.
49. Fitness reports, 1895–1898, RG 125, Entry 62, Box 785, NA; Military records, WFP.
50. Henry C. Taylor to Secretary of the Navy, Annual Report of the Commanding Officer of the Indiana, September 10, 1898, reprinted in William G. Cassard, *Battleship Indiana and Her Part in the Spanish-American War* (New York: The Indiana Ship's Company, 1898), 1–5; Department of the Navy, Naval History Division, *Dictionary of American Fighting Ships*, volume 3, 1977, 429–430.
51. On the recommendation of a medical board, the Navy Department relieved Admiral Montgomery Sicard of his fleet command at Key West and invalided him home on March 26. Captain William T. Sampson, soon to be promoted to temporary rear admiral in April, assumed command of the fleet. Sicard died in September 1900 at

his home in New York. He was sixty-six years old. "Navy Commands Change," *New York Times*, March 25, 1898, 2; "Sampson for Rear Admiral," *New York Times*, April 23, 1898, 2; "Rear Admiral Sicard Dead," *New York Times*, September 15, 1900, 6.
52. Taylor to Secretary of the Navy, September 10, 1898, 5–6.
53. Taylor to Secretary of the Navy, September 10, 1898, 6.
54. Taylor to Secretary of the Navy, September 10, 1898, 6.
55. Taylor to Secretary of the Navy, September 10, 1898, 9.
56. Taylor to Secretary of the Navy, September 10, 1898, 9–10.
57. Taylor to Secretary of the Navy, September 10, 1898, 10.
58. Taylor to Secretary of the Navy, September 10, 1898, 10, 13.
59. Taylor to Secretary of the Navy, September 10, 1898, 13.
60. Taylor to Secretary of the Navy, September 10, 1898, 13–14.
61. Taylor's report described the organization of the expedition. The escorts included "the Indiana, Detroit, Annapolis, Castine, Helena, Wasp, Wompatuck, Manning, Bancroft, Rodgers, Kricsson, Dupont, Osceola, Hornet, and Eagle." Taylor organized the transports into "three columns, twelve in a column, with three men-of-war as column leaders." Taylor to Secretary of the Navy, September 10, 1898, 14–21.
62. Taylor to Secretary of the Navy, September 10, 1898, 21.
63. Taylor to Secretary of the Navy, September 10, 1898, 21–22.
64. David F. Trask, *The War with Spain in 1898* (Lincoln: University of Nebraska Press, 1981), 261–262; French Ensor Chadwick, *The Relations of the United States and Spain: The Spanish-American War*, Volume 2 (New York: Charles Scribner's Sons, 1911) 129; Taylor to Secretary of the Navy, September 10, 1898, 22; *Annual Report of the Secretary of the Navy*, 1898, 13.
65. *Annual Report of the Secretary of the Navy*, 1898, 13–14; Taylor to Secretary of the Navy, September 10, 1898, 22.
66. Taylor to Secretary of the Navy, September 10, 1898, 22; Department of the Navy, *Annual Report of the Secretary of the Navy*, 1898, 14.
67. Taylor to Secretary of the Navy, September 10, 1898, 26; Military records, WFP.
68. Fitness reports, 1895–1898, RG 125, Entry 62, Box 785, NA.

**CHAPTER 3**
1. Allan R. Millett, *Semper Fidelis: The History of the United States Marine Corps* (New York: The Free Press, 1991), 155–156; U.S. Senate, *Story of Shansi Massacres of Foreign Missionaries,* in Serial Set No. 4029, Senate Document 30, 56th Congress, 2nd Session (Washington, D.C.: U.S. Government Printing Office, 1900), 1–5.
2. Serial No. 4029, *Ibid.*; Nat Brandt, *Massacre in Shansi* (New York: Syracuse University Press, 1994), xiii–xvi; Eva Jane Price, *China Journal 1889–1900: An American Missionary Family during the Boxer Rebellion, with the Letters and Diaries of Eva Jane Price and Her Family* (New York: Scribner and Sons, 1989).
3. Millett, *Semper Fidelis*, 155–156; Littleton W. T. Waller to Charles Heywood, October 23, 1899, Letters Received, Commandant, 1899, RG 127, Entry 10, Box 401, National Archives (hereafter cited as NA), Washington, D.C.
4. Waller to Heywood, October 20, 1898, November 20, 1898, Letters Received, Commandant, 1899, RG 127, Entry 10, Box 399, NA.

5. Waller's reputation grew as he matured as an officer and with the fame that came from his success before the Supreme Court. See Chapter 2 for details regarding his law school training and his work on the Sayre case.
6. Proceedings of a Marine Examining Board Convened at the Marine Barracks, Washington, D.C., July 31, 1899, RG 125, Entry 62 (HM1988), Box 785, NA.
7. Certificate of Birth, August 19, 1899, Commonwealth of Virginia, Bureau of Vital Statistics, State Board of Health, copy in Vernon Williams Archives, Abilene, Texas.
8. Norfolk images, Reid Family Photograph Albums, George C. Reid Historical Collection, PC144, Marine Corps Historical Center(hereafter cited as MCHC), Washington Navy Yard, Washington, D.C.
9. Waller to Heywood, October 23, 1899, Box 401.
10. Waller to Heywood, October 23, 1899, Box 401; Charles Heywood to Littleton W. T. Waller, October 28, 1899, Waller Family Papers, La Jolla, California (hereafter cited as WFP).
11. General Heywood wrote Waller that the Battalion would be composed of seventeen officers and four companies, but the officer assignments actually included only sixteen named officers (see Figure 10). Nothing in Waller's papers or in RG127 was found to explain the increase of one officer in Heywood's communication or why only sixteen officers were listed by name.
12. Littleton W. T. Waller to [first name unknown] West, March 7, 1910, WFP.
13. Annual Report of the Brigadier-General, Commandant of the United States Marine Corps to the Secretary of the Navy, 1900, in Serial Set No. 4098, Senate Document 3, 56th Congress, 2nd Session (Washington, D.C.: U.S. Government Printing Office, 1900), 1099–1101, 1109–1110.
14. Lowell Thomas, *Old Gimlet Eye* (Quantico, Virginia: The Marine Corps Association, a reprint of the 1933 edition, 1981), 36–41; Smedley D. Butler to mother, June 17, 1900, Butler Historical Collection (hereafter cited as BHC), copies in the author's files; Hans Schmidt, *Maverick Marine: General Smedley D. Butler and the Contradictions of American Military History* (Lexington, : The University Press of Kentucky, 1987), 12–13.
15. Millett, *Semper Fidelis*, 156; John T. Myers to Commander-in-Chief, U.S. Naval Forces on the Asiatic Station, September 26, 1900, Annual Report of the Commandant, 1901.
16. This number varies from account to account. In 1959, Marine historian R. D. Heinl, Jr., published a detailed accounting of each national force, which totaled "21 officers and 431 enlisted men." R.D. Heinl, Jr., "Hell in China," *Marine Corps Gazette*, November 1959, 58.
17. Millett, *Semper Fidelis*, 137; Heinl, "Hell in China," 58–59; Elbridge Colby, "Tientsin and the Boxer Rebellion, *Military Engineer* 29, no. 164 (May–June 1937): 191.
18. Millett, *Semper Fidelis*, 137; Heinl, "Hell in China," 59; Diana Preston, *The Boxer Rebellion: The Dramatic Story of China's War on Foreigners that Shook the World in the Summer of 1900* (New York: Walker & Company, 2000), 89–101; Colby, "Tientsin and the Boxer Rebellion," 191.
19. Millett, *Semper Fidelis*, 137; Heinl, "Hell in China," Preston, *The Boxer Rebellion*, 89–101; Colby, "Tientsin and the Boxer Rebellion," 191.
20. Robert L. Meade to Charles Heywood, March 19, 1901, Robert L. Meade Historical Collection (hereafter cited as RLM), Marine Corps Research Center, Quantico,

Virginia; China Diary, William C. Powell Papers, Marine Corps Historical Center, Washington Navy Yard, Washington, D.C. (hereafter cited as WCP); Waller to Meade, June 28, 1900. Additional copies of this document come from RG 127, Entry 26, Box III, National Archives, National Archives, Washington, D.C., and RLM. Since there are some small differences in these copies, I have referred to all three versions in each case and this document will hereafter be cited as WFP/RLM/NA. This communication was also published in the Annual Report of the Commandant of the Marine Corps in 1901; Colby, "Tientsin and the Boxer Rebellion," 194.
21. Littleton W. T. Waller to Charles Heywood, June 18, 1900, RG 127, Entry 26, Box III, National Archives, National Archives, Washington, D.C.; Waller to Meade, June 28, 1900, WFP/RLM/NA; Smedley D. Butler to mother, July 2, 1900, BHC; Powell China Diary, WDP; Colby, "Tientsin and the Boxer Rebellion," 194.
22. Waller to Heywood, June 18, 1900; Waller to Meade, June 28, 1900; Butler to mother, July 2, 1900; Powell china Diary; Colby, "Tientsin and the Boxer Rebellion," 194.
23. Waller to Meade, June 28, 1900, WFP/RLM/NA.
24. Waller to Meade, June 28, 1900; Waller to Clara Waller, June 22, 1900.
25. Waller to Meade, June 28, 1900; Waller to Clara Waller, June 22, 1900; Powell China Diary; Dagget, *America in the China Relief Expedition*, 21; Colby, "Tientsin and the Boxer Rebellion," 94.
26. "7th Endorsement," Meade to Heywood, not dated, RLM; Heinl, "Hell in China," 60; Waller to Heywood, June 18, 1900, NA; Waller to Meade, June 28, 1900, WFP/RLM/NA; Powell China Diary, WCP.
27. Waller to Meade, June 28, 1900, WFP/RLM/NA; Powell China Diary, WCP; Preston, *The Boxer Rebellion*, 102–104. Preston's account leaves the American Marines out, content to emphasize the British and Russian forces who counted for fourteen hundred of the eighteen hundred officers and men in the rescue force; Colby, "Tientsin and the Boxer Rebellion," 194.
28. Waller to Meade, June 28, 1900; Preston, *The Boxer Rebellion*, 102–104; Colby, "Tientsin and the Boxer Rebellion," 194.
29. Waller to Meade, June 28, 1900, WFP/RLM/NA.
30. Waller to Meade, June 28, 1900.
31. Charles Heywood to R. Page Waller, June 26, 1900, WFP; R. Page Waller to Charles Heywood, not dated, WFP. It is not known how the erroneous report and drawing came to appear in the newspaper or the source for the story.
32. *Ibid.*; Butler to mother, August 2, 1900, BHC; William C. Harllee to Amelia Harllee, August 3, 1900, William C. Harllee Papers, Marine Corps Historical Center, Washington Navy Yard, Washington, D.C. (hereafter cited as WCH); George M. Palmer Papers, Marine Corps Historical Center, Washington Navy Yard, Washington, D.C. (hereafter cited as GMP).
33. Waller to Heywood, June 28, 1900, WFP/RLM/NA; Francis X. Holbrook, "Brave Hearts and Bright Weapons," *Marine Corps Gazette,* November 1973, 50–61; Robert Debs Heinl, Jr., *Soldiers of the Sea: The United States Marine Corps, 1775–1962* (Annapolis, Maryland: United States Naval Institute, 1963) 133–134; Colby, "Tientsin and the Boxer Rebellion," 194–195.
34. Waller to Heywood, June 28, 1900; Millett, *Semper Fidelis*, 160.

35. Louis McCarty Little to unknown, not dated, Louis M: Little Papers (hereafter cited as LML), PC 143, MCHC; Meade to Heywood, March 19, 1901, RLM.
36. Waller to Clara Waller, June 30, 1900, WFP; Waller to Heywood, July 30, 1900, WFP; Waller to Louis Kempff, July 2, 1900, RG 127, Entry 26, Box III; Schmidt, *Maverick Marine*, 16–17; Colby, "Tientsin and the Boxer Rebellion," 195–196.
37. Waller to Clara Waller, June 30, 1900; Waller to Heywood, July 30, 1900; Waller to Kempff, July 2, 1900; Schmidt, *Maverick Marine*, 16-17.
38. Little to unknown, not dated, LML; Harry W. Edwards, "Memory of a Day with the-Royal Welch," *Leatherneck Magazine*, March 1979, 78–79. This is a copy of the article located in the Waller Family Papers.
39. Robert L. Meade to Charles Heywood, July 16, 1900, RLM. While the Marines engaged the Chinese to the south of the Walled City, the Russians initiated an independent attack on the northern perimeter. While not attacking in concert with Dorward and his forces, the Russian operation did draw Chinese defenders from the South Wall and aided the taking of the South Gate on the morning of July 14; Colby, "Tientsin and the Boxer Rebellion," 196–197.
40. Meade to Heywood, July 16, 1900; Robert H. Dunlap to C. G. Long, July 16, 1900, RLM; C. G. Long to Meade, July 16, 1900, RG 127, Entry 26, Box 3, NA; P. M. Bannon to Meade, July 15, 1900 and July 24, 1900, RG 127, Entry 26, Box 3, NA; Butler to mother, July 23, 1900, BHC; Ben Fuller to C. G. Long, July 16, 1900, RG 127, Entry 26, Box 3, NA; R. F. Wynnee to Meade, July 17, 1900, RLM; C. G. Anderson to Meade, July 30, 1900, RG 127, Entry 26, Box 3, NA; Colby, "Tientsin and the Boxer Rebellion," 197–199.
41. Dunlap to Long, July 16, 1900; Long to Meade, July 16, 1900; Bannon to Meade, July 15, 1900 and July 24, 1900; Butler to mother, July 23, 1900; Fuller to Long, July 16, 1900; Wynnee to Meade, July 17, 1900; Anderson to Meade, July 30, 1900; Colby, "Tientsin and the Boxer Rebellion," 197-199; Waller to Heywood, date unknown, reprinted in Annual Report of the Commandant of the Marine Corps, Serial Set 4287 (Washington, D.C.: Government Printing Office, 1901), 1275.
42. Harllee to Amelia Harllee, August 3, 1900, WCH; Charles A. Coolidge to Adjutant General of the Army, July 26, 1900, Annual Report of the Secretary of War, 1900, House Document 2, 56th Congress, Session 2, Serial Set 4078, 26–27 (hereafter cited as Serial 4078); Waller to Adna R. Chaffee, July 26, 1900, Serial 4078; Colby, "Tientsin and the Boxer Rebellion," 197–198.
43. Meade to Heywood, July 16, 1900, RLM.
44. Meade to Heywood, July 16, 1900.
45. Meade to Heywood, July 16, 1900; Little to unknown, undated, LML.
46. Meade to Heywood, July 16, 1900, RLM; Dorward to Meade, July 15, 1900, RLM.
47. Waller to Heywood, not dated, Annual Report of the Secretary of the Navy, 1901, House Document 3, 57th Congress, Session 1, Serial Set 4287, 1275 (hereafter cited as Serial 4287).
48. Cochrane Diary, October 16, 1900; Schmidt, *Maverick Marine*, 17; Oliver D. Norton to Medical Officer in charge, U.S. Naval Hospital, Mare Island, California, July 27, 1900, RLM; Report on the Fitness of Officers, Robert L. Meade, July 28, 1900, RLM; Meade to Secretary of the Navy, October 22, 1900, RLM; Waller to Heywood, 1275, Serial 4287.

49. Cochrane Diary, October 16, 1900; Schmidt, *Maverick Marine*, 17; Norton to Medical Officer in charge, July 27, 1900; Report on the Fitness of Officers, Robert L. Meade, July 28, 1900; Meade to Secretary of the Navy, October 22, 1900; Waller to Heywood, 1275, Serial 4287.
50. Waller to Meade, July 28, 1900, RLM.
51. Waller to Heywood, Serial Set 4287, 1275.
52. Harllee to Andrew T. Harllee, August 20, 1900, and August 27, 1900, WCH; Adna R. Chaffee to Commandant, September 1, 1900, RG 127, Entry 26, Box 3, NA.
53. Littleton W. T. Waller to W. P. Biddle, August 20, 1900, WFP; W. P. Biddle to Adna R. Chaffee, August 20, 1900, WFP; A.D.L. Cary and Stouppe McCance, comp., *Regimental Records of the Royal Welch Fusiliers*, volume. 2, 1816–1914 (London: Forster Groom and Company, Ltd., 1923), 263–264.
54. Littleton W. T. Waller to W. P. Biddle, August 20, 1900, WFP; W. P. Biddle to Adna R. Chaffee, August 20, 1900, WFP; Daniel Blake, "Diary," August 4–5, 1900, Daniel Blake Papers, PC 1196, Marine Corps Historical Center, Washington Navy Yard, Washington, D.C.
55. Waller to Biddle, August 20, 1900; Blake, Diary, August 5, 1900.
56. james Bevan, "From Filipinos to Boxers in 1900," *Leatherneck*, 18, no. 4 (April 1935): 6–7; Waller to Biddle, August 20, 1900; Butler to mother, August 19, 1900, BHC; Schmidt, *Maverick Marine*, 22–23; Biddle to Chaffee, August 19, 1900.
57. Harllee to Harllee, August 20, 1900, and August 27, 1900; Chaffee to Commandant, September 1, 1900.
58. Biddle to Chaffee, August 20, 1900, RG 127, Entry 26, Box 3; Thomas, *Old Gimlet Eye*, 75.
59. Adna R. Chaffee to Adjutant General, U.S. Army, September 1, 1900, Reports re to Engagements in the Philippines and China, RG 127, Entry 26, Box 3 (hereafter referred to as Engagements); Thomas Butler to Littleton W. T. Waller, August 15, 1900, WFP; General Y. Fukishima to Littleton W. T. Waller, March 8, 1901, Littleton W. T. Waller Sr. Papers, PC 942, Box 1, Folder 4, MCHC (hereafter WSR MCHC); Promotion citations, Engagements; Biddle to Commandant, Serial 4287; Thomas Butler to Littleton W. T. Waller, August 26, 1901, PC 942, Box 2B24, Folder 3, WSR MCHC.

## CHAPTER 4

1. Joseph L. Schott, *The Ordeal of Samar* (New York: Bobbs Merrill, 1964), 52.
2. Affairs in the Philippine Islands: Hearings before the Committee on the Philippine Islands (January 31–June 28, 1902) 57th Congress, 1st session, Senate Document 331, volume 2, 1591–1592 (Washington, D.C.: Government Printing Office, 1902); John Gates, *Schoolbooks and Krags: The United States Army in the Philippines, 1898–1902* (Westport, Connecticut: Greenwood Press, 1973), 250.
3. Brian M. Linn, 'We Will Go Heavily Armed: The Marines' Small War on Samar, 1901–1902," in William R. Roberts and Jack Sweetman, eds., *New Interpretations in Naval History*, Ninth Naval History Symposium (Annapolis, Maryland: Naval Institute Press, 1991), 278.
4. For accounts of the Balangiga Massacre, Smith, and the events surrounding the decision to initiate punitive operations on Samar see: Stanley Karnow, *In Our Image:*

*America's Empire in the Philippines* (New York: Random House Publishing Co., Inc., 1989), 191–192; Gates, *Schoolbooks and Krags*, 248–256; Brian Linn, *The U.S. Army and Counterinsurgency in the Philippine War, 1899–1902* (Chapel Hill, North Carolina: University of North Carolina Press, 1989), 226–27; Linn, "We Will Go Heavily Armed," 273–292; Schott, *Ordeal*, 7–66. Another interesting source includes various accounts by some of the twenty-six survivors. A popular edited volume privately printed is James O. Taylor, ed. and comp., *The Massacre of Balangiga* (Joplin, Missouri: McCarn Printing Company, 1931).

5. Schott, *Ordeal*, 3, 62–65; J. Robert Moskin, *The U.S. Marine Corps Story*, second revised and updated edition (New York: McGraw-Hill Book Company, 1987), 94.
6. Quoted in Schott, *Ordeal*, 65.
7. The bolo was a principal weapon for the Filipino guerillas in the U.S.-Philippine War. There were many designs for the bolo, depending on the tribe or the island from which the fighter came from. A "common distinguishing characteristic" of the Philippine bolo "is its blade that widens and curves towards the tip. With more weight at the end of the blade, chopping becomes forceful and efficient." Perry Gil Mallari wrote a brief history and discussion of the bolo in Philippine history, and the article can be found online at https://fmspulse.com/fma-corner-bolo-filipino-utility-tool-and-weapon/.
8. Schott, *Ordeal*, 65.
9. Schott, *Ordeal*, 65.
10. Schott, *Ordeal*, 66; Moskin, *The U.S. Marine Corps Story*, 335; Charles Heywood to John Long, "Annual Report of the Commandant of the United States Marine Corps," Annual Report of the Navy Department for the Year 1901, House Document No. 3, Part 2, 57th Congress, 1st Session (Washington, D.C.: Government Printing Office, 1901), 1226–1227.
11. General Order 76, October 10, 1901, Headquarters, Department of the Visayas, Senate Document 331, Part 2, 1561. Washington: Government Printing Office, 1902; General Order 65, October 10, 1901, Headquarters, Department of the Visayas, Senate Document 331, Part 2, 1561–1562; General Order 66, November 1, 1901, Headquarters, Department of the Visayas, Senate Document 331, Part 2, 1562–1564; Adna Chaffee to Adjutant-General of the Army, First endorsement dated October 8, 1901 to R. P. Hughes to Adjutant General, Division of the Philippines, October 4, 1901, Senate Document 331, Part 2, 1598–1599. General Order 66 established a system of separate brigades in the command and listed Brigadier General Jacob H. Smith as commander of the Sixth Separate Brigade. The order indicated that Smith's command included the islands of Leyte, Samar, and all adjacent islands.
12. Schott, *Ordeal*, 66.
13. Fred Rodgers to Littleton W. T. Waller, October 21, 1901, Waller Report to the Commandant of the Marine Corps, May 25, 1902, copy in WFP (hereafter Samar Report); Waller testimony, Records of the Office of the Judge Advocate General, Record Group 153, Waller G.C.M 30313. The report to the Commandant was compiled by Waller while on board the U.S. Army transport *Warren* en route to the United States after the courts-martial. The report is a compilation of telegrams, after action reports, letters, and other documents relating to Waller's service on Samar. It also includes brief com-

mentaries to introduce sections of the report or to clarify Waller's position on various questions or events.
14. Rodgers to Waller, October 22, 1901.
15. Schott, *Ordeal*, 67–68.
16. Schott, *Ordeal*, 69–70.
17. Littleton W. T. Waller to Clara Waller, October 27, 1901, WFP; Rodgers to Littleton W. T. Waller, November 1, 1901, Littleton W. T. Waller, Sr., Papers, PC 942, Box 1, Folder 4, Marine Corps Historical Center, Washington, D.C.
18. Schott, *Ordeal*, 69–70.
19. Quoted in Waller to Clara Waller, October 27, 1901. WFP.
20. Schott, *Ordeal*, 70; Waller to Clara Waller, October 27, 1901..
21. Testimony by Littleton W. T. Waller, David Porter, and Jacob Smith in the Waller, Day, and Smith courts-martial, RG 153, Waller G.C.M. 30313, Day G.C.M. 10196, and Smith G.C.M. 30739, NA.
22. *Ibid.*; Waller to Porter, October 23, 1901, Samar Report.
23. Waller testimony, Smith testimony, F. M. Halford testimony, Hiram I. Bearss testimony and Porter testimony, Waller, Day, and Smith courts-martial, RG 153, Waller G.C.M. 30313, Day G.C.M. 10196, and Smith G.C.M. 30739, NA. Smith testified at the Waller court-martial that he did not give any such instructions and indicated that he disagreed with Waller's more militant instructions to his men. Waller was recalled to the stand to refute Smith's testimony using specific quotations of Smith's instructions to him. The defense then recalled Captain David D. Porter, Second Lieutenant F. M. Halford, and Captain H. I. Bearss, who corroborated Waller's recollection of Smith's verbal orders.
24. Littleton W. T. Waller, "Brief Account of the Samar incident," typescript, eleven pages, copy in WFP. This statement was made some time after all three courts-martial were completed and when Waller had returned to the United States. In the document he refers to a meeting with the "then" President of the United States [Theodore Roosevelt]. Waller reported that Roosevelt "informed me that I had the legal right to perform the act [shoot the prisoners on Samar]; [but that] it came at an inopportune moment." Waller privately groused that "I knew nothing of the political situation. I was in the jungle six thousand miles away. My duty was to my men and my colors. I did what I thought was right."
25. Waller, "Brief Account of the Samar Incident.".
26. Waller to Clara Waller, October 27, 1901.
27. Waller to Clara Waller, October 27, 1901.
28. Rodgers to Waller, November 1, 1901, MCHC.
29. Waller to Clara Waller, October 27, 1901, WFP.
30. Waller to Clara Waller, October 27, 1901, WFP; Littleton W. T. Waller to Adjutant General, Sixth Separate Brigade, November 10, 1901, copy in WFP; George B. Clark, *Hiram Iddings Bearss, U.S. Marine Corps* (Jefferson, North Carolina: McFarland & Company, Inc., 2005), 47; Schott, *Ordeal*, 79–85.
31. Littleton W. T. Waller to Adjutant General, Sixth Separate Brigade, October 31, 1901, copies in WFP.
32. Waller to Adjutant General, November 10, 1901.

33. Waller to Adjutant General, November 10, 1901.
34. Telegram, Littleton W. T. Waller to Adjutant General, November 5, 1901, WFP; Waller to Adjutant General, November 10, 1901, WFP.
35. Telegram, Littleton W. T. Waller to Adjutant General, November 13, 1901, WFP; Telegram, Littleton W. T. Waller to Frederick Rodgers, November 14, 1901, WFP.
36. Littleton W. T. Waller to Frederick Rodgers, November 14, 1901, WFP; Littleton W. T. Waller to Adjutant General, November 14, 1901, November 19, 1901, November 23, 1901, WFP. Waller report to the Commandant, copy in WFP; Littleton W. T. Waller to Clara Waller, November 21, 1901, WFP.
37. Waller refers to the "left bank" as he describes Porter's progress toward the cliffs area. Based on Waller's description of Porter's next efforts going up the trail through the insurgent's abandoned camps and positions, "left bank" probably should be "right bank," as Porter continued up the river on the eastern side to position his men and his Colt gun opposite the main insurgent camp on the Panhulugan Cliff across the river. See the inset box in Map 4.3 that marks Porter's and the insurgent main camp positions. Waller to Adjutant General, November 23, 1901, WFP.
38. Waller to Adjutant General, November 23, 1901, WFP.
39. Waller to Adjutant General, November 23, 1901, WFP.
40. Waller to Adjutant General, November 23, 1901, WFP.
41. Waller to Adjutant General, November 23, 1901, WFP.
42. Telegram, Littleton W. T. Waller to Adjutant General, November 30, 1901, WFP; Telegram, Littleton W. T. Waller to Adjutant General, November 26, 1901, WFP;
43. Linn, "'We Will Go Heavily Armed,'" 281; Waller G.C.M. 30313; Schott, *Ordeal*, 104.
44. Linn, "'We Will Go Heavily Armed,'" 281; Waller G.C.M. 30313; *Ordeal*, 104; Waller to Adjutant General, January 25, 1902, WFP.
45. Waller and the Marines on Samar were supported by a small fleet of shallow-drafted gunboats along the coastline, placed there by the Navy to interdict resupply efforts from other nearby islands and deny insurgent control of coastal settlements along the Samar coast where they operated against American efforts to subdue the area. Waller's reports include references to four gunboats, *Vicksburg, Panay, Aryat*, and *Isle de Cuba*, and their support of his operations ashore. These gunboats, many of them former Spanish vessels, were built with shallow drafts and contained armament that enhanced their suitability for river work in Samar. See the *Dictionary of American Fighting Ships* for details regarding their draft, armament characteristics, and historical data relating to their deployment in the Philippines.
46. Littleton W. T. Waller to Adjutant General, December 18, 1901, WFP; Schott, *Ordeal*, 99–100.
47. Littleton W. T. Waller to Adjutant General, December 18, 1901, WFP; Schott, *Ordeal*, 99–100; Annual Report of the Navy Department for the Year 1902, (Washington, D.C.: Government Printing Office, 1902), 969-970.
48. Waller to Adjutant General, December 18, 1901, WFP.
49. Waller to Adjutant General, December 18, 1901, WFP.
50. A baroto, also sometimes referred to in Waller's reports as a banca, is a small dugout boat with a flat bottom that allows it to be used on shallow rivers in the islands. One authority explained that "a boroto [usually] 120 centimeters wide may be hewn out

of a single trunk. Its capacity varied." Waller often found himself on rivers that were too shallow for his steam launches and had to resort to using barotos or bancas with paddles to travel on many of the inland riverways on Samar. The names of these crafts were used interchangeably by Waller, and the difference in names may refer to the capacity of a particular boat. Henry F. Funtecha, "The History and Culture of Boats and Boat-building in the Western Visayas," *Philippine Quarterly of Culture and Society* 28 (June 2000): 115; Merriam-Webster, https://www.merriam-webster.com/dictionary/baroto. Accessed June 16, 2022.

51. Littleton W. T. Waller to Adjutant General, December 21, 1901, WFP; Schott, *Ordeal*, 101; Clark, *Hiram Iddings Bearss*, 54.
52. Littleton W. T. Waller to Adjutant General, January 25, 1902, WFP; Schott, *Ordeal*, 103–105; Clark, *Hiram Iddings Bearss*, 54–55; Edwin H. Simmons, "Stand, Gentlemen, He Served on Samar," *Shipmate* (Annapolis, Maryland: United States Naval Academy Alumni Association), November 1976, 26; Paul Melshen, "He Served on Samar," *Proceedings* (Annapolis, Maryland: United States Naval Institute), November 1979, 45.
53. Littleton W. T. Waller to Adjutant General, January 25, 1902, WFP.
54. Waller to Adjutant General, December 25, 1901, WFP.
55. Waller to Adjutant General, December 25, 1901, WFP.
56. Waller to Adjutant General, December 25, 1901, WFP.
57. Littleton W. T. Waller to Adjutant General, January 25, 1902, WFP; Annual Report of the Commandant of the Marine Corps, in the Annual Report of the Navy Department for the Year 1902 (Washington, D.C.: Government Printing Office, 1902), 970.
58. Littleton W. T. Waller to Adjutant General, January 25, 1902, WFP.
59. A. S. Williams to Littleton W. T. Waller, February 18, 1902, WFP; Waller G.C.M. 30313.
60. Waller to Adjutant General, January 25, 1902; Waller testimony, Waller G.C.M. 30313.
61. Littleton W. T. Waller to Frederick Rodgers, January 24, 1902; Littleton W. T. Waller to Adjutant General, First Marine Brigade, January 29, 1902, January 25, 1902; Waller G.C.M. 30313.
62. Littleton W. T. Waller, Summary Statement, Waller G.C.M. 30313.
63. Littleton W. T. Waller to Jacob Smith, February 5, 1902, copy in WFP.
64. Littleton W. T. Waller to Charles Heywood, May 24, 1902, Samar Report.
65. Waller to Commandant, July 1, 1902, Samar Report.
66. Transcript, Waller G.C.M. 30313, WPF; "Results of the Philippine 'Atrocities' at Washington," *Literary Digest*, May 10, 1902, 630–631; Richard E. Welch, Jr., "American Atrocities in the Philippines: The Indictment and Response," *Pacific Historical Review* 43 (May 1974): 233–253.
67. Instructions for the Government of Armies of the United States in the field, originally issued as General Orders No. 100, Article 82, Adjutant General's Office, April 24, 1863 (Washington: Government Printing Office, 1864), 111.
68. General Orders no. 100, Article 82, April 24, 1863, 111.
69. Defense summation, Waller G.C.M. 30313.
70. Waller's papers contain numerous orders and official commendations for service on courts-martials, certificates for admission to the bar in Virginia and to the U.S. Supreme Court—all dated before 1900, WFP.

71. Smith testimony, Porter testimony, Waller testimony, Waller G.C.M. 30313, NA; Waller summation, Waller G.C.M. 30313, NA.
72. Waller G.C.M. 30313; Day G.C.M. 10196; Smith G.C.M. 30739.
73. Moskin, *The U.S. Marine Corps Story*, 340–341; Schott, *Ordeal*, 283; Millett, *History of the United States Marines*, 154.
74. Schott, *Ordeal*, 146.
75. Millett, *History of the United States Marines*, 154.
76. Marcus Howell, "Soldier and Carper," signed typescript copy in WFP.
77. Waller testimony, Smith G.C.M. 30739.
78. Findings, Waller G.C.M. 30313.

## CHAPTER 5

1. Clara Wynne Waller to Charles Heywood, March 13, 1902, WFP.
2. The Army transport ship *Warren*, originally the Hamburg American Line vessel *Scandia*, sold to the U.S. Army in 1898 and converted for transport duty. Online histories of passenger ships, http://www.theshipslist.com/ships/descriptions/ShipsS.html; Baggage Declaration and Entry, no date, Port of San Francisco, WFP; Littleton W. T. Waller to [first name unknown] West, March 7, 1910, WFP.
3. Littleton W. T. Waller to Clara Wynne Waller, April 11–12, 1902, WFP; Littleton W. T. Waller to Commandant, August 21, 1903, WFP.
4. "Major Waller Back among His Friends," clipping, unknown newspaper, unknown date, clipping file, WFP.
5. Littleton W. T. Waller to Charles Heywood, June 23, 1902, June 24, 1902, Letters Received, Commandant, 1902, RG 127, Box 408, National Archives; Littleton W. T. Waller to William H. Moody, June 29, 1902, WFP.
6. Program, "Complimentary Banquet Tendered to Major L. W. T. Waller by Norfolk Light Artillery Blues," July 15, 1902, WFP; Littleton W. T. Waller to Charles Heywood, July 18, 1902, Letters Received, Commandant, 1902, RG 127, Box 408, National Archives.
7. Waller's personal papers are filled with correspondence from old colleagues with whom he had served during the previous twenty years. American Army and Marine officers from over the years, together with British and Japanese officers who remembered Waller from China, maintained a long correspondence with him over the years. In the period following the Samar expedition, many wrote of their support for him in the face of the courts-martial and later added their congratulations at the news of the acquittal. These welcome missives added to the pleasant times at Warm Springs.
8. Two years earlier, Waller received a brevet [temporary or honorary] promotion to lieutenant colonel for his service at Tientsin in China. Throughout his career, Waller received brevet promotions or advancement in numbers that allowed him to move ahead on the seniority list. His permanent promotions moved steadily up in rank, influenced by his record in difficult situations in the field. Rufus H. Lane, "Military History of Littleton W. T. Waller," July 18, 1926, WFP.
9. Littleton W. T. Waller to Charles Heywood, October 9, 1902, October 12, 1902, November 7, 1902, November 15, 1902, November 20, 1902, Letters Received, Commandant, 1902, RG 127, Box 409–410, National Archives; The Major General Commandant to

Index and Record Section, Veterans Bureau, "Military History of Former Major General Littleton W. Waller, U.S.M.C.," October 13, 1926, Major General Littleton W. T. Waller personnel file, National Personnel Records Center at St. Louis, Missouri.
10. Charles Heywood to W. H. Moody, September 25, 1902, September 22, 1903, Letters to the Secretary of the Navy, RG 127, National Archives; Littleton W. T. Waller to Charles Heywood, October 10, 1902, October 12, 1902, November 7, 1902, November 15, 1902, November 20, 1902, Letters Received Commandant, 1902–1903, Box 409–410, RG 127, National Archives; Millett, *Semper Fidelis*, 163–164.
11. The historiography is vast and varied for the story of United States' efforts to secure a treaty with Columbia for rights to build and operate a canal in Panama to connect the Caribbean Sea and the Atlantic Ocean, and why those efforts failed. Those efforts led to the Panama Revolution and a few days later, an immediate American diplomatic recognition. For a good background to events in Columbia and Panama preceding the decision to send a Marine expeditionary force to Panama in 1903–1904, consider the following historical accounts. Charles K. Rockwell, "A Brief History of the Panama Canal," *Society of American Military Engineers* 1, no. 2 (April–June 1909): 164–174. Rockwell's article was written in the period and contains the story of the Panama Canal as it unfolded, but the author's imperial bias comes through in the article as well. Among the textbooks available, see latest editions in "Theodore Roosevelt, the Big Stick, and U.S. Hegemony in the Caribbean," in Dennis Merrill and Thomas G. Paterson, *Major Problems in American Foreign Relations*, volume 1 (Boston: Wadsworth, 2010); and Thomas G. Paterson, et al., *American Foreign Relations: A History/ Since 1895*, Volume 2 (Stamford, Connecticut: Cengage Learning, 2015).
12. Millett, *Semper Fidelis*, 164–165; Dana G. Munro, *Intervention and Dollar Diplomacy in the Caribbean, 1900–1921* (Princeton, N.J.: Princeton University Press, 1964), 37–60; George F. Elliott to Assistant Secretary of the Navy, January 11, 1904, RG 127, Entry 43, Box 4, National Archives.
13. Annual Report of the Commandant of the Marine Corps, in the Annual Report of the Navy Department for the Year 1904 (Washington, D.C.: Government Printing Office, 1904), 1231.
14. Annual Report, 1904, 1166.
15. Annual Report, 1904, 1166, 1193.
16. Annual Report, 1904, 1193.
17. Annual Report, 1904, 1193.
18. Annual Report, 1904, 1166, 1193–1194 ; Annual Report, 1905, 1206–1207; Harry A. Ellsworth, *One Hundred Eighty Landings of United States Marines, 1800–1934* (Washington, D.C.: History and Museums Division, Headquarters, U.S. Marine Corps, 1974), 134–136.
19. Annual Report, 1904, 1194; Annual Report, 1905, 1206–1207; Harry A. Ellsworth, *One Hundred Eighty Landings of United States Marines, 1800–1934* (Washington, D.C.: History and Museums Division, Headquarters, U.S. Marine Corps, 1974), 134–136.
20. "Military History of Littleton W. T. Waller," various dates and levels of detail produced for Headquarters, U.S. Marine Corps. Copies of these histories were found in the Waller Family Papers, the Marine Corps Historical Center Collections, and in the National Personnel Records Center at St. Louis, Missouri; "Waller's Home Coming," *Times Dispatch*, April 5, 1904, 5; "Colonel Waller Arrives," *Times Dispatch*, April 13, 1904, 5.

21. Annual Report, 1904, 1182; Annual Report, 1905, 1232; Annual Report, 1906, 1083; Ellsworth, *One Hundred Eighty Landings*, 62.
22. James H. Hitchman, "U.S. Control Over Cuban Sugar Production, 1898–1902," *Journal of Interamerican Studies and World Affairs* 12, no. 1 (January 1970): 96–97; Ellsworth, *One Hundred Eighty Landings*, 62; Allan Millett, *The Politics of Intervention: The Military Occupation of Cuba, 1906–1909* (Columbus, Ohio: Ohio State University Press, 1968), 70–80.
23. At the time of his trip to Cuba with Taft, Bacon was temporarily Acting Secretary of State due to Elihu Root's travels to the Pan-American Conference at Rio de Janeiro and tour through South America. "Robert Bacon," in *Dictionary of American Biography* (New York: Charles Scribner's Sons, 1936). Gale online entry https://go.gale.com/ps/i.do?p=GPS&u=wikipedia&id=GALE|BT2310018466&v=2.1&it=r&sid=G-PS&asid=afdbbd9a (accessed July 16, 2022).
24. Millett, *The Politics of Intervention*, 59–63; Ralph Eldin Minger, "William H. Taft and the United States Intervention in Cuba in 1906," *Hispanic American Historical Review* 41, no. 1 (February 1961): 76–77; Christopher A. Abel, "Controlling the Big Stick: Theodore Roosevelt and the Cuban Crisis of 1906," *Naval War College Review* 40, no. 3 (Summer 1987): 91–93; Allan R. Millett, "The General Staff and the Cuban Intervention of 1906," *Military Affairs* 31, no. 3 (Autumn 1967): 114–117. For a comprehensive view of events leading up to American intervention, see Millett's chapter "The August Revolution," in *The Politics of Intervention*, 59–88.
25. Millett, *The Politics of Intervention*, 74–75, 77–78.
26. Roosevelt wire to Bacon is quoted in Millett, *The Politics of Intervention*, 78.
27. Millett, *The Politics of Intervention*, 78.
28. Ellsworth, *One Hundred Eighty Landings*, 62; Millett, *The Politics of Intervention*, 78, 91–92; "Getting Ready to Land in Cuba," *Evening Star*, September 26, 1906, 1–2; "Moving of Marines," *Chattanooga Daily Times*, September 27, 1906, 4; "Storm is Interfering," *Boston Globe*, September 28, 1906, 1.
29. Ellsworth, *One Hundred Eighty Landings*, 62; Millett, *The Politics of Intervention*, 78, 91–92; Glenn M. Harned, *Marine Corps Generals, 1899–1936: Volume 1 of a Marine Corps Biographical Encyclopedia*, 2nd. ed. edition (North Charleston, South Carolina: CreateSpace Independent Publishing, 2017), 55.
30. For a comprehensive overview of the Army's pacification operations in Cuba, see Millett's chapters 3–5 in *The Politics of Intervention*, 89–168.
31. "Statement of Facts and Arguments Presented by the Major-General Commandant of the Marine Corps, Urging the Disapproval by the Department of the Proposed Reduction of the Strength of and Ultimate Removal of the Marine Detachment from the Vessels of the Navy," in House of Representatives, Hearings before the Subcommittee on Naval Academy and Marine Corps, Committee on Naval Affairs, House of Representatives on the Status of the Marine Corps (hereafter cited as Hearing 1909) (Washington, D.C.: Government Printing Office, 1909), 22.
32. An example of the newspaper stories appearing in the 1890s that attempted to demonstrate derogatory Marine attitudes toward sailors on ships appeared in the New York Times in 1892. "Major ---------, United States Marine Corps, advances the following: The sailors, in my long experience, have always shirked military duty, and are now,

and always will be, lax in everything pertaining to military discipline. They not only try to circumvent the Marines on duty, but also the officers and petty office3rs of the ship. On more than one occasion I have known the chief petty officers of a ship to be the leaders in mutinous conduct, and if there had been no Marine guard on board there is no telling what would have become of the ship." The writer continued, "it would be impossible to imagine a more complete condemnation of the seamen and petty officers of the navy than this." *New York Times*, February 22, 1892, 3.

33. Hearing 1909; Littleton W. T. Waller to Charles Heywood, July 17, 1894, RG 127, Letters Received Commandant, Box 393, National Archives; typescript, [petition relating to removal of Marines], "To the Congress of the United States, no date, Letters Received Commandant, Box 393, National Archives; [quotations and arguments relating to the removal of Marines], typescript, no title, no date, Letters Received Commandant, RG 127, Box 393, National Archives; Allan Millett, *Semper Fidelis: The History of the United States Marine Corps*, rev. and expanded edition (New York: The Free Press, 1991), 138-144.
34. Waller to Heywood, July 17, 1894, WFP.
35. Millett, *Semper Fidelis*, 138-144; Hearing 1909, 24.
36. Heinl, Jr., *Soldiers of the Sea*, 102-103.
37. Quoted in Robert Debs Heinl, Jr., "An Association was Formed," *Marine Corps Gazette*, April 1963, 15; Matthew M. Oyos, "Theodore Roosevelt, Congress, and the Military: U.S. Civil-Military Relations in the Early Twentieth Century," *Presidential Studies Quarterly* 30, no. 2 (June 2000), 316-317.
38. Hearing 1909, 3-4.
39. Hearing 1909.
40. Hearing 1909, 3. Representative Sydney E. Mudd, chairman of the subcommittee on the Status of U.S. Marines, was ill, and Butler assumed the role of acting chairman as the next ranking Republican on the subcommittee.
41. Testimony by Truman H. Newberry, John E. Pillsbury, William A. Marshall, John C. Fremont, J. M. Helm, C. McR. Winslow, William S. Sims, W. F. Fullam, Frederick Rodgers, Royal R. Ingersoll, R. D. Evans, Hearing 1909; Millett, *Semper Fidelis*, 138-144.
42. Robert Debs Heinl Jr., *Soldiers of the Sea*, 104-105.
43. Act of March 3, 1909 (35 Statute, 773), as quoted in Senate Document 238, 67th Congress, 2nd Session (Washington, D.C.: Government Printing Office, 1922), 954.
44. R. D. Heinl, Jr., "An Association was Formed," *Marine Corps Gazette*, April 1963, 14-17; Douglas C. McDougal to Randolph McCall Pate, January 18, 1956, MCHC; Randolph McCall Pate to Douglas C. McDougal, January 27, 1956, MCHC.
45. For an account of the political fight between Elliott and Colonel Charles H. Lauchheimer, see Wayne A. Wiegand, "The Lauchheimer Controversy: A Case of Group Political Pressure during the Taft Administration," *Military Affairs*, April 1976, 54-59.
46. Merrill L. Bartlett, "Old Gimlet Eye," *Proceedings of the U.S. Naval Institute* 112 (November 1986), 66; Schmidt, *Maverick Marine*, 36; Archibald Butt to Clara Butt, February 2, 1911, in Archibald Butt, *Taft and Roosevelt: The Intimate Letters of Archie Butt, Military Aide*, volume 2 (New York: Doubleday, Doran & Company, Inc., 1930), 587-588.
47. Butt to Clara Butt, February 2, 1911, in Butt, *Taft and Roosevelt*, 587.

48. Butt to Clara Butt, February 2, 1911, in Butt, *Taft and Roosevelt*, 587-588.
49. There were only thirty-one signatures on the petition.
50. Claude Swanson to Woodrow Wilson, January 17, 1914, Josephus Daniels Papers, Library of Congress, Washington, D.C. (hereafter cited as JDP); Boies Penrose to Josephus Daniels, December 17, 1913, JDP.
51. Henry Cabot Lodge to Josephus Daniels, December 3, 1913, JDP.
52. Henry Cabot Lodge to Claude Swanson, January 16, 1914, JDP; Swanson to Wilson, January 17, 1914, JDP.
53. Daniels's reference to Waller as a general was in error. Waller was not promoted to brigadier general until 1916.
54. Josephus Daniels, *The Wilson Era: Years of Peace, 1910–1917* (Chapel Hill, North Carolina: University of North Carolina Press, 1944), 322.
55. Daniels, *The Wilson Era*, 322-323.
56. Merrill L. Bartlett, "Ouster of a Commandant," *Proceedings*, November 1980, 60; Commandant Letter File, 1913-1914, JDP. The Karmandy file contains over thirty-four letters of support, which includes some former Waller supporters who signed Swanson's petition, among them Senators Shafroth and Ashust.
57. Munro, *Intervention and Dollar Diplomacy*, 469, 472. Munro's chapter "The Relations with Cuba, 1909–1921" (pages 469–487) gives a full account of a series of corrupt and unwise economic missteps in Cuba between 1909 and 1911 that produced the need for the occasional dispatch of Marines to Cuba.
58. Rufus H. Lane, "Military History of Littleton W. T. Waller," July 18, 1926, entry for 1911, WFP; John H. Johnstone, *A Brief History of the 1st Marines* (Washington, D.C.: U.S. Marine Corps, 1968), 8.
59. John S. D. Eisenhower, *Intervention: The United States and the Mexican Revolution, 1913–1917* (New York: W. W. Norton & Company, 1993), 82, 99; Millett, *Semper Fidelis*, 171–172.
60. For background on President Woodrow Wilson's position on President Victoriano Huerta and how events leading up to the Tampico incident influenced Wilson to take decisive action at Veracruz, see J. Robert Moskin, *The U.S. Marine Corps Story*, rev. and updated (New York: McGraw Hill Book Company, 1987), 157–159; Millett, *Semper Fidelis*, 171–172; John Eisenhower, *Intervention*, 70–82.
61. For an additional overview of President Wilson's Mexican policies and his attitudes toward Victoriano Huerta, see John Eisenhower, *Intervention*, 19-68.
62. For an examination of the events surrounding the Ypiranga and the arms cargo, see Michael C. Meyer, "The Arms of the Ypiranga," *The Hispanic American Historical Review* 50, no. 3 (August 1970) 543-556; and Thomas Baecker, "The Arms of the Ypiranga: The German Side," *Americas* 30, no. 1 (July 1973): 1-17.
63. Moskin, *The U.S. Marine Corps Story*, 158–159; Millett, *Semper Fidelis*, 172–173; John Eisenhower, *Intervention*, 113–114.
64. Millett, *Semper Fidelis*, 173.
65. *New York Times*, April 24, 1914, 3.
66. Lane, "Military History of Littleton W. T. Waller," July 18, 1926, entries for April 1914, WFP; John Eisenhower, *Intervention*, 82, 99; *New York Times*, April 22, 1914, 3; *New York Times*, April 26, 1914, 4.

67. "Ports of Tampico and Vera Cruz Will Be Seized," *Liberty Vindicator*, April 24, 1914, 1; "Marine Intelligence," *Houston Daily Post*, April 24, 1914, 16; "Fifth Brigade Sails for Vera Cruz Today, *Houston Daily Post*, April 24, 1914, 1, 3; "Troop Movement Toward Mexico," *Austin American-Statesman*, April 21, 1914, 1–2; "Soldiers Sail for Veracruz," *New York Sun*, April 25, 1914, 3. At the time of the initial landings at Veracruz, elements of the Marine brigade under Lejeune were located at New Orleans and Pensacola and able to move quickly across the Gulf of Mexico to join the fleet anchored off Veracruz.
68. Millett, *Semper Fidelis*, 173–174.

## CHAPTER 6

1. For a detailed account of the events leading up to the coup and murder of President Jean Vilbrun Guillaume Sam and the massacre surrounding the attack on the government, see Robert D. Heinl and Nancy G. Heinl, newly revised and expanded by Michael Heinl, *Written in Blood: The Story of the Haitian People, 1492-1995* (Lanham, Maryland: University Press of American, Inc., 2005), 323-375. *Written in Blood* is also a good reference for an overview of the culture of violence that surrounded the Haitian society for most of its history. The revised edition by Robert and Nancy Heinl's son, Michael Heinl, added two new chapters (Chapters 15 and 16) that brought the original edition's coverage to an additional twenty-four years.
2. Ivan Musicant, *The Banana Wars* (New York: Macmillan Publishing Company, 1990), 159.
3. Barnett to Daniels, "Report on Affairs in the Republic of Haiti," 2; Robert Lansing to James Oliver, January 30, 1918, Robert Lansing Papers, Library of Congress, Manuscript Division and Lansing, Diary, July 11, 1915, LC in Lester D. Langley, *The Banana Wars: An Inner History of American Empire, 1900–1934* (Lexington, Kentucky: The University Press of Kentucky, 1983), 125.
4. The Caco was a northern Haitian bandit who in time of peace made his living by simple thievery and in times of political unrest made the most of it by selling his mercenary talents to the highest bidder. Haitian revolutions began in the north when a political contender had the financial clout to purchase a sufficient Caco army to sweep him south and to the power of the presidential palace at Port-au-Prince. Usually within weeks the new president had competition in the north who began to follow the strategic plan that he himself had just successfully concluded. The first task for the newest sovereign usually was to deal with the Cacos of the old regime in Port-au-Prince and scattered around the countryside. He used his Caco army for this task while his future ouster was busy in the north raising a third Caco army. It was a vicious cycle that contributed to the anarchy of the times and provided a certain predictability to Haitian politics.
5. Edward Beach, *Admiral Caperton in Haiti*, 6 in Musicant, *The Banana Wars*, 162.
6. Robert D. Heinl and Nancy G. Heinl, *Written in Blood: The Story of the Haitian People, 1492–1971* (Boston: Houghton Mifflin, 1978), 390–392; Musicant, *The Banana Wars*, 163–164; David Healy, *Gunboat Diplomacy in the Wilson Era: The U.S. Navy in Haiti, 1915–1916* (Madison, Wisconsin: The University of Wisconsin Press, 1976), 34, 128–129.
7. Langley, *The Banana Wars: An Inner History*, 121–122; Musicant, *The Banana Wars*, 163; Healy, *Gunboat Diplomacy*, 54–57; R. B. Davis to Robert Lansing, "Summary of

Conditions Existing in the Republic of Haiti Immediately Prior to the Overthrow of the Government of President Vilbrun Guillaume Sam and of Events Attending the Overthrow of that Government," January 12, 1916, in Department of State, *State Papers Relating to the Foreign Relations of the United States* (Washington, D.C.: Government Printing Office, 1916), 313–314 (hereafter cited as *Foreign Relations, 1916*). A full online version of *Foreign Relations* is available from the University of Wisconsin at http://digital.library.wisc.edu/1711.dl/FRUS.
8. *Foreign Relations, 1916*, 315; Musicant, *The Banana Wars*, 165–166. Musicant interviewed Major General Walter Greatsinger Farrell in October 1987. Farrell was a Marine aviator whose early service coincided with the last years of Waller's career.
9. 67th Congress, U.S. Senate, Inquiry into the Occupation and Administration of Haiti and Santo Domingo, volume 1 (Washington, D.C.: Government Printing Office, 1922), 306–307; *Foreign Relations*, 1916, 314; Heinl and Heinl, *Written in Blood*, 397.
10. *Foreign Relations, 1916*, 316.
11. George Barnett to Josephus Daniels, "Report on Affairs in the Republic of Haiti," June 1915 to June 30, 1920, 2–8, Littleton W. T. Waller, Jr., Historical Collection, PC 224, Box 3, Folder 31, Marine Corps Historical Center, Washington, D.C. (hereafter cited as LWJR).
12. Barnett to Daniels, "Report on Affairs in the Republic of Haiti," 2.
13. Barnett to Daniels, "Report on Affairs in the Republic of Haiti," 6–7; Diary, Adolph B. Miller, July 30–31, 1915, A. B. Miller Papers, PC 196, Box 2, Marine Corps Historical Center, Washington, D.C. (hereafter cited as Miller Diary).
14. Miller Diary, August 1–3, 1915; Barnett to Daniels, "Report on Affairs in the Republic of Haiti," 7; Secretary of the Navy, Annual Report, 1915, 763; Annual Report, 1920, 249–50.
15. Miller Diary, August 4, 1995.
16. Barnett, "Report on Affairs," 14.
17. Walter H. Posner, "American Marines in Haiti, 1915–1922," *Americas* 20, no. 3 (January 1964), 251.
18. See Chapter 2, "The Embattled Old Corps," for an examination of the emerging new generation of Marine officers competing with Waller and officers of the old corps. These inter- and intraservice rivalries are outside the primary story of Haiti, but they remain an integral part of the intrigue underway within the Marine Corps establishment and are critical parts of the interweaving struggle going on within the command ashore in Port-au-Prince and elsewhere in Haiti.
19. Littleton W. T. Waller to John A. Lejeune, August 26, 1915, WFP.
20. Acting Secretary of the Navy to Littleton W. T. Waller, August 6, 1915, WFP; Musicant, *The Banana Wars*, 165–167; Langley, *The Banana Wars: An Inner History*, 127–129; Posner, "American Marines in Haiti," 231.
21. Littleton W. T. Waller to John Beresford Wynne Waller, August 10, 1915, WFP.
22. Littleton W. T. Waller to George Barnett, August 16, 1915, WFP; Charles Lee Lewis, *Famous American Marines* (Boston: L.C. Page & Company), 170.
23. Allan R. Millett, *Semper Fidelis*, 185–186; Richard Lee Schreadley, "Intervention—The Americans in Haiti, 1915–1934" (doctoral dissertation, Fletcher School of Law and Diplomacy, 1972), 121–122.

24. Millett, *Semper Fidelis*, 185–186; Schreadley, "Intervention," 122–124.
25. Littleton W. T. Waller to John A. Lejeune, August 21, 1915, John A. Lejeune Papers (hereafter cited as JAL), Library of Congress, Washington, D.C.; William B. Caperton to Littleton W. T. Waller, September 1, 1915, WFP.
26. Littleton W. T. Waller to John A. Lejeune, July 1, 1916, JAL.
27. Han Schmidt, *Maverick Marine*, 85; Littleton Waller to John A. Lejeune, July 1, 1916, JAL.
28. George Barnett to Josephus Daniels, "Report on Affairs," 24.
29. Littleton W. T. Waller to John A. Lejeune, October 8, 1915, John A. Lejeune Papers; Littleton W. T. Waller to John A. Lejeune, October 13, 1915, JAL and WFP; Littleton W. T. Waller to John A. Lejeune, October 13, 1915, JAL and WFP; William B. Caperton to Josephus Daniels, September 21, 1915, WFP.
30. U.S. Congress, Senate, Select Committee on Haiti and Santo Domingo, 67th Congress, 1st and 2nd sessions, 1922, Inquiry into the Occupation and Administration of Haiti and Santo Domingo, 1682–1683; Moskin, *The U.S. Marine Corps Story*, 177.
31. Moskin, *The U.S. Marine Corps Story*, 178.
32. Moskin, *The U.S. Marine Corps Story*, 178; U.S. Congress, Senate, Inquiry into the Occupation and Administration of Haiti and Santo Domingo, 1684.
33. William B. Caperton to Josephus Daniels, October 1, 1915, WFP; Barnett to Daniels, "Report on Affairs in the Republic of Haiti," 28–29; Posner, "American Marines," 248–249; Littleton W. T. Waller to William B. Caperton, November 9, 1915, WFP.
34. Eli Cole to Littleton W. T. Waller, November 17, 1915, WFP; Barnett to Daniels, "Report on Affairs in the Republic of Haiti," 35–37; William B. Caperton to Josephus Daniels, November 19, 1915, WFP.
35. Moskin, *The U.S. Marine Corps Story*, 180–181.
36. Posner, "American Marines in Haiti," 261.
37. Much of the material on Waller and his relationship with naval and Marine officers was first presented as a paper at the Naval Academy's Tenth Naval History Symposium in 1991 and is available in the proceedings under the title "Politics of Command," in Jack Sweetman's (et al., eds.) *New Interpretations in Naval History* (Annapolis, Maryland: Naval Institute Press, 1993); Millett, *Semper Fidelis*, 153; Littleton W. T. Waller, II Interview, March 11, 1990, La Jolla, California; Smedley Butler to mother, July 23, 1900, Butler Family Papers, Newtown Square, Pennsylvania.
38. Gerard M. Kincade to Littleton W. T. Waller, Jr., September 29, 1930, WFP. For a good example of personal attack leveled at Waller, see untitled manuscript, n.d., n.s., fifteen pp., WFP. Another copy is in Ben H. Fuller Papers, Marine Corps Historical Center, Washington, D.C.
39. Commandant Barnett had established an "unofficial" correspondence route for Waller through Assistant Commandant Lejeune to ensure a clear line of communications free of the Naval command on station—meaning Admiral Caperton. These letters were sent to Lejeune, giving Lejeune and Barnett an uncensored account of activities ashore.
40. John A. Lejeune to Littleton W. T. Waller, October 1, 1915, JAL.

41. Littleton Waller to John A. Lejeune, August 21, 1915, August 26, 1915, September 21–24, 1915, October 20, 1915, JAL and copies of same in WFP.
42. Waller to Clara Waller, September 8, 1915; Waller to Lejeune (annotated copy sent to son Littleton Waller, Jr., October 10, 1915, WFP). Negative references to Cole and others do not appear in Waller's letters to Lejeune after Lejeune's censure earlier in October. Waller continued to write such observations, but only in the personal postscripts added to carbon copies of the letters he sent to his sons.
43. Waller to Littleton Waller, Jr., January 25, 1916, WFP.
44. Littleton W. T. Waller to John A. Lejeune, February 8, 1916; October 10, 1915, JAL.
45. U.S. House of Representatives, Committee on Naval Affairs, Marine Corps Personnel Hearing, February 29–March 2, 1916. House Document 159-0.9, 2169 (Washington: Government Printing Office, 1916), For Waller and his fellow colonels, every proposal included an increase in the brigadier general category, representing future promotion opportunities for many of these senior colonels. As it stood in 1916, the only avenue to general's stars was to be named commandant, the only general officer in the Marine Corps. That would soon change.
46. Littleton W. T. Waller to John Beresford Wynne Waller, March 7, 1916, WFP.
47. Edwin N. McClellan, *The United States Marine Corps in the World War* (Washington, D.C.: Historical Branch, G-3, Headquarters, U.S. Marine Corps, 1920; 1968 reprint), 11.
48. Waller to John Beresford Wynne Waller, March 7, 1916, WFP.
49. Waller to John Beresford Wynne Waller, March 7, 1916, WFP; Waller to Clara Waller, February 17, 1916, WFP; Waller to Littleton W. T. Waller, Jr., John Beresford Wynne Waller, and Henry Tazewell Waller, March 12, 1916, WFP.
50. Waller to Clara Waller, February 17, 1916, WFP.
51. George Barnett to Littleton W. T. Waller, Orders #35F, March 27, 1916, Headquarters, U.S. Marines Corps, Washington, D.C., copy in WFP.
52. Waller to Lejeune, April 12, 1916, JAL.
53. William B. Caperton to George Barnett, December 3, 1915, Waller Fitness Report File, RG127, National Archives, College Park, Maryland (hereafter cited as WFRF).
54. William B. Caperton to Josephus Daniels, January 3, 1916, WFRF.
55. George Barnett to William B. Caperton, November 15, 1916, WFRF; William B. Caperton to George Barnett, November 16, 1916, WFRF.
56. Healy, *Gunboat Diplomacy*, 206–228.
57. Waller to John Beresford Wynne Waller, July 22, 1916, WFP.
58. Waller to John Beresford Wynne Waller, July 22, 1916, WFP..
59. Waller to John Beresford Wynne Waller, May 12, 1916, WFP.
60. Record of Proceedings of a Marine Examining Board in the case of Colonel Littleton [W.] T. Waller, November 22–24, 1916, WFRF.

## CHAPTER 7

1. Littleton W. T. Waller to the men of the Third Battalion, Fifth Regiment, Marine Corps AEF, July 15, 1918. WFP.
2. Littleton W. T. Waller to the men of the Third Battalion, Fifth Regiment, Marine Corps AEF, July 15, 1918. WFP.

3. George Barnett to Littleton W. T. Waller, March 17, 1920, March 28, 1920, WFP.
4. Robert Debs Heinl, Jr., and Nancy Gordon Heinl, *Written in Blood: The Story of the Haitian People, 1492–1971* (Boston: Houghton Mifflin Company, 1978), 465.
5. Heinl and Heinl, *Written in Blood*, 464–465; U.S. Senate, Hearings before a Select Committee on Haiti and Santo Domingo, 67th Congress, 1st and 2nd Sessions, S. Res. 112 (Washington, D.C., 1922), 423–455, 607–647.
6. Hearings on Haiti, 607–647; Littleton W. T. Waller to Littleton W. T. Waller, Jr., July 8, 1923, WFP; Waller to children, circa 1923, WFP.
7. U.S. Senate, Inquiry into the Occupation and Administration of Haiti and Santo Domingo, 67th Congress, 2nd Session, Senate Report No. 794.1 (Washington, D.C., 1922), 22–23.
8. Inquiry into Occupation, 23.
9. Inquiry into Occupation, 241.
10. Littleton W. T. Waller to sons, July 4, 1923, WFP.
11. Littleton W. T. Waller to sons, July 4, 1923, WFP.
12. Littleton W. T. Waller to sons, July 4, 1923, WFP.
13. Littleton W. T. Waller to Tazewell Waller, July 8, 1923, WFP.
14. Littleton W. T. Waller to Tazewell Waller, July 8, 1923, WFP; Agnes Waller to Beresford Waller, July 13, 1926, WFP.
15. Littleton W. T. Waller Jr. to Beresford Waller, July 25, 1926, WFP.
16. Littleton W. T. Waller Jr. to Beresford Waller, July 25, 1926, WFP.
17. Littleton W. T. Waller Jr. to Beresford Waller, July 25, 1926, WFP; Agnes Waller to Beresford Waller, July 13, 1926, WFP.
18. Littleton Jr. to Beresford, July 13, 1926, WFP.
19. Littleton Jr. to Beresford, July 13, 1926, WFP.
20. Littleton Jr. to Beresford, July 13, 1926, WFP.
21. Littleton Jr. to Beresford, July 13, 1926, WFP.
22. Agnes Waller to Beresford Waller, July 16, 1926, WFP; Littleton to Beresford, July 13, 1926.
23. Agnes to Beresford, July 16, 1926.
24. Littleton Jr. to Beresford, July 13, 1926.
25. Littleton Jr. to Beresford, July 13, 1926, WFP.

# BIBLIOGRAPHY

### GOVERNMENT DOCUMENTS AND PUBLICATIONS

Department of the Navy. *Annual Report of the Brigadier-General, Commandant of the United States Marine Corps to the Secretary of the Navy, 1900.* Serial Set No. 4098, Senate Document 3, 56th Congress, 2nd Session. Washington, D.C.: U.S. Government Printing Office, 1900.

Department of the Navy. *Annual Report of the Brigadier-General, Commandant of the United States Marine Corps to the Secretary of the Navy,* House Document 3, 57th Congress, Session 1, Serial Set 4287. Washington, D.C.: Government Printing Office, 1901.

Department of the Navy. *Annual Report of the Commandant of the Marine Corps,* in the *Annual Report of the Navy Department for the Year 1904.* Washington, D.C.: Government Printing Office, 1904.

Department of the Navy. *Annual Report of the Commandant of the Marine Corps,* in the *Annual Report of the Navy Department for the Year 1905.* Washington, D.C.: Government Printing Office, 1905.

Department of the Navy. *Annual Report of the Commandant of the Marine Corps,* in the *Annual Report of the Navy Department for the Year 1915.* Washington, D.C.: Government Printing Office, 1915.

Department of the Navy. *Annual Report of the Commandant of the Marine Corps,* in the *Annual Report of the Navy Department for the Year 1920.* Washington, D.C.: Government Printing Office, 1920.

Department of the Navy. Records of the Office of the Judge Advocate General, RG 125. College Park, Maryland: National Archives.

Department of the Navy. Records of the Office of the U.S. Marine Corps, RG 127. College Park, Maryland: National Archives.

Department of the Navy. *Register of the Commissioned and Warrant Officers of the Navy of the United States and of the Marine Corps.* Washington, D.C.: Government Printing Office, 1885, 1895.

Department of State. *State Papers Relating to the Foreign Relations of the United States.* Washington, D.C.: Government Printing Office, 1916.

Department of War. *Annual Report of the Secretary of War, 1900,* House Document 2, 56th Congress, Session 2, Serial Set 4078. Washington, D.C.: Government Printing Office, 1900.

Department of War. General Orders No. 100, Article 82, Adjutant General's Office, April 24, 1863, Washington: Government Printing Office, 1864.

Department of War. Records of the Office of the Judge Advocate General, RG 153, College Park, Maryland: National Archives.

*Passenger Lists of Vessels Arriving at New York, New York, 1820–1897.* Microfilm Publication M237, roll 483. Washington, D.C.: National Archives.

U.S. Congress. House of Representatives. "Statement of Facts and Arguments Presented by the Major-General Commandant of the Marine Corps, Urging the Disapproval by the Department of the Proposed Reduction of the Strength of and Ultimate Removal of the Marine Detachment from the Vessels of the Navy," in House of Representatives, *Hearings before the Subcommittee on Naval Academy and Marine Corps, Committee on Naval Affairs, House of Representatives on the Status of the Marine Corps (hereafter cited as Hearing 1909).* Washington, D.C.: Government Printing Office, 1909.

U.S. Congress. House of Representatives. Committee on Naval Affairs. Marine Corps Personnel Hearing, February 29–March 2, 1916. House Document 159-0.9, 2169. Washington: Government Printing Office, 1916.

U.S. Congress. Senate. *Affairs in the Philippine Islands: Hearings before the Committee on the Philippine Islands [Jan. 31–June 28, 1902].* 57th Congress, 1st session, Senate Document 331, Volume 2, 1591–1592. Washington, D.C.: Government Printing Office, 1902.

U.S. Congress. Senate. *Inquiry into the Occupation and Administration of Haiti and Santo Domingo,* Volume 1, 67th Congress. Washington, D.C.: Government Printing Office, 1922.

U.S. Congress. Senate. *Hearings before a Select Committee on Haiti and Santo Domingo,* 67th Congress, 1st and 2nd Sessions, S. Res. 112. Washington, D.C., 1922.

U.S. Congress. Senate. "Naval Appropriations," Senate Document 238, 67th Congress, 2nd Session. Washington, D.C.: Government Printing Office, 1922.

U.S. Congress. Senate. *Story of Shansi Massacres of Foreign Missionaries,* in Serial Set No. 4029, Senate Document 30, 56th Congress, 2nd Session. Washington, D.C.: U.S. Government Printing Office, 1900.

U.S. Congress. *U.S. Statutes at Large,* Volume 22, Chapter 391, 47th Congress, 1881–1883. United States. https://www.loc.gov/item/llsl-v22/.

**MANUSCRIPTS AND ARCHIVAL MATERIALS**

Blake, Daniel Papers. PC 1196, Archives Branch, Marine Corps History Division, Quantico, Virginia.

Butler, Smedley D. PC3124, Archives Branch, Marine Corps History Division, Quantico, Virginia.

Cochrane, Henry C. Papers. PC1, Archives Branch, Marine Corps History Division, Quantico, Virginia.

Daniels, Josephus Papers. Library of Congress, Washington, D.C.

Fuller, Ben Papers. PC713, Archives Branch, Marine Corps History Division, Quantico, Virginia.

Grigsby, Hugh Blair Papers. Mssl-G878263091-3094, Virginia Historical Society, Richmond, Virginia.

Harllee, William C. Papers. PC1140, Archives Branch, Marine Corps History Division, Quantico, Virginia.

Jones, Mary H. Byrd Claiborne Papers. Mssl-J735b23-40, Virginia Historical Society, Richmond, Virginia.
Lansing, Robert Papers. Library of Congress, Manuscript Division.
Lejeune, John A. Papers. Library of Congress, Washington, D.C.
Little, Louis Mc. Papers. PC 143, Archives Branch, Marine Corps History Division, Quantico, Virginia.
Logbooks of U.S. Navy Ships, ca. 1801–1940, RG 24, National Archives, College Park, Maryland.
Marine Corps Data Base, Vernon L. Williams Historical Collection, Old Primero Historical Foundation, Abilene, Texas.
Meade, Robert L. Papers. PC2216, Archives Branch, Marine Corps History Division, Quantico, Virginia.
Miller, A. B. Papers, PC 196. Archives Branch, Marine Corps History Division, Quantico, Virginia.
Norfolk Light Artillery Blues Historical Collection, Sergeant Memorial Room, Norfolk Public Library, Norfolk, Virginia.
"Norwood School," Vertical file, Jefferson-Madison Regional Library, Charlottesville, Virginia.
Palmer, George M. Papers. Archives Branch, Marine Corps History Division, Quantico, Virginia.
Powell, William C. Papers. Archives Branch, Marine Corps History Division, Quantico, Virginia.
Reid, George C. Papers. PC144, Archives Branch, Marine Corps History Division, Quantico, Virginia.
Service Records, National Personnel Records Center, St. Louis, Missouri.
Waller Family Papers. San Diego, California and Boston, Massachusetts.
Waller, Littleton W. T. Papers. PC 942, Archives Branch, Marine Corps History Division, Quantico, Virginia.
Waller, Littleton W. T., Jr. Papers. PC 224, Archives Branch, Marine Corps History Division, Quantico, Virginia.

### INTERVIEWS
Oral Interview, Littleton W. T. Waller II by Vernon L. Williams, March 22, 1990, La Jolla, California.

### BOOKS AND ARTICLES
Abel, Christopher A. "Controlling the Big Stick: Theodore Roosevelt and the Cuban Crisis of 1906." *Naval War College Review* 40, no. 3 (Summer 1987): 88–98.
Allen, Gardner Weld, ed. *Papers of John Davis Long.* Boston: The Massachusetts Historical Society, 1939.
Baecker, Thomas. "The Arms of the Ypiranga: The German Side." *Americas* 30, no. 1 (July 1973): 1–17.

Baedeker, Karl. *Egypt and the Sudan: A Handbook for Travelers.* 7th edition. Leipzig, Germany: Karl Baedeker, 1914.

Bartlett, Merrill L. *Lejeune: A Marine's Life, 1867–1942.* Columbia, South Carolina: University of South Carolina Press, 1991.

Bartlett, Merrill L. "Old Gimlet Eye." *Proceedings of the U.S. Naval Institute* 112, no. 11 (November 1986): 65–72.

Bartlett, Merrill L. "Ouster of a Commandant." *Proceedings of the U.S. Naval Institute* 106, no. 11 (November 1980): 60–65.

Bevan, James. "From Filipinos to Boxers in 1900." *Leatherneck* 18, no. 4 (April 1935): 5–7, 65–55.

Brandt, Nat. *Massacre in Shansi.* New York: Syracuse University Press, 1994.

Butt, Archibald. *Taft and Roosevelt: The Intimate Letters of Archie Butt, Military Aide,* volume 2. New York: Doubleday, Doran & Company, Inc., 1930.

Cary, A.D.L. and Stouppe McCance, compilers. *Regimental Records of the Royal Welch Fusiliers* volume 2, 1816–1914. London: Forster Groom and Company, Ltd., 1923.

Cassard, William G., ed. *Battleship Indiana and Her Part in the Spanish-American War.* New York: The Indiana Ship's Company, 1898.

Chadwick, French Ensor. *The Relations of the United States and Spain: The Spanish-American War, volume 2.* New York: Charles Scribner's Sons, 1911.

Clark, George B. *Hiram Iddings Bearss, U.S. Marine Corps.* Jefferson, North Carolina: McFarland & Company, Inc., 2005.

Clark, Harold P., et al. *History of the Tazewell House: Talisman from the Wishing Oak.* Virginia Beach, Virginia: W. S. Dawson Company, 1991.

Colby, Elbridge. "Tientsin and the Boxer Rebellion." *Military Engineer* 29, no. 165 (May–June 1937): 191–199.

Collum, Richard S. *History of the United States Marine Corps.* New York: L. R. Hamersly Company, 1903.

Daggett, A. S. *America in the China Relief Expedition.* Nashville, Tennessee: The Battery Press, a reprint of the 1903 edition, 1997.

Daniels, Josephus. *The Wilson Era: Years of Peace, 1910–1917.* Chapel Hill, North Carolina: University of North Carolina Press, 1944.

Editor. *Norfolk City and Business Directory, 1866.* Baltimore, Maryland: Webb and Fitzgerald, 1866.

Editor. *Norfolk City Directory.* Norfolk, Virginia: J. F. Milligan & A. J. Dalton, 1869, 1872.

Editors. *Norfolk and Portsmouth Directory, 1872–1873.* Norfolk, Virginia: Chataigne & Boyd, 1872.

Editor. *Norfolk City Directory for 1869, 1972.* Norfolk, Virginia: Jas. F. Milligan & Co., 1869, 1872.

Editor. "Results of the Philippine 'Atrocities' at Washington." *Literary Digest,* May 10, 1902.

Edwards, Harry W. "Memory of a Day with the Royal Welch." *Leatherneck Magazine* 56, no. 3 (March 1979).

Eisenhower, John S. D. *Intervention: The United States and the Mexican Revolution, 1913–1917.* New York: W. W. Norton & Company, 1993.

Ellsworth, Harry A. *One Hundred Eighty Landings of United States Marines, 1800–1934.* Washington, D.C.: History and Museums Division, Headquarters, U.S. Marine Corps, 1974.

Ferslew, W. Eugene. *Vickery's Norfolk City Directory, 1859.* Norfolk, Virginia: Vickery & Company, 1859.

Funtecha, Henry F. "The History and Culture of Boats and Boat-building in the Western Visayas." *Philippine Quarterly of Culture and Society* 28, no. 2 (June 2000): 111–132.

Gates, John. *Schoolbooks and Krags: The United States Army in the Philippines, 1898–1902.* Westport, Connecticut: Greenwood Press, 1973.

Harned, Glenn M. *Marine Corps Generals, 1899–1936: Volume 1 of a Marine Corps Biographical Encyclopedia.* 2nd edition. North Charleston, South Carolina: CreateSpace Independent Publishing, 2017.

Healy, David. *Gunboat Diplomacy in the Wilson Era: The U.S. Navy in Haiti, 1915–1916.* Madison, Wisconsin: The University of Wisconsin Press, 1976.

Heinl, Robert Debs, Jr. "An Association Was Formed." *Marine Corps Gazette* 47, no. 4 (April 1963): 14–17.

Heinl, Robert Debs, Jr. "Hell in China." *Marine Corps Gazette* 43, no. 11 (November 1959): 55–58.

Heinl, Robert Debs, Jr. *Soldiers of the Sea: The United States Marine Corps, 1775–1962.* Annapolis, Maryland: United States Naval Institute, 1963.

Heinl, Robert Debs, Jr., and Nancy G. Heinl. *Written in Blood: The Story of the Haitian People, 1492–1971.* Boston: Houghton Mifflin, 1978.

Hitchman, James H. "U.S. Control Over Cuban Sugar Production, 1898–1902." *Journal of Interamerican Studies and World Affairs* 12, no. 1 (January 1970): 90–106.

Holbrook, Francis X. "Brave Hearts and Bright Weapons." *Marine Corps Gazette* 57, no. 11 (November 1973): 56–65.

Janowitz, Morris. *The Professional Soldier: A Social and Political Portrait.* New York: The Free Press, 1971.

Johnstone, John H. *A Brief History of the 1st Marines.* Washington, D.C.: U.S. Marine Corps, 1968.

Karnow, Stanley. *In Our Image: America's Empire in the Philippines.* New York: Random House Publishing Co., Inc., 1989.

Karsten, Peter. *The Naval Aristocracy: The Golden Age of Annapolis and the Emergence of Modern American Navalism.* New York: The Free Press, 1972.

Langley, Lester D. *The Banana Wars: An Inner History of American Empire, 1900–1934.* Lexington, Kentucky: The University Press of Kentucky, 1983.

Lewis, Charles Lee. *Famous American Marines.* Boston: L.C. Page & Company, 1950.

Linn, Brian. *The U.S. Army and Counterinsurgency in the Philippine War, 1899–1902.* Chapel Hill, North Carolina: University of North Carolina Press, 1989

McClellan, Edwin N. *The United States Marine Corps in the World War.* Washington, D.C.: Historical Branch, G-3, Headquarters, U.S. Marine Corps, 1920 (1968 reprint).

Melshen, Paul. "He Served on Samar." *Proceedings of the United States Naval Institute* 105, no. 11 (November 1979).

Merrill, Dennis, and Thomas G. Paterson, ed. *Major Problems in American Foreign Relations*, volume 1. Boston: Wadsworth, 2010.

Meyer, Michael C. "The Arms of the Ypiranga." *Hispanic American Historical Review* 50, no. 3 (August 1970): 543–556.

Millett, Allan R. "The General Staff and the Cuban Intervention of 1906." *Military Affairs* 31, no. 3 (Autumn 1967): 114–117.

Millett, Allan R. *The Politics of Intervention: The Military Occupation of Cuba, 1906–1909.* Columbus, Ohio: Ohio State University Press, 1968.

Millett, Allan R. *Semper Fidelis: The History of the United States Marine Corps.* New York: Macmillan, 1980, 1991.

Minger, Ralph Eldin. "William H. Taft and the United States Intervention in Cuba in 1906." *Hispanic American Historical Review* 41, no. 1 (February 1961): 75–89.

Moskin, Robert. *The U.S. Marine Corps Story*, second revised and updated edition. New York: McGraw-Hill Book Company, 1987.

Munro, Dana G. *Intervention and Dollar Diplomacy in the Caribbean, 1900–1921.* Princeton, N.J.: Princeton University Press, 1964.

Musicant, Ivan. *The Banana Wars.* New York: Macmillan Publishing Company, 1990.

Oyos, Matthew M. "Theodore Roosevelt, Congress, and the Military: U.S. Civil-Military Relations in the Early Twentieth Century." *Presidential Studies Quarterly* 30, no. 2 (June 2000): 312–330.

Paterson, Thomas G., et al. *American Foreign Relations: A History since 1895.* Volume 2. Stamford, Connecticut: Cengage Learning, 2015.

Posner, Walter H. "American Marines in Haiti, 1915–1922." *Americas* 20, no. 3 (January 1964): 231–266.

Preston, Diana. *The Boxer Rebellion: The Dramatic Story of China's War on Foreigners that Shook the World in the Summer of 1900.* New York: Walker & Company, 2000.

Price, Eva Jane. *China Journal 1889–1900: An American Missionary Family during the Boxer Rebellion, with the Letters and Diaries of Eva Jane Price and Her Family.* New York: Scribner and Sons, 1989.

Roberts, William R., and Jack Sweetman, eds. *New Interpretations in Naval History*, Ninth Naval History Symposium. Annapolis, Maryland: Naval Institute Press, 1991.

Robinson, Robert L. "Gunboat Diplomacy 1882: The United States Navy and the Bombardment of Alexandria." *Warship International* 19, no. 1 (1982): 47–56.

Rockwell, Charles K. "A Brief History of the Panama Canal." *Society of American Military Engineers* 1, no. 2 (April–June 1909): 164–174.

Schmidt, Hans. *Maverick Marine: General Smedley D. Butler and the Contradictions of American Military History.* Lexington, Kentucky: The University Press of Kentucky, 1987.

Schott, Joseph L. *The Ordeal of Samar.* New York: Bobbs Merrill, 1964.

Sheriff, B.R. *Sheriff & Co's Norfolk and Portsmouth Directory.* Norfolk, Virginia: Sheriff & Company, 1875–1877.

Shulimson, Jack. *The Marine Corps' Search for a Mission, 1880–1898.* Lawrence, Kansas: University Press of Kansas, 1993.

Simmons, Edwin H. "Stand, Gentlemen, He Served on Samar." *Shipmate* (November 1976): 24–28.

Stewart, William H., ed. and comp. *History of Norfolk County, Virginia and Representative Citizens.* Chicago, Illinois: Biographical Publishing Company, 1902.

Sweetman, Jack, et al. *New Interpretations in Naval History*. Annapolis, Maryland: Naval Institute Press, 1993.
Taylor, James O., ed. and comp. *The Massacre of Balangiga*. Joplin, Missouri: McCarn Printing Company, 1931.
Thomas, Lowell. *Old Gimlet Eye*. Quantico, Virginia: The Marine Corps Association, a reprint of the 1933 edition, 1981.
Trask, David F. *The War with Spain in 1898*. Lincoln, Nebraska: University of Nebraska Press, 1981.
Venzon, Anne Ciprano. *General Smedley Darlington Butler: The Letters of a Leatherneck, 1898–1931*. New York: Praeger, 1992.
Welch, Richard E. Jr. "American Atrocities in the Philippines: The Indictment and Response." *Pacific Historical Review*, 43, no. 2 (May 1974): 233–253.
Wiegand, Wayne A. "The Lauchheimer Controversy: A Case of Group Political Pressure during the Taft Administration." *Military Affairs* 40, no. 2 (April 1976): 54–59.
Wise, Frederic M. *A Marine Tells It to You*. New York: J. H. Sears & Company, Inc., 1929. 1981 reprint by the Marine Corps Association.

## DISSERTATIONS AND THESES

Schreadley, Richard Lee. "Intervention—The Americans in Haiti, 1915–1934." Doctoral dissertation, Fletcher School of Law and Diplomacy, 1972.

## WEBSITES

*Dictionary of American Naval Fighting Ships*, online version. Naval Historical Center, Washington Navy Yard, Washington, D.C. http://www.history.navy.mil/danfs.
Gallia history, http://www.theshipslist.com/ships/descriptions/ShipsG.html.
Gallia tow attempt, February 23, 1885 entry. http://www.norwayheritage.com/p_ship.asp?sh=geise.
Fisk, Charles. "Graphical Portrayal of New York Central Park Daily Temperatures, Precipitation, and Snowfall, by Year (1876–Present)." http://home.att.net/~ny_climo/NY1885.gif.
Hill, Brian T. February 1885 entries, "Ice Charts and Ship/Iceberg Database." http://researchers.iot.nrc.ca/~hillb/icedb/ice/ice_charts/1885jf.htm.
Holmes, Conrad biographical essay, Department of Justice website. https://web.archive.org/web/20081009072131/http://www.usdoj.gov/osg/aboutosg/holmescbio.htm.
Johnson v. Sayre, Case Summary, FindLaw Corporation. http://findlaw.com/us/158/109.html.
Merriam-Webster.com *Dictionary, Merriam-Webster*. https://www.merriam-webster.com/dictionary/baroto. Accessed June 16, 2022.
Online histories of passenger ships. http://www.theshipslist.com/ships/descriptions/ShipsS.html.
"Robert Bacon." In *Dictionary of American Biography*. New York: Charles Scribner's Sons, 1936. Gale online entry https://go.gale.com/ps/i.do?p=GPS&u=wikipedia&id=GALE|BT2310018466&v=2.1&it=r&sid=GPS&asid=afdbbd9a. Aaccessed July 16, 2022.

## NEWSPAPERS

*Austin American-Statesman* (Austin, Texas)
*Chattanooga Daily Times* (Chattanooga, Tennessee)
*The Boston Globe* (Boston, Massachusetts)
*Houston Daily Post* (Houston, Texas)
*The Liberty Vindicator* (Liberty, Texas)
*The New York Sun*
*The New York Times*
*The New York World*
*Norfolk Virginian* (Norfolk, Virginia)
*The Times Dispatch* (Richmond, Virginia)
*Virginia Pilot* (Norfolk, Virginia)

# INDEX

Bacon, Robert, 152, 155
Balangiga, Samar, 106, 108–110, 114, 116–117, 122–123, 125–127, 131
Balboa, Panama Canal, 146
Banglay, Samar, 124
Barnett, George, 41, 167, 182, 201, 203–204, 211, 229, 236, 254–256
barotos, 126
Bas Obispo, Panama Canal, 146–147, 150
Basey, Samar, 110, 116–119, 120, 123, 127–128, 130–131–136
Beach, Edward, 199–200
Bearss, Hiram, 119, 121, 123, 125-126, 138, 220
Beresford, Lord Charles, 24–25
Biddle, William F., 97–99, 101–102, 149–150, 161–163, 167
Blockage of Cuba Operations, 61–63
Bobo, Rasalvo, 178, 181
Bombardment of Alexandria, Egypt, 21–25
area of Marine operations ashore, 23
Boxers, 70–71, 75–76, 79, 84, 86
operations against the Boxers in Tientsin, 75–97
operations against the Boxers in Peking, 98–105
Bradford, Anne E. T., 7
Butler, Smedley, 79, 91, 97, 104, 159, 161, 194–198, 201–202, 240–241
Butler, Thomas, 159, 161, 201
Butt, Archibald, 158, 161-163
Caco, 177–178, 191–196, 204, 212
Camp Columbia, Cuba, 155–156
Camp Elliott, Panama Canal, 146
Caperton, William B., 176, 178–179, 181, 184–185, 189–193, 195–196, 199–200, 203–207
Cap-Häitien, Haiti, 178, 181, 187, 189, 192, 194

Casey, Silas, 73
Catbalogan, Samar, 114
Chaffee, Adna R., 98–99, 104, 107–110, 133
Changing Career Patterns in the Corps, 37–45
Chien-men Gate, Peking, 100, 103–104
China Merchants Steam Navigation Company, Tientsin, China, 82, 84, 92
China Relief Expedition
first American response, 75–79
Tientsin operations, 75, 97
march on Peking, 98–105.
Cochrane, Henry C., 10–11, 13, 15–17, 19, 21–22, 24–25, 27, 29–32, 36–37, 45–47, 49, 53, 59, 97
Cogswell, James K., 125
Cole, Eli K., 149–150, 182–184, 187, 194, 197–199
Colon, Panama Canal, 146–147, 149
Concessions at Tientsin, China, 83
Craddock, Christopher, 82, 88
Cuban Pacification Campaign (1906), 143, 147, 150–153, 155–157
Cuban Pacification Campaign (1911), 154, 167–168
Cuevan de Sojoton, Samar, 124
Daniels, Josephus, 164, 166-167
Dartiguenave, Philippe-Sudré, 187, 189
Davis, Robert B., 187
Day, J. H. A., 116, 133–134, 136
Deer Point, Cuba, 154, 160
Denny, Frank L., 21–24, 29, 32, 34
Dorward, A. R. F., 93, 95–96
Draper, H. L., 73
Dunlap, Robert H., 96
Elliott, G. F., 147, 149–150, 160–161
Empire, Panama Canal, 146–147, 149–150
Etienne, Charles-Oscar, 179

Executive Order 969, 159–160
Faunt Le Roy, R. P., 73
Forney, James, 45
Fort Berthol, Haiti, 195
Fort Riviere, Haiti, 194–195
Fort Selon, Haiti, 195
Franck, Harry, 211
Fullam, W. F., 157–158
Galveston, Texas, 173
General Order 100, 134–135
Gherardi, Bancroft, 13, 15
Glenn, Harry, 119
Gómez, Josó Miguel, 152, 168
Goodrich, C. F., 13
Gibbs, B. F., 9
Grigsby, Hugh Blair, 5–9
Guantanamo Bay, Cuba, 47, 150, 160, 168, 181, 203
Guiuan, Samar, 124, 126–127
Harding, A. E., 88
Harding, Warren G., 211
Haitian custom houses, 189–190
Haitian Gendarmerie, 196, 207
Haiti Expedition
    Unrest and Chaos, 177–182
    the expedition begins, 182–200
Haiti-US Treaty, 187
Haut Obispo, Panama Canal, 146, 149
Hay-Bureau-Varilla Pact, 145
Hemani, Samar, 124–125
Heywood, Charles, 71
Hinojosa, Ramón, 168
Hitchman, James H., 151–152
Hogg, John W., 9
Hsi Ku Arsenal, 70, 79, 84, 99
Huntington, R. W., 73
Jolly, W. L., 88
Karmandy, Lincoln, 167
Kempff, Louis, 86–87
King, Campbell, 125–126
Lagtiao, Samar, 124, 128
Lanang, Samar, 123, 127–128, 130–131, 136
League Island, Philadelphia, 147–148, 155, 172, 174
Leary, Richard P., 49

Lejeune, John A., 147, 150, 173–174, 182, 198, 201, 203, 209, 211
Liruan, Samar, 119–120
Little, Louis M., 90, 96
Lodge, Henry Cabot, 164–166
Luaan, Samar, 124–125
Lucas, Lewis C., 147–148, 150
Mahoney, James, 148, 153
Mare Island, California, 141, 168, 172
Marine Corps Association, 160–161
Marine Corps expansion-1916, 200–203
Marines on ships, 157–161
Matthews, A. J., 126–128
Mayo, Henry T., 168–169
McCalla, Bowman H., 76
McCawley, Charles G., 9
Meade, Robert L., 79, 90–99
Mercedes, Samar, 124
Miller, Adolph B., 182–184
Millett, Allan R., 136
Missionaries (from Oberlin College) in Shansi, 70–71
Moody, William H., 147
*Morro Castle* (chartered transport), 172
Moses, F. J., 99, 101–103
Moses, R. M., 172
Myers, John T., 75–76
Neville, Wendell C., 133, 169, 170–171, 174, 182
Newberry, Truman H., 159
Ninth U.S. Infantry, 91, 93, 101, 108, 116, 122, 127–128
Nipa Nipa, Samar, 123, 125
Odoc, Samar, 119–120
Omagongong, Samar, 124, 126–128
Palma, Tomás Estrada, 152–153, 155
Pambujan, Samar, 124–128
Panama Canal Company, 149–150
Panama Canal Expedition, 144–151
Panhulugan Cliff in the Sojohan district, Samar, 120
Peitsung, China, 99, 100–102
Penrose, Boies, 162–164
Pershing, John J., 209
Pickering, James N., 127–128

## INDEX | 269

Pillsbury, John E., 159
Point Capines, Samar, 124
Pond, Charles, 205–206
Port-au-Prince, Haiti, 176–179, 181–182, 184, 187, 189–192, 196–197, 203, 206–207
Porter, David D., 81–82, 116–117, 119, 121, 123, 130–132
Posner, Walter H., 196, 254–255, 264
Quick, John Henry, 126
Quinapundan, Samar, 124, 126–127
Reilly, Henry J., 103–104
racial bias, 177, 185, 192
Rodgers, Frederick W., 109–111, 113–114, 116–117, 119
Roosevelt, Theodore, 143, 145, 151–153, 155, 157–161
Root, Elihu, 108–109
Ryther, Dwight W., 126
Salcedo, Samar, 124
Sam, Jean Vilbrun Guillaume, 177–179, 181, 187
Samar Expedition
    early coastal operations on Samar, 114–118
    Sojoton River Expedition, 118–119, 121–123, 127
    march across the Samar Wilderness, 122–132
    assessment of the Samar Expedition, 136–139
Seymour Relief Expedition (Edward Seymour), 76–79, 84–86, 88
Schott, Joseph, 111
Sixth Separate Brigade, 109–110
Smith, Jacob, 106, 109–111, 114, 116–119, 122–123, 132–136
Sojoton Trail, Samar, 129
SS *Gallia*, 35–36
Swanson, Claude, 164–166
Taft-Chaffee conflict, 107–109
Taft, William Howard, 152, 157, 160–163
Tacloban, Leyte, 109, 118, 124–126
Tampico, Mexico, 168–169, 170, 172
Tazewell, Ella, 5
Tazewell, John, 5
Tazewell, Littleton Waller, 4–5
Tazewell, Sally, 5, 7
Théodore, Davilmar, 178
Thompson, Richard W., 9
Tungchow, China, 100, 102
Underwood, R. O., 194
Upshur, William P., 18
USAT *Warren*, 140–141
USS *Aryat*, 126–127
USS *Connecticut*, 180, 182–184, 194, 199
USS *Denver*, 153, 155
USS *Detroit*, 158
USS *Dixie*, 145, 147, 149, 151
USS *Dolphin*, 168
USS *Eagle*, 181
USS *Indiana*
    Battle of Santiago Operations, 63–68
    Bombardment of San Juan, Puerto Rico, 62–63
    Maintenance Problems, 59–61
USS *Iroquois*, 47–49
USS *Isla de Cuba*, 125
USS *Kearsarge*, 50–51
USS *Lancaster*, 59
    cruise narrative, October 29, 1881–June 6, 1886, 13–19
    cruise narrative, June 6–July 20, 1882, 20–22
    cruise narrative, July 20–August 10, 1883, 25–27
    cruise narrative, August 15, 1883–July 18, 1884, 27–28
USS *Marietta*, 153, 155
USS *Miami*, 155
USS *Newark*, 59
USS *New York*, 111, 113–114, 132–133, 136, 148, 173–174
USS *Nipsic*, 17–18, 21
USS *Ontario*, 192
USS *Panay*, 123, 125
USS *Pensacola*, 49–50
USS *Powhatan*, 27, 29–30, 32
USS *Prairie*, 147, 168–169, 171
USS *Quinnebaug*, 18, 21

USS *Solace*, 74–75
USS *Tallapoosa*, 50–52
USS *Tennessee*, 180, 184, 186
USS *Waller* commissioning, 1–3
USS *Washington*, 176, 178, 180–181
USS *Vicksburg*, 118
Vandegrift, Alexander A., 194
Veracruz Expedition, Mexico, 168–175
Victor, Filipino guide, 131
Meyer, George von Lengerke, 161–162
Waller, Clara Wynne, 1, 3, 6, 27, 29–32, 35–37, 116, 140–141, 183, 186, 198, 202–203
Waller, Henry T. Waller, 3, 71
Waller, John Beresford Wynne, 1, 3, 54
Waller, Littleton W.T. Waller,
    appointed provost at Peking, 104–105
    Argentine Revolution, 52–53
    attitudes towards changing career patterns, 45
    beginning of Marine Corps career, 8–10
    boar hunt, coast of Africa, 18–19
    Commandant of the Marine Corps, 161–167
    courtship and marriage, 19, 27, 29–31
    courts-martial for murder, 132–136
    Cuban Pacification Campaign (1906), 151–157
    Cuban Pacification Campaign (1911), 154, 167–168
    death, 215–222
    detached to the USS *Lancaster*, 11–13
    duties on European Station, 15–16
    early life, 3–7
    early coastal operations on Samar, 114–118
    erroneous report of Waller's death in China, 87
    final assignment, 209–210.
    gunnery at Battle of San Juan, 63
    gunnery at Battle of Santiago, 63–68
    Haiti, 182–200
    hearing (1920) on atrocities in Haiti, 211–213
    landing at Alexandria, Egypt, 21–25
    leave in Lisbon, 1890–1891, 53
    links to aristocratic Virginia, 6–7
    march across the Samar Wilderness, 122–13
    march from Taku to Tientsin, 79–84
    march on Peking, 98–105
    marriage, 34–37.
    military law, 53, 55–58
    Norfolk Light Artillery Blues, 8, 142
    Panama Canal, 144–151
    post-courts-martial assignments in the U.S., 140–144
    promotion to brigadier general, 207–208
    recruiting, 143–144, 147, 151
    rescue of the Seymour Expedition in China, 84–86, 88
    retirement, 211, 213–215
    return to Philippines from China, 109
    Samar operations begin, 109–118
    service overview, 3
    Sojoton River Expedition, 118–119, 121–123, 127
    temporary transfer to the USS *Nipsic*, 17, 25
    Tientsin, China operations, 75–97
    to the Philippines, 71, 73–75
    troubles with Cochrane, 17
    Veracruz, Mexico, 168–175
    Warm Springs recouperation, 141–142
Waller, Littleton W. T. Waller, Jr., 3, 45
Waller, Mary Tazewell, 4–8, 34–35, 46
Waller, Matthew Page, 4–5
Weeks, John, 167
Williams, Alexander S., 131
Williams, Kenneth, 127
Wilson, Woodrow, 164–165, 177–178, 184, 186
Winthrop, Robert Charles, 8–9
Wise, Frederic M., 25
Wynne, John Beresford, 19
Yangtsun, China, 100–102
*Ypiranga*, 169
Zamor, Oreste, 179

www.ingramcontent.com/pod-product-compliance
Lightning Source LLC
Chambersburg PA
CBHW021340230426
43666CB00006B/357